I0819275

ALSO BY ISAAC FITZGERALD

Dirtbag, Massachusetts
How to Be a Pirate
Knives & Ink: Chefs and the Stories Behind Their Tattoos
Pen & Ink: Tattoos and the Stories Behind Them

AMERICAN RAMBLER

AMERICAN RAMBLER

WALKING THE TRAIL *of* JOHNNY APPLESEED

ISAAC FITZGERALD

ALFRED A. KNOPF · NEW YORK · 2026

A BORZOI BOOK

FIRST HARDCOVER EDITION PUBLISHED BY ALFRED A. KNOPF 2026

Map by David Lindroth Inc.

Part opener image (apple) by Vintage Studio / Adobe Stock

Published by Alfred A. Knopf, a division of Penguin Random House LLC, 1745 Broadway, New York, NY 10019.

Library of Congress Cataloging-in-Publication Data

Names: Fitzgerald, Isaac author

Title: American rambler : on the trail with Johnny Appleseed / by Isaac Fitzgerald.

Description: First hardcover edition. | New York : Alfred A. Knopf, 2026. |

Identifiers: LCCN 2025036590 | ISBN 9780593537794 hardcover | ISBN 9780593537800 ebook

Subjects: LCSH: Appleseed, Johnny, 1774–1845 | Fitzgerald, Isaac—Travel | Travel—Psychological aspects | Self-actualization (Psychology) | Apple growers—United States | LCGFT: Biographies | Autobiographies

Classification: LCC S417.C45 F58 2026

LC record available at https://lccn.loc.gov/2025036590

penguinrandomhouse.com | aaknopf.com

Printed in the United States of America

1st Printing

The authorized representative in the EU for product safety and compliance is Penguin Random House Ireland, Morrison Chambers, 32 Nassau Street, Dublin D02 YH68, Ireland, https://eu-contact.penguin.ie.

For Kelly Farber, my home

Like Johnny Appleseed, Dionysus was a figure of the fluid margins, slipping back and forth between the realms of wildness and civilization, man and woman, man and god, beast and man.

—MICHAEL POLLAN,
The Botany of Desire

What I fundamentally mean when I say "walking" is "moving at human pace." Moving through the world and absorbing the world in its rich detail. At human pace. At human scale. And inscribing your personality, your character, your sensibility, your thoughts, your conversations, your stories onto the place you are moving through.

—GARNETTE CADOGAN,
said to me while on a long nighttime walk

There ain't no home and there is no cure
For a no-good ramblin' man

—ZACH BRYAN,
"No Cure"

CONTENTS

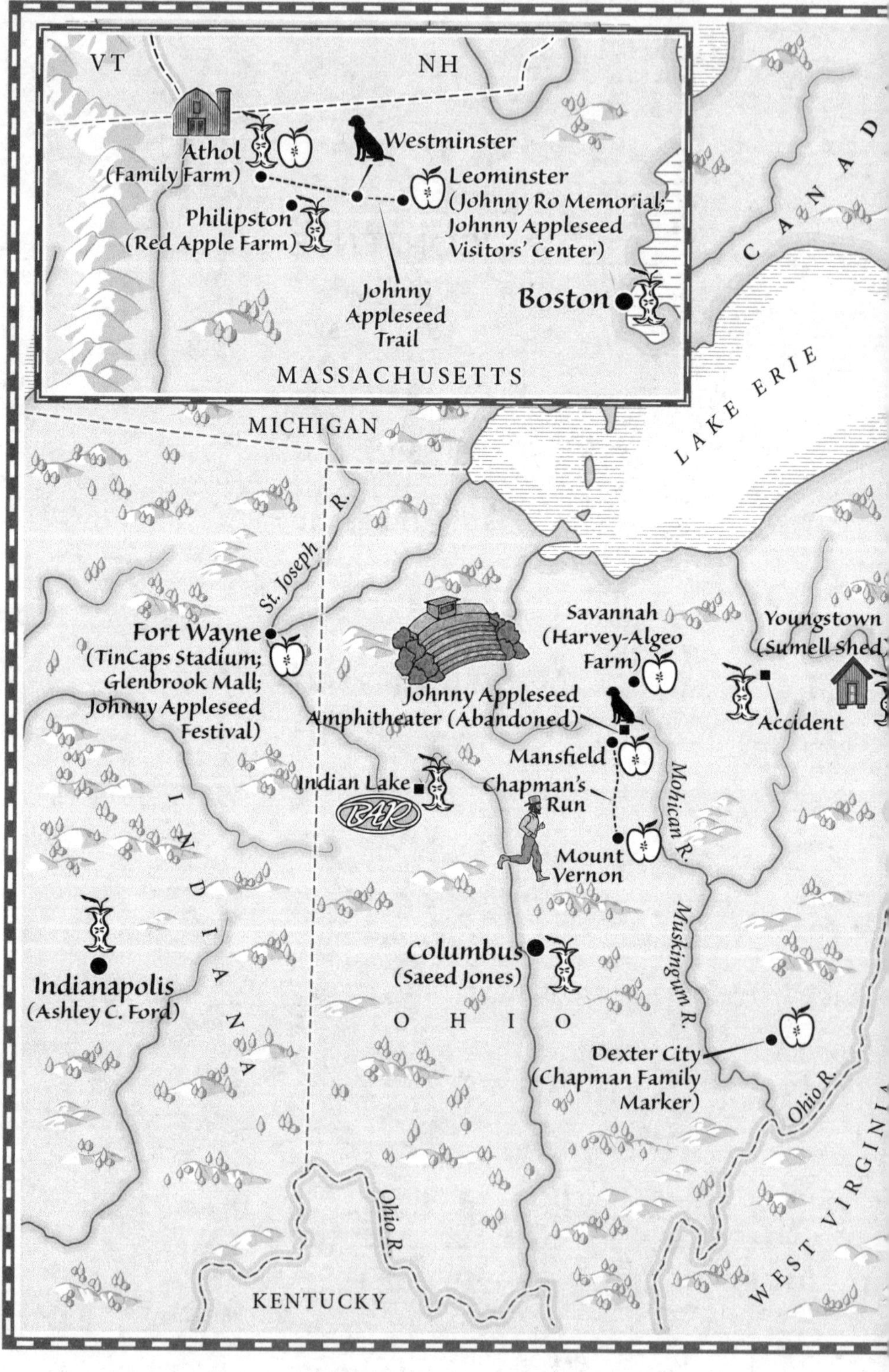
VT
NH
Athol
(Family Farm)
Westminster
Leominster
(Johnny Ro Memorial;
Johnny Appleseed
Visitors' Center)
Philipston
(Red Apple Farm)
Johnny
Appleseed
Trail
Boston
MASSACHUSETTS
CANADA
LAKE ERIE
MICHIGAN
St. Joseph R.
Fort Wayne
(TinCaps Stadium;
Glenbrook Mall;
Johnny Appleseed
Festival)
Savannah
(Harvey-Algeo
Farm)
Youngstown
(Sumell Shed)
Johnny Appleseed
Amphitheater (Abandoned)
Accident
Mansfield
Indian Lake
Chapman's
Run
Mohican R.
Mount
Vernon
INDIANA
Muskingum R.
Columbus
(Saeed Jones)
Indianapolis
(Ashley C. Ford)
OHIO
Dexter City
(Chapman Family
Marker)
Ohio R.
Ohio R.
WEST VIRGINIA
KENTUCKY

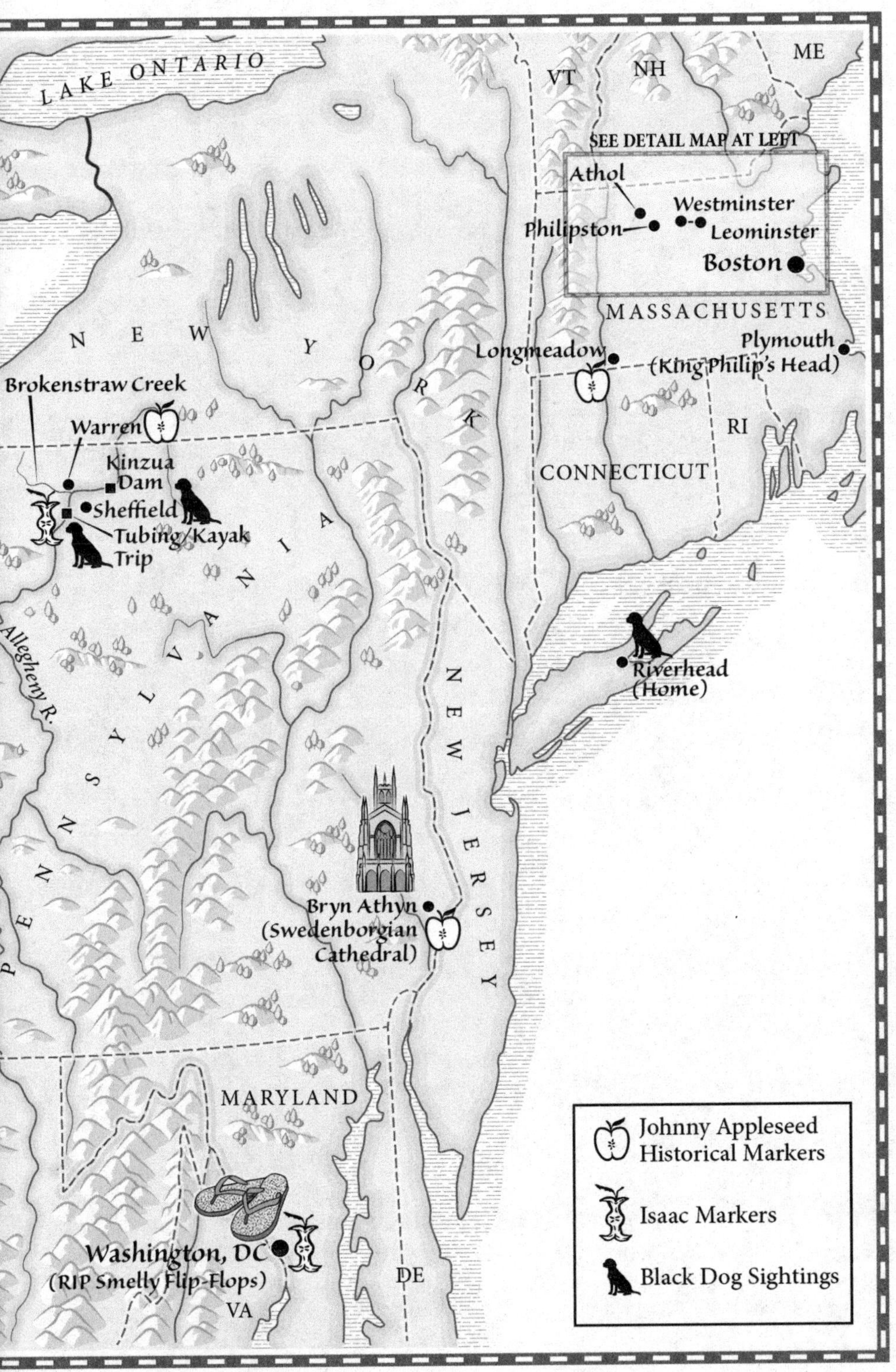
LAKE ONTARIO
VT
NH
ME
SEE DETAIL MAP AT LEFT
Athol
Westminster
Philipston
Leominster
Boston
MASSACHUSETTS
Longmeadow
Plymouth
(King Philip's Head)
RI
CONNECTICUT
NEW YORK
Brokenstraw Creek
Warren
Kinzua
Dam
Sheffield
Tubing/Kayak
Trip
Allegheny R.
PENNSYLVANIA
Riverhead
(Home)
NEW JERSEY
Bryn Athyn
(Swedenborgian
Cathedral)
MARYLAND
Washington, DC
(RIP Smelly Flip-Flops)
VA
DE
Johnny Appleseed
Historical Markers
Isaac Markers
Black Dog Sightings

· SPRING ·

1

I'VE BEEN DRINKING a bit less and praying a lot more than I used to.

Now, that's not to say I'm drinking less than most people—I'm not—nor that a doctor would sign off on my lifestyle as a healthy one—they wouldn't—but self-betterment has to start somewhere, and for me that means choosing sobriety occasionally. More often than I'm used to, which is to say more often than any sane person living in these modern times would want to.

As for the praying? It's not that I'm praying some saintly amount, but it's another habit I'm developing, a healthier one. Like most of my habits, I picked this one up from my parents—only to abandon it for decades—taking prayer out on semi-rare occasions like car accidents, late rent payments, or particularly bad hangovers. But over the past few years I've found myself doing it more and more, and not only when I'm in trouble. Sometimes in moments of happiness. Other times, contentment. Every once in a rare while, during a moment of peace, I find myself with my knees in the dirt reciting the Lord's Prayer.

Which is what I'm doing right now—though it should be noted that I'm on my knees because I'm hiding behind a bush, and that this is very much one of those vintage "Oh shit, I'm in trouble" prayers, not one of contentment or peace.

On top of all that, yes, I'm sober at the moment, though I'd rather not be, as I'm trying to avoid a railway police officer—known as a bull—who is slowly but steadily heading my way, and the stress of the situation is getting to me.

In my mind, I put an emphasis on "And forgive us our trespasses . . ."

The plan was never to walk miles and miles on train tracks during a freezing day in early March—and it certainly wasn't to hide from a cop, trying not to get picked up on loitering charges for strolling along a railroad that up until very recently I believed to be abandoned. There was supposed to be a trail.

The Johnny Appleseed Trail of North Central Massachusetts, to be exact.

My interest in Johnny Appleseed, whose real name was John Chapman, was born of another habit I picked up from my parents but have only recently rediscovered: walking.

In a way, prayer and walking have a bit in common. A repetition. A solitude. They're both ways of getting out of one's own head—or at least away from one's more perilous thoughts, if only for a little while. (Drinking, come to think of it, has a similar effect.)

During the early years of my life, my family lived in Boston. We were poor, and we walked everywhere, rarely taking public transportation. My father biked to work, and my ma's job at a local cathedral was a short stroll from the Catholic homeless shelter where we lived. My parents were working to get back on their feet after being dealt a few tough hands by life, and then making a few questionable decisions on top of that. One of those decisions was having me.

Our vacations were walks, too, my father taking me into the White Mountains in our beat-to-shit, hand-me-down, rust-tinged Toyota truck—the bed covered in a crumbling plastic shell. We'd backpack for days at a time in New Hampshire and Maine, sleeping in the makeshift camper if a thunderstorm rolled in, my small body curled into my father's musty chest as water leaked in through the roof.

But if the weather was right, my da and I would spend our nights in the woods, sleeping in a cheap, lightweight tent—or sometimes, when the temperature was *perfect,* in our sleeping bags under the stars. Once the sun came up, we would hike. Just the two of us, for miles and miles. My father telling long, elaborate stories to make sure my little legs kept pumping, putting one small foot in front of the other.

"Moonlight gleams off the sword of the red knight as he raises his weapon high above his head, the sharp blade whistling through the air as he brings it down with *crushing* force upon the green knight's great helm."

"Oh no!"

"Oh yes! And do you know what happened next?"

"No! Tell me!"

"Well, if you follow me to that next bend in the trail—do you see it? That one right up there. If we get past that curve, then I can tell you the fate of our hero, the gallant green knight."

Dry, dead leaves crunched under my father's boots as he turned his back to me and hiked ahead. All I could do—my head spinning, my spirit *aching* with a desire to know what would happen to the green knight—was follow him.

Those legends, so often tales woven on the fly in my father's mind—using bits of *Sir Gawain and the Green Knight, Beowulf, Seven Samurai,* stories from the Bible, *Lord of the Rings,* and always, always, at least a *touch* of *Star Wars*—kept me moving. When the stories of knights eventually dried up, maybe on day two or three of our hikes, I would learn history. None of it accurate. The shot heard round the world, fired by a Minuteman, known famously for being so quick that they could run faster than said bullet that was shot—

"Which actually traveled around the *whole* world before it crashed into the chest of an unlucky British soldier, mind you."

"I don't think that's how it went, Da."

"That's how it went. Don't you believe me?"

By the fifth day of hiking, colonial history gave way to stories of how the West was won (violently, which, to be fair to my father, was accurate). Tall tales of Pecos Bill, which then made way for other American legends. John Henry. Paul Bunyan. Johnny Appleseed. Tornadoes were ridden and giant iron pans were greased by lumberjacks wearing blocks of butter as ice skates.

Apple trees got haphazardly planted across the vast expanse of the American frontier.

It's no wonder that, as far back as I can remember, I've been seduced by stories—legends of all kinds—but especially tales of people on permanent quests. You know the ones. They loom large. The lone wanderer, or a group of stragglers, rambling toward an endless horizon, either riding an old steed, like Rocinante (Don Quixote's horse, or Steinbeck's camper van named in tribute, take your pick), or on foot.

Fiction or nonfiction—when you're a child, you don't know the difference. A book is a book. A story is a story. All you hear is your father's voice.

It's a difficult thing to separate legend from story from memory from fact. Especially when you're young, surrounded by adults doing their best to hide a tough living situation—eventually my parents and I left the homeless shelter and moved into John Leary House, a halfway house run by the Catholic Worker for unhoused people trying to find a permanent place to live—with fantasies and self-made lore in hopes of distracting a child from his surroundings.

To put it one way, I grew up with a sense of magic and wonder.

To put it another, I grew up never really sure what was real and what was myth.

The walking, though. Out there on a trail, following my father and listening to his stories. My feet on the ground.

The walking was real.

Now that I'm older, the things I love about walking, other than fond memories of my father—hell, maybe I'd go so far as to say the things I love about living—are freedom and solitude.

The two are inextricably linked in my mind. If you're walking in a group, there will be discussions of the best way to go, and your body will almost subconsciously start to keep in step with the herd. On your own, though? You set the pace. You map out the journey.

There are so few things one has control over in this life. But out for a walk? Alone? With enough time? You start to feel like the captain of your own ship again.

It's those little, subtle joys that make walking such a pleasure—a lukewarm happiness. Satisfying and steady. Moments of euphoria can be stumbled upon, sure, along with moments of catastrophe (such as getting arrested for trespassing on train tracks by a railway cop). But for the most part, if you keep your pace constant and your feet dry, your contentment will be consistent and light.

Now, are you *totally* in control? Of course not. We're not gods. As soon as you walk out your front door—on a journey either long or short—you are opening yourself up to the elements, to the spontaneity of life. But on your own you get to choose how you respond. Leave your phone at home? All the better, communication itself is a way others can exert control. When you are alone, walking through the world, your concerns become immediate. Will it rain? Snow? Is there a river that might prove difficult to cross? The issues you face are elemental. How lucky that one can access such a drastic change in reality simply by going outside.

Freedom and solitude.

Escape.

All that said, too much freedom? Too much solitude? Too much escape?

A man does get lonely.

When I was growing up, my ma was always more down to earth than my father. Less of a dreamer would be one way to put it, negative might be a more critical framing—though it was understandable, raised as she was in the chilly northern hills of Massachusetts by two strict puritanical realists. My mother's family lived off the land. Grew their own food. Wasted nothing. No wonder she was so charmed by my father's storytelling—an Irish Catholic who was raised next to the sea. A religion filled with relics and idols and tales of faith-fueled magic. Giant stained-glass windows, so different from the plain white Protestant churches that dotted my ma's part of the state.

My mother, a teacher, would do her best to counterbalance my father's tales of fancy. Johnny Appleseed wasn't a legend, nor was he the mythical pagan god my father made him out to be. He was simply a man: a man named John Chapman. And he grew up just down the road from my ma's run-down family farm.

Born right before the American Revolution in Leominster, Province of Massachusetts Bay, on September 26, 1774, John Chapman was a pioneer nurseryman, planting apple trees across the American Midwest during the early nineteenth century. He was deeply religious, leading a simple—often barefoot—life, guided by spiritual convictions and a strong respect for nature.

Rather than randomly scattering seeds across the land as the legends suggest, though, Chapman strategically established nurseries—fencing them in to protect the saplings from animals—and partnered with local caretakers who would look after the trees, often selling them on Chapman's behalf long after he had left town. His efforts helped supply apple trees to settlers expanding westward, especially in Western Pennsylvania, Ohio, and Indiana, where Chapman would die in the mid-1800s not far from Fort Wayne.

"Knowing what's true is important," my ma would tell me. Like any child who hears that they have a tenuous (at best) connection to somebody famous, I became obsessed with both the man and the myth. My father filled my head with stories, while my mother brought me dusty encyclopedias full of primary sources, like this tidbit from author and poet Rosella Rice, who met Chapman when she was young:

> His personal appearance was as singular as his character. He was a small, "chunked" man, quick and restless in his motions and conversation; his beard, though not long, was unshaven, and his hair was long and dark, and his eye[s] black and sparkling. He lived the roughest life, and often slept in the woods. His clothing was mostly old, being generally given to him in exchange for apple-trees. He went bare-footed, and often traveled miles through the snow in that way. . . . [He] wore on his head a tin utensil which answered both as a cap and a mush pot.

Another from historian Paul Aron in his more modern book *American Stories* adds further nuance to the entertaining but embellished tall tales: "Chapman was actually a successful businessman. He bought many of the parcels of land on which he planted his seeds and ultimately accumulated about twelve hundred acres across three states. . . . He wore pauper's clothing by choice and not out of necessity."

As a child who grew up in a homeless shelter, but wasn't aware yet how that had affected him—something I maybe still haven't totally figured out—who was obsessed with the outdoors thanks to hikes with my father, and also raised religious, Johnny Appleseed became a personal hero.

A patron saint.

I got older, and my trips to the mountains with my father became less frequent. My family finally found a stable home—it was in an old, dilapidated house on my ma's parents' aforementioned ramshackle farm. The house was far from the city, which I missed immediately. Out in north central Massachusetts, past Leominster, where John Chapman was born. My ma had spent her whole life escaping that farm; imagine her disappointment about having to return. My grandparents' house was big, bright, and red, with a fresh coat of paint, while our maybe-gray house languished, the paint peeling away. The color of the wooden cladding outside matched the dreary atmosphere inside.

It was a home of charity, at best—boiling over with resentment and anger on its worst days.

My parents would fight, the stress of their lives finally catching up with them. Yelling built like a symphony, with other sections joining in. Crashing plates. Tearing clothes. Flying hands turned into closed fists and subsequent wails.

Sometimes the wails were mine.

But when I could, I would walk in the forested hills that surrounded the farm. Taking the chaos of the elements over the human-made confusion of my home.

No wonder I became an outdoor cat.

I escaped that home at the age of fourteen, and by my early twenties I lived on the other side of the country. Not once during that time did I own—nor could I afford—a car. So I did my damnedest to live in a bunch of walkable cities, subconsciously avoiding rural landscapes, which I associated with the harder parts of my childhood. I walked everywhere for the same reason my parents had back when they were my age, a simple lack of funds, but I never thought much of it. The same way that you never think to breathe.

But more recently? After the locked-in, stifling indoor months of 2020 I needed to break out into the open air, walking more and more each day. The apple doesn't fall far from the proverbial tree. It's a funny thing, growing older. Often realizing—so slowly that you barely notice—that the fascinations of your parents are now your fascinations, too. Walking. Storytelling. Prayer.

In the back half of my thirties, though, I found myself walking with purpose. The same way breathing can become meditation, if you focus on each inhale and exhale. I would slip on a pair of beat-up Vans, old running shorts, and a loose-fitting Hawaiian shirt with a few rips in it and set out into New York City—where I'd moved a handful of years before—the most walkable place I'd ever lived. Every morning, as the sun clawed its way into the sky, and every evening, as dusk set in on the buildings surrounding me.

It felt good to move my body. Accomplishing something gave me a jolt of mood-lifting dopamine. I became addicted to the activity. I had recently abandoned a well-paying job, and a fiancée had abandoned me. I was broke and unhealthy. In the middle of an achingly difficult year, here was a small task I could complete—something good for me. Simple.

Every morning after I woke, and every evening before bed, rain or shine I headed to the park near my apartment and put one foot in front of the other.

Soon I was walking twenty thousand steps a day, or about ten miles. Days turned into weeks turned into months.

Not surprisingly, walking day in and day out had positive, if subtle, effects on my body. I grew sturdier. My leg muscles got a little bigger and harder, and I felt generally stronger and more resilient.

It also had a positive effect on my mind. I felt sharper, more alert. My morning walks got me charged up for the day, and my sunset walk gave me a boost going into the evening, whereas before, I would just lie about, wondering why I was so tired.

While I kept my phone on me—wanting to keep track of my step count—I swore not to look at it while I was walking. Taking a break from the tiny, upsetting digital universe I keep in my pocket freed me up to be attentive to the world my body moved through, to notice and connect with other walkers I encountered. One man always wore goggles. Another carried a large ball, sometimes bouncing or kicking or throwing it forward before running to catch up with it. There was a group of women who must have kept to the exact same schedule I did, given how often we ran into each other. We'd all give each other the nod when we crossed paths, and it felt oh so good. "Hello, fellow traveler."

The nod I valued most came from a rail-thin, bearded old man who always stood out to me. Regardless of the weather, I'd see him walking or running. A full sweat suit. Trash bags keeping him dry if it rained. His name was Luis Rios, and he'd been circling the park since 1977. Luis was my second patron saint of walking.

Always, on those walks, in the back of my mind, this whispering idea: What if I kept walking west and didn't stop?

Camaraderie with other walkers provided a wholesome substitute for something I desperately missed during those personally dark days: the sense of community I'd always enjoyed while hanging out in bars—or working in them, as I did for years. In a way, the park became my new, *much healthier* bar.

Walking helped me to transform much of a terrible year into a tolerable one. The following year was the same. So much ahead that would continue to test us, to traumatize us, to stretch to the breaking point our capacity for madness and uncertainty and horror.

So I kept on walking. *No reason to stop now,* I thought to myself.

"Why are you doing this again?"

My father and I are standing in his kitchen. It's a fair question. The truth is, I'm worried. My parents have been growing older. My ma and da still live in the area where I grew up, and now they're taking care of ma's mother—she's one hundred years old and still living on that family farm—alongside my ma's sister. My aunt, my ma, and my father are all in their seventies. I wanted to visit, to come up and see how everyone was doing. But you can't say that to a parent. "I'm worried that I should be taking care of you, but you're still taking care of a woman who refuses to die."

It's the night before I head out for what I think is the trailhead of the misleadingly named Johnny Appleseed Trail. Walking Chapman's trail is just a cover—to come up north and see how my folks are doing—except that more and more the way the man lived his life seems appealing to me. Feet on the ground, sleeping outside. Taking life's problems one at a time, away from a desk, from responsibilities. My brain still full of those books and stories from my youth of people who go a-wandering. You only get one life. You can't wait for some wizard to show up at the door of your hobbit-hole and invite you on an adventure.

The masculine urge to go out for a pack of cigarettes and never come back.

My father asks another question before I can answer his first one, which is probably for the best. Often the dreams in one's head sound foolish at best—and gravely worrisome at worst—when spoken aloud.

"And your plan is to walk all the way back here? That's something like forty or so miles."

Thirty-four-point-two miles, to be exact. But I don't correct him, and take a different approach.

"You used to go on long backpacking trips all the time." Which is true. Even before my father took *me* hiking, when my parents first started seeing each other—back when they were married to different people—they would drive out of Boston up to the White Mountains and go on long hikes together. A love of getting outdoors, the natural world, a desire to spend some romantic time together in the woods, and, you know, a logistical solve for the affair they were having.

They figured it out, eventually. Not exactly in what one might deem the "correct" order, but in their defense, who does? Rumor is I was conceived at the top of one of those mountains. They got around to getting divorced and remarrying each other when I was roughly three years old. By the time my father and I are talking in their kitchen, he and my ma have been married for almost forty tumultuous years. But things had been calming down, now that I was—we *all* were—older.

"When I go hiking, I bring proper gear. What gear do you have?"

I point to an old, beat-up, green JanSport backpack that I've had since middle school—so far it has a sweatshirt and some toiletries in it. The number of safety pins holding the bag together is . . . troubling.

"Christ." My father whispers the word, almost under his breath. A prayer for me or a prayer for patience, I can't tell. "Do you at least have some boots?"

I look down at the Timberlands I'm wearing—a footwear staple where I live in Brooklyn—and gesture at my feet as if to say, "Look. Boots."

"So, no. Okay, come with me," my father says, as he heads down to the basement.

This is a familiar dance for me and my father. He often finds himself a bit bewildered by me, especially as I haven't opened up to him about my recent growing interest in spirituality. I'm a drinker, whereas he is sober. A man of faith—best described as a practicing Catholic with healthy servings of Buddhism, Eastern Philosophy, and a deep understanding of Judaism and the Old Testament. It's where my parents met all those years ago, in an Old Testament class taught by a scholar, Dr. William L. Holladay. Later, when they had a bastard child out of wedlock—or rather, while in wedlock with other people—my parents and baby me lived at Dr. Holladay's apartment for a spell, before the homeless shelter, having nowhere else to go.

My ma would tell me Dr. Holladay and I used to have long conversations when I was a toddler, about anything, really. Two verbose souls trying to outtalk each other—like a radio show hosted by a child and a sixtysomething-year-old man. Sometimes we'd even talk religion, she told me—a bit delusionally, as even the most realistic mother's love often is. "Like young Jesus with the teachers at the temple. Or John Chapman, talking about God with children by the hearth of whatever cabin generous settlers allowed him to sleep in that night."

Later in life, when I asked Dr. Holladay about this, he grunted and said, "More than likely I needed a break from your endless yapping and was reading passages from the Bible to you in hopes that you'd fall asleep."

But he said it with a chuckle.

"Here, take these." My father hands me a pair of tough-looking, well-broken-in leather hiking boots. Walking in my father's shoes felt a little on the nose, but then again, it would beat the blisters my Timberlands would give me.

Like I said, this is a familiar dance between me and my father. He doesn't quite know what to do with my choices, most of the time, but if he can help me be less of an idiot, he tries to.

"And you're going to need a sleeping bag. Maybe my bivouac tent, too. Which'll mean a proper rucksack—not that rag you're still pretending is a functional bookbag. Do you have a tarp?"

I shake my head no.

"Alright. Well, take this all upstairs and set up the tent in the living room. We want to make sure it isn't missing any poles. I'll grab a few more things that might prove useful and come right up."

When my father joins me in the living room a few minutes later, he lets out a heavy sigh.

"I don't know, I," he says, using his abbreviated, single-letter nickname for me, as he gestures at the half-assembled bivouac tent sitting in the center of the room, which more resembles a modern art piece than a functional shelter. "This isn't looking too good."

Whether he means the tent or the chances that my walk is going to end in disaster or not, I'm not sure. Either way, he stays up late into the night with me, showing me how to assemble the bivvy and properly use the rest of his equipment.

"I promise to return it all safely," I say, assuming he's worried I might damage or wreck something.

"Nah, keep it. Not sure I've got too many camping trips left in me, anyhow."

The statement sits there for a moment. The reality of death and loss and the passing of time. The fear of the unknown while contemplating this *extremely* common occurrence that each one of us will experience, but which none of us—not a single one of us throughout our entire human history—has ever fully understood.

My father and I look at each other.

"You should get some sleep," he says. "I'll drive you to the trailhead in the morning."

After my father turns out the lights, I sneak a flask of whiskey into my pack, among all his camping gear. I didn't know it yet, but the next day I would start a journey that would end up consuming the next year of my life.

2

THE NEXT MORNING I find myself shivering in front of the Johnny Appleseed Visitors' Center between exits 35 and 34 on westbound Route 2 at the Lancaster/Leominster town line. It's a cold day in early March, and after I watch my father drive away, I shoulder my backpack loaded with camping gear, tighten the shoelaces on his boots, and begin looking for the start of the Johnny Appleseed Trail of North Central Massachusetts.

Like all children who grew up in Massachusetts—John Chapman's home state—I was raised on the myth of the apple-seed-spreading, tin-pot-hat-wearing, animal-loving, Bible-thumping frontiersman who brought apples to the early pioneers not just by my parents, but by my teachers, too. Even the priests were in on it. An old short from Disney's 1948 film *Melody Time* titled "The Legend of Johnny Appleseed" was an after-service favorite in the church basement, all of us donut-fueled kids encouraged to sing:

Oh, the Lord's been good to me
And so I thank the Lord
For giving me the things I need:
The sun and the rain and the appleseed;
Oh, the Lord's been good to me.

You likely know the rest.

The Johnny Appleseed Visitors' Center is that Disney song come cheerily to life. Right out front, where I'm standing, there is "The Big Apple of New England," a ten-foot-tall red apple that is "the largest apple sculpture of its kind in all of New England." Although how many others could there really be? Painted in white on the front of the apple is a message: "Visit North Central Massachusetts, Johnny Appleseed Country."

There is also a patina sculpture of a young, barefoot John Chapman in a tricornered hat holding a basket of apples. In front there are actual apple trees, plus a plaque claiming they are descendants of the "last surviving Rambo apple tree planted in Nova, Ohio, around 1840 by John Chapman." The image of a 'roided-out apple tree wearing a red headband while holding an M60 machine gun briefly flickers in my mind—what I don't yet know is that I will visit that very tree myself before the year is through, and that my Sylvester Stallone–inspired vision is more on point than I could imagine.

A sign is nailed into one of the trees. "Please Do Not Climb," it reads, along with "Or Pick the Apples."

Inside the center there is hot cider for sale, and a diorama portraying an older Johnny Appleseed walking while reading the Good Book. There are knickknacks and old publications of all sorts, all under glass, along with less-Appleseed-related items available for purchase: cookies, stuffed animals, and maple syrup. There is an antique hand-crank apple press and a bearded visage carved into a large tree trunk, which looks more like Gandalf the Grey than a nineteenth-century pioneer.

Maybe wizards do show up after all, I think to myself.

"May I help you?"

The woman behind the desk is every bit as New England as one would hope. A large wool sweater, gray unfussed hair, eyeglasses hanging from a chain around her neck. At first I think she's being judgmental—I have a large beard and beat-up boots on, and am gripping a backpack with a sleeping bag attached. Perhaps she's worried I might knock over the row of ceramic mugs emblazoned with a Johnny Appleseed emblem that looks like it was designed by whoever switched the New England Patriots logo from "Pat the Patriot" to the "Flying Elvis." Johnny is more cartoon than man—smooth, a bag floating behind him with his legs spread wide, midstride, an arm enthusiastically thrusting forward.

"I'm looking for the head of the trail," I say, motioning to my rucksack.

"The head of the trail?"

"The Johnny Appleseed Trail of North Central Massachusetts," I clarify, though I'm wondering why I should need to. There's only one trail, and from what I read online, this visitors' center is supposedly where it starts.

"Well, yes, the Johnny Appleseed Trail does indeed start here, but it's simply what we call this stretch of highway. It's to encourage tourism in the area," she says, before adding, with an almost concerned tenor in her voice, "for motorists."

"So there's no hiking?"

"There's hiking all around here, to be sure. But any trails that head out from this very spot? No."

I wonder for a moment if the woman saw my father drop me off and then drive away—through the window, from her perch behind her desk. If the concern in her voice stems from the fact that she knows I have no vehicle, and thus no way out of this rest stop.

I ask a few more questions—half to put her at ease and half to buy myself time to think. The Johnny Appleseed Trail was founded in 1996 by the JATA (Johnny Appleseed Trail Association) to help "promote tourism and travel in the North Central Massachusetts region." Like much of America as you stray from its major urban hubs, this part of my home state has been historically overlooked, despite the relative proximity to Boston and the picturesque Berkshires to the west. The tourism campaign is showing signs of progress, as there are now many popular orchards in the area, not to mention restaurants, breweries, and . . . the aforementioned hiking trails, all of which are nowhere near where I am currently standing.

I thank the woman for her hospitality, buy a hot cider plus a couple of children's books about Appleseed for my niece and nephews, and stuff them in my bag before heading out. The March sky is bleak, and the air outside seems harsher after some time spent indoors. Despite it technically being spring, winter isn't quite over here in Massachusetts.

3

THE JOHNNY APPLESEED Visitors' Center is surrounded by a tall chain-link fence. I know this because I walked the entire perimeter while I sipped my already-cooling—nonalcoholic—hot cider.

But, if you should ever find yourself in the position I find myself in now, know this: There's a hole in the fence. Right by the green dumpsters in the back.

After finishing my cider and tossing the empty cup in the large metal bin overflowing with trash, I throw my gear through the hole in the chain-link fence and scurry after my belongings.

The forest behind the visitors' center is still covered in fallen leaves from the previous autumn. No buds are out on the trees yet, and the air is frigid and damp. There are also a surprising number of tires littered around. Many people in these parts choose to dump their tires in order to avoid disposal fees. Or, even worse, individuals offer to collect and haul other people's unwanted tires for a fee—promising to take them to a landfill or recycling center—but instead save money on both disposal fees and gas by simply tossing the tires in the woods. That all-American tradition of exchanging money for someone else to commit a sin for you.

Still, the tires are beautiful, in their way. A smattering of black rubber circles dotting the forest floor. I look at my iPhone's compass and walk west, following the sound of passing cars on Route 2.

The legend of Johnny Appleseed is as large as the life of John Chapman is multifarious, a testament to which the trinket-filled Johnny Appleseed Visitors' Center I was leaving behind stands as proof.

A son of the American Revolution, his father was a Minuteman—apparently known for being ready for battle in a minute's notice, *not* for how quickly they could run the fifty-yard dash, despite what my father told me as a child.

In his late teens, after a rather impoverished childhood, John Chapman was one of many colonists who pushed westward from the East Coast, which was becoming more crowded post-Revolution. That's where the legend of the apple-tossing, rag-wearing, no shoes on his feet and a cooking pot on his head man began—though the embellishments about his life wouldn't come until years after his death. But the true story of John Chapman is much more complex—and booze-fueled—than even my ma's history books had led me to believe.

For starters, despite what the Disney short portrays, Chapman's Christianity was . . . complex. He was a devout follower of Swedish theologian Emanuel Swedenborg, and practiced a small, unique, *mystic* Christian faith with one tenet at its center: the more we suffer in this life, the more we will be blessed in the next. This belief system is why many say Chapman embraced the difficulties of his transient lifestyle with such jubilation in his heart. As a person who was raised Catholic and still thinks if something in my life is going right something else surely must be going wrong, I can relate.

Speaking of his nomadic way of living, you should also know that the whole "rags for clothes" thing (sometimes wearing old coffee sacks as shirts, though probably *not* the legendary tin pot as a cap, it pains me to say) and the owning of very little in terms of belongings was all a personal choice. As noted previously, Chapman had 1,200 acres across three states to his name when he died. Those orchards he planted throughout the area? Well, he was technically the owner of the land those trees were planted on. Which is all to say, Johnny Appleseed died—at least on paper—a rather wealthy man. But it was wealth he himself never touched, in accordance with his belief in Swedenborgianism.

In his book *Johnny Appleseed: The Man, the Myth, the American Story,* historian Howard Means says of Chapman, "He ached for land but couldn't settle down long enough to claim it." An inability to stay in one place, another feeling I'm all too familiar with.

Means puts forth a theory that Chapman's notions of land ownership rested somewhere between those of his colonial brethren and those of the Indigenous peoples whose lands those brethren were stealing, often violently. Chapman "loved land," Means writes, "but was never meant to own it." His devout beliefs gave him, as Means puts it, a "missionary's zeal," alongside "a missionary's disregard for dollar signs."

As to the booze of it all? Those apple seeds Chapman roamed the land with—well, he got them from cideries, pulling them from the excess pulp produced while creating the ubiquitous alcoholic beverage—widely consumed due to the nonpotability of most water during that time. That brings us to our boozy second fact, which is that the trees that were planted from said seeds, and more particularly the fruit that they bore, were *not* used for apple pies and apple tarts and applesauce to feed the pioneers moving west—no matter what Disney's *Melody Time* would have you believe—nor were the apples used as snacks for said pioneers' horses. No, those apples were mainly used to create alcoholic cider, and the harder liquor known as applejack, an apple brandy high in alcohol content.

The thought of applejack—or more so the Johnny Appleseed Trail turning out to be a regular stretch of highway—has me feeling for the whiskey flask in my bag. Nobody likes being wrong straight out of the gate. But given the long walk I still have in front of me, I decide to leave it be for now.

I climb over rusted, long-forgotten wire fences and carefully avoid deer scat, tromping through the woods until I come to a clearing, which I quickly realize is a parking lot. There's a sign: Orchard Hills Athletic Club. A large building nearby has "Laser Storm" written on its side, along with "Fun America" in large block letters colored red, white, and blue—but the place looks abandoned. A mustached man leaving the gym scans me quizzically as I walk out of the woods.

I follow the parking lot to a service road, which leads to an on-ramp. Route 2 was the highway of my youth—the first one I drove on, behind the wheel of friends' trucks even before I had a license. The road runs east to west, cutting across the entire northern part of the state. Starting at the Common in downtown Boston, Route 2 goes all the way to the Berkshires at the New York line, before it continues on as NY Route 2.

Constructed in the early 1900s, certain sections of Route 2 were previously called New England Interstate Route 7, and before that it was a Native American path that was known as the Mohawk Trail—a trade route which connected Atlantic tribes with tribes in upstate New York and beyond. Those paths, of course, followed animal trails that once crisscrossed the thick forests of the Northeast.

In their own language, the Mohawk people call themselves the "people of the flint"—Kanien'kehá:ka—which they traded with other tribes who needed the sedimentary rock for tools and weapons. Their Algonquian-speaking neighbors—and sometimes trade competition—the people of Muh-heck Haeek Ing ("food area place"), often known as the Mohican, referred to the people of Ka-nee-en Ka as Maw Unk Lin, meaning "bear people." The Dutch heard the phrase Maw Unk and bastardized the term into "Mohawk."

A stretch of Route 2, on the *western* side of my childhood hometown, Athol, Massachusetts, is still referred to as the Mohawk Trail for tourism purposes—despite the fact that some claim this area was historically inhabited by the Mohican, not the Mohawk—much as this stretch of Route 2 I'm walking along is now referred to as the Johnny Appleseed Trail.

It's here that I also find a welcoming-looking set of train tracks. Well, perhaps *not* welcoming, as there are multiple Do Not Enter signs posted, but certainly more manageable than the tire-filled forest I was walking in before. The railway seems to stick relatively close to the highway, so I assure myself that those warnings look pretty old, and that the railroad is probably long abandoned. I pretend not to see the postings and make my way down the gravelly path of wood and metal.

A few miles into my journey I stop to drink some water from my canteen and look at a red-tailed hawk circling above me. My mind is clear, in the way that only steady walking can provide.

Walking on the train tracks has proved a little more difficult than I imagined, on account of the gap between sleepers—the wooden sections that the track is spiked into—being a bit wider than my natural gait, meaning I'm more hopping from track to track than striding across them. Eventually I decide to simply walk *beside* the train tracks, and it's there that I find my rhythm.

As I cap my water and start to move again, the earth beneath my feet begins to vibrate ever so slightly. I was so caught up in my beautiful moment of outdoorsy Americana that I forgot train tracks aren't just for self-appointed ramblers but, you know, for trains—and it turns out these tracks aren't as abandoned as I'd hoped.

Luckily this train isn't moving very fast, because I'm slow to realize what's happening and even slower in figuring out what I should actually do. It's clear the conductor sees me—the train horn blasts a few times just as I decide the best of my options is to scramble up the embankment and into the woods.

A train with a black locomotive and more than thirty cars of varying yellows, maroons, oranges, and blues passes by—each one covered in blazing, brilliant graffiti. Crouched in the underbrush I almost feel like I'm seeing a wild animal pass. A giant steel never-ending moose made up of different colors, while I hide behind pine branches.

After the behemoth passes, I get back out on the tracks and walk on.

After twenty minutes or so of walking I see a truck—a standard-seeming pickup—and I rub my eyes. At first I think there must be a road crossing up ahead, but the truck is clearly making its way toward me on the tracks—which is when I notice that the truck has lights on its roof. Security. Train police. Railway cops. Or, to use proper hobo terminology, a bull.

In previous centuries, it's said, bulls used to murder drifters and train jumpers in the thousands. In the modern era, I am in no way fearing for my life, but the idea of getting brought into some holding cell just a few hours into my Johnny Appleseed walk doesn't appeal to me. Neither does trying to explain why I have an as-of-yet untouched flask of whiskey in my backpack along with a stack of children's books. The embankment here is higher than before, though, plus there's a fence. Instead of making a run for it, I kneel in a nearby bush and mouth the Lord's Prayer.

"And forgive us our trespasses . . ."

The truck gets closer, and I can see that instead of rubber tires, it has metal wheels—similar to those you'd see on a train—that allow it to travel along the rusted tracks.

There's no way this bush is covering both me and my rucksack. The conductor driving the train that passed me earlier must have radioed in that they saw a weird-looking fella with a bag walking along the rails. Now security was out looking for me. I figure it's best to step up and put on a smile instead of being caught cowering in some shrubbery. I pray they don't search my bag and swing out toward the approaching truck, giving my friendliest wave.

I only see into the truck's cab for a moment. There is indeed a bull inside, with a security uniform and some semblance of a badge—but whether the man is sleeping, or looking down at his phone so hard that his eyes *seem* closed, or perhaps praying himself, I'll never know. You don't need to steer a truck that's running on tracks. The bull's lights don't light, and his alarm doesn't sound. He simply rolls blissfully along as my friendly wave drops to my side.

With the exhilaration of the minor but thrilling near miss warming me a bit against the cold, I continue down the railway, which passes close to a cluster of homes and backyards. Again I'm startled, but this time by a massive, furious dog. I can't make out the breed, perhaps a cane corso, mastiff, or Great Dane. All I know is that it seems as big as a horse, is dark gray, and its barking scares me more than the bull and the previous train combined. As the dog leaps up on its hind legs, it pushes its paws against the straining metal of the fence, which I am grateful to for keeping us separated.

"What's going on?" I hear a voice call out. "What's that, Susie Q?"

Is this dog's name Susie Q?

"Susie Q, what's out there, girl?"

"Hi, Susie Q," I whisper. Susie Q stops barking momentarily, but only to look at me puzzlingly and then goes right in again.

"Susie Q! Come here, girl!" The voice belongs to a man, who steps out onto his back porch and puts me in his sights.

I wait for him to start yelling at me. Or to call the police, or at least threaten to. Or maybe go get a gun. Susie Q is still barking, and I don't move, looking back at the man from the other side of the fence.

After what must have been only a few moments, but which felt like an eternity, the man slowly raises his hand, which is holding a bottle of beer. My hand is empty, but I pull the flask I've been carrying from my bag, and raise it up in return.

"Come back, Susie Q! Leave that poor guy alone!" he yells, and the dog lets go of the fence and allows herself to be called back inside. The man gives one last long-distance cheers and closes his sliding glass porch door behind the lumbering beast as I pour a slug of whiskey into my mouth and raise a cheers back.

The sun is lower in the sky than it was, but the small amount of friendliness offered by Susie Q's owner heartens me. I feel a flicker of appreciation for the kindness that John Chapman looked for in all of God's creatures, and walk on.

4

IF ONLY FRIENDLY salutes could actually keep you warm.

The wind picks up, turning the already-freezing air sharp as heavy clouds move in. I can't decide what would be worse, if it started raining or snowing. I'm lost again—or as lost as you can be with a digital map in your pocket, which I'm now learning is still pretty lost. The Johnny Appleseed Trail turning out to be simply a section of highway was confusing. It would appear the same was true of the highway's on-ramps and off-ramps, designed for cars and not pedestrians. With each step, it becomes more and more evident: Most of this country is no longer made for walking.

I have decided I will walk the length of the Johnny Appleseed Trail, despite the raw weather and there being no actual trail to speak of—whether in people's backyards or the woods along the side of the highway. The deceptively named stretch of road ends in Athol, where my parents still live. The town is over thirty miles away, but I'll be damned if I call my father and ask him to come pick me up.

If I can make it back to Athol, I'll at least have managed to do *something*.

Plus, despite the elements and impending weather, I'm somewhat enjoying my chaotic, poorly-thought-out adventure. The usual benefits of walking—an active but undistracted mind, fresh air in my lungs, the meditative rhythm of my steps—are all there, sure. But there's something more. Chasing John Chapman out here in the same place where he started his venturesome life, well, I feel alive. Motivated. In a way I haven't in quite some time.

The whiskey probably helps.

I decide to take a detour and stop by John Chapman's birthplace—and even begin to play with the idea of not stopping in Athol at all, but taking this 34.2-mile hike and stretching it farther, out across the four states that Chapman himself traversed, planting his apples and proselytizing and living off the generosity of friends and strangers alike. What would a month of living that way feel like? A year?

Was it this same restlessness and itchy feet that drove Chapman out into the surrounding wilderness almost 250 years ago? Who hasn't wanted to simply walk out the front door and see what's out there?

After my run-in with the train, the napping bull, and Susie Q and her friendly owner, I decide to stop walking the tracks, a feat easier said than done. Soon I was pressing up against a sound wall, which is the purpose of those large barriers you see on the sides of highways—to lower the noise pollution for nearby residents.

The thick concrete wall is good in the sense that it is between me and the speeding cars, but on the other side of me, the fence I was walking along simply stopped, and I found myself in the backyard of a housing development. Worrying about what might happen if another dog like Susie Q comes out—this time with no barrier between us—or perhaps a local who doesn't take as kindly to backpackers on their property, I run as fast as I possibly can to a nearby road. I try not to picture how ridiculous I must seem to someone looking up from washing their dishes, the world's most hapless traveler jumping over their child's Tonka trucks left in the backyard, running away from nothing other than the threats in his mind.

To give myself a moment of respite, I take shelter under an overpass. I am, as almost all walkers are when they stop to check their progress, disappointed in how little ground I've covered. But I will press on to Appleseed's birthplace, if I can figure out a way across this highway.

Leominster, Massachusetts, wasn't always known as the birthplace of Johnny Appleseed. Many years after his death—as often happens when legend mixes with fact, time quietly chipping away at the truth—folks had guesses, saying he was from Boston, or Springfield, while others went so far as to say Connecticut, Maryland, or even Pennsylvania or Ohio—the latter two places where John Chapman had indeed lived, but not where he was born. There were rumors of a Harvard education, and others about a Native American mother.

But all these legends were put to rest, as many legends often are, by a fastidious librarian who wanted nothing more than to get some facts straight. In the 1930s Florence E. Wheeler, charter member of the Leominster Historical Society, discovered genealogical records that proved John Chapman was born to Nathaniel Chapman and Elizabeth Simonds—who had been married on February 8, 1770—on September 26, 1774, in, yes, Leominster. Chapman's ancestors on both sides of his family hailed from England and had been in America since the 1630s—one of his mother's forebears, William Simonds Sr., having come over on a vessel coincidentally christened *The Planter.*

As I mentioned, Chapman's father, Nathaniel, was a Minuteman, a member of the local militia made up of farmers ready to fight on a "minute's notice." That call came for Nathaniel on April 19, 1775, when he participated in the legendary Battle of Concord.

I learn all this while reading a rather lengthy, sun-bleached sign that stands next to a much more succinct stone marker, which simply reads "Near this site was born John Chapman, known as Johnny

Appleseed." The marker reminds me more of a gravestone than a celebratory birthplace plaque.

Carved into the stone is a familiar logo. It's a bit more detailed, but it's the same as the one at the Johnny Appleseed Visitors' Center. An outline of John Chapman, legs outstretched, a seedbag in his hand, his feet bare and his head balding, with wild hair coming off the sides. I feel regret for mocking it earlier—the cartoonish logo is growing on me. The marker also reads "Sept 26, 1774–March 18, 1845," the day Chapman was born and the supposed day he died (though the accuracy of the latter is still up for debate).

The worn, yellowing sign next to the stone goes on:

> John's mother Elizabeth succumbed to tuberculosis before he was two years old. John lived in Leominster until he was six years old, then moved with the family to Longmeadow, [Massachusetts] following his father's second marriage.
>
> Johnny began his western pilgrimage in about 1797. Appleseed has been depicted as a somewhat deranged character wearing a tin pot for a hat, who spread apple seeds in Ohio and Indiana. In reality, this pioneer orchardist was an astute and practical nurseryman, who set out orchards and sold or gave trees to the pioneers. He was accepted by white men as an eccentric and by the [American] Indians as a medicine man because he grew and distributed herbs to them—herbs that still grow wild near his old nurseries.
>
> A deeply religious follower of Emanuel Swedenborg, he became a self-appointed missionary, sharing his religious tracts and Bible with settlers, who listened in awe to his interpretations. During the War of 1812 he saved countless lives by being a peacemaker between the [American] Indians and settlers.
>
> After braving nearly fifty wilderness winters in peace and harmony with the land, Johnny Appleseed died in Fort Wayne, Indiana on March 18, 1845. He had planted the seeds of love as an itinerant preacher, as well as apple trees, throughout much of the Midwest.

Of course the sign doesn't tell the whole story. How could it? For starters, some believe that Chapman's mother, Elizabeth, died in childbirth—that it wasn't tuberculosis. But either way, Captain Nathaniel Chapman moved to Longmeadow, where he then married one Lucy Cooley (who was eighteen at the time) and had ten more children, according to records discovered by the Longmeadow Historical Society. Those same records note that a young boy received a delivery of rum and sugar for his father in 1781, which would have been then seven-year-old John Chapman. They also show that after being relieved of his duties guarding the nearby Springfield Arsenal, Nathaniel fell on hard times, often trading labor for goods like the aforementioned rum and sugar, along with molasses, tobacco, coffee, salt, turnips, and nails. But he must have skimped on *his* end of the bargain, as he served a stint in a debtor's prison in 1785.

Now is as good a time as any to mention that, aside from these few findings—mostly based on a shopkeeper's book—we don't know much about Chapman's childhood. We can clearly assume that he lived a lean life, which might well have been a motivating factor in his heading west. But outside of that, the history books go rather blank on Chapman until he shows up in *another* shopkeeper's ledger out in Western Pennsylvania in 1797. It would seem the only folks motivated to keep their paperwork in order at the time were the ones tasked with keeping track of who owed them money.

The sign in Leominster ends by saying that in 1966 the United States Postal Service issued "the Johnny Appleseed stamp," the first stamp in the American Folklore Series. On the stamp is another artist's rendition of Chapman—with a shovel over one shoulder and a seedbag at his side, no longer skinny or bald, but absolutely shredded, as one would expect a frontiersman to be, with a beard and a hat that is very much *not* a tin pot—and in the background a large, red apple. It's hard to explain why, but the stamp-Chapman seems to be tall, almost of Paul Bunyan–esque stature.

Here is John Chapman as seen through the lens of local history.

Certainly more complex than my mother's facts-based Chapman, and more grounded in reality than the stories of my father's Johnny Appleseed. That said, I was suspicious of certain things that were stated as fact—such as his "acceptance" by "[American] Indians" as a "medicine man"—and curious about others. Plus I wanted to find out how the hell this nature-and-religion-loving legend was involved in the War of 1812.

But first, I had to walk home.

Johnny Appleseed Lane—which one assumes was named around the time these markers went up—is a perfectly normal suburban street. When I was a teenager, this area was covered in forest, but clearly there's been some development since then. Today, there's a small wooden shed that looks more like where you'd keep a lawn mower than the colonial home of John Chapman and his family; either that, or they were a very small people. But no, it's clear that this is a miniature replica built by some well-meaning citizen. If you peek inside you find a single empty room. The perfect place for local kids to smoke cigarettes or huff inhalants—as my childhood best friend Conner and I once did in old, rusted metal cylindrical rail cars we found abandoned in the woods.

As I'm about to walk on I notice two things. First, someone has placed a smooth oval rock—painted almost entirely in black save a few colorful swirls and flowers, along with the words "Be kind"—on the front porch of the small wooden shack. The item seems like something one would find in the 1990s, at that time being a throwback to the '60s, rather than something you would see nowadays. But the paint seems somewhat fresh. I put the rock back where I found it. Which is when I notice that, on the back of the original Johnny Appleseed marker, are the words "Located by Florence E. Wheeler, 1935." I'm happy the librarian got her name engraved in stone.

It's always a gamble, who gets remembered and who doesn't. Whose story gets told correctly, and whose story is warped over time. History is never definitively what happened—it's a human construct, with human biases, perspectives, and agendas. Like all things human, history is flawed, and forgetful, and at times overly optimistic.

Statues are erected, and statues are torn down. Memorials are built and then dismantled. Especially in a country as young as ours, and as big as ours—with such a lugubrious and contentious past—history isn't so much history as it is a never-ending narrative that is constantly being amended, erased, added to, and often ignored.

Still, ya gotta try. I'm glad people like Florence E. Wheeler do.

The sky is still threatening, but whatever precipitation is up there has managed to stay in the clouds. Nevertheless, the temperature continues to drop—I can feel the icy air cutting into my hands, and I regret not bringing gloves—as I walk away from the memorial and head farther west.

5

The tank is the first thing I see as I walk down Johnny Appleseed Lane to where it intersects with Mechanic Street. It is much larger than the small wooden house that stands nearby at the John Chapman birthplace memorial. By the tank is a parking lot, and statues, and a wall with photographs of slain soldiers. One of those statues, made by sculptor Robert Shure, is of Jonathan Roberge.

Roberge—better known as Johnny Ro—was killed in Iraq on February 9, 2009. Born and raised in Leominster, Ro was assigned to a cavalry division out of Fort Hood, Texas. He died of wounds sustained from a suicide car bomb detonation near Mosul while on patrol in a Humvee. Lieutenant Colonel Garnet R. Derby, Sergeant Joshua A. Ward, and Private First Class Albert R. Jex also died in the attack.

On February 19, 2009, more than 1,200 people attended Jonathan Roberge's funeral at St. Cecilia's Church in his hometown. Children stayed home from school in order to stand in the crowd and wave American flags. His godmother, Rita Sheridan, spoke of Johnny fondly, saying, "We had a special bond between us. We were both kind of rebels in our own way. He was a larger-than-life person who just lit up the room when he walked in."

Ro graduated in 2005 from Leominster High School's Center for Technical Education. After working as an auto mechanic for a bit, he enlisted in the army and was sent to basic training at Fort Knox in Kentucky. Ro's uncle, Frank Richard, remembered "getting agitated" with Johnny while coaching him in Little League when he was a boy because "it's so hard to coach somebody who is just smiling all the time."

Sheridan went on to say, "He was a magnet. He just drew people towards him. How could you ever forget a kid like that?"

We fear forgetting those we love. Time eases the pain of grief, but that lessening of hurt comes at a cost. Slowly, the faces of the ones we lost begin to fade. Their habits, the small idiosyncrasies that made them who they were, that information is replaced, as we—the ones left behind—make new memories.

In terms of not forgetting, a memorial helps. A memorial with a tank? Even better.

What began with the question "How could you ever forget a kid like that?" turned into a shrine for all Massachusetts soldiers who have given their lives in the wars in Iraq and Afghanistan. But Johnny Ro Veterans Memorial Park isn't funded by the federal government or the Commonwealth of Massachusetts. After his death, Roberge's family formed a committee, which solicited donations from individuals and local businesses to help fundraise for the memorial.

Johnny Ro was trained as a tank driver, so the committee decided to see if they could get a tank, which they did after two years of requests. An M60A3 tank to be exact, which they procured from the North Carolina National Guard Armory and brought up to New England. Statues of helmets and boots and rifles, along with Shure's statue of Ro, were added over the years, plus blast walls covered with photos.

Welcoming signs tell visitors that the memorial to these Massachusetts soldiers was modeled after elements of their daily lives in Iraq and Afghanistan and the markers they crafted themselves while serving there to honor their fallen. A memorial to memorials, in a way, a re-creation of their war zone cenotaph.

Posted nearby, drilled into a telephone pole, is a sign labeled "Helpful Information" under which a twenty-four-hour VA crisis suicide hotline number is listed along with the number of the Massachusetts Department of Veterans Services S.A.V.E. team.

As I walk between the blast walls, pausing to read each of the names, and over to Ro's statue, something catches my eye. There, I find a little rock, covered in bits of dirt and sitting on a wall. It's painted purple, with "Smile" scrawled on it in a lambent yellow, along with dots and smiley faces. The handwriting is the same as on the black-painted rock that read "Be Kind," which I found at the John Chapman memorial. I put the rock back where I found it.

I don't pretend to know the intricacies of war—or what makes a "good" death. All I know is that to die far from home must be a lonely experience, and to die so young a tragedy. As I walk out of the park, I look up at the full-sized tank. "I'm kind of a big deal" is painted on the side of its main gun barrel. I don't need to research that one. It's from the 2004 Will Ferrell vehicle, *Anchorman*. Ro apparently loved that bit of dialogue and would repeat it often.

As I leave the memorial behind me, the sky opens up and finally makes good on its promise to rain.

There are plenty of reasons to build a memorial. One is to say, "Look! Here is an important figure. They are from here, like us! Something about this area produced this incredible person. This makes us proud to be from here, too." Then there are those that mark a loss or dramatic incident. "Something truly terrible happened here, let us never forget." And then there are the ones that most of us will receive, in one small way or another, at the end of our lives: "Here is a marker to remember this person, who once lived." John Chapman's memorial in Leominster, Massachusetts, is the former, but there is one for him that is the latter, as well. It can be found in Fort Wayne, Indiana. It's not clear to me yet, as I walk away from both Chapman and Ro's memorials—Ro's, in my opinion, being all three types wrapped into one—but I am, in a way, walking toward Johnny Appleseed's resting place. I have stood at the marker of where he was born, and I will stand at the marker commemorating his death: A journey that will take me the entire year. And that will bear witness to another death I can't yet see coming.

America itself is a memorial to ideas—a rose-colored view on history, not to mention human civility. A yearning for people to be the best, most democratic versions of themselves. For us to view each other as equals. Dreams and ideals that we as a people, and as a country, fall short of time and time again. Even the idea of the small town. Quaint. Contained. But more often than not nowadays, merely places to pass through while we get to somewhere else.

Not when you're walking, though. Not when you're viewing America at eye level, moving at human pace. Which is what I do now, in the rain, slowly making my way through Leominster.

There are no sidewalks. Like this entire country, the infrastructure is built for that great invention—which was initially dreamed up in Europe but was, like so many things, perfected in terms of mass production here in America—the automobile. In the 1960s, it was estimated that the average American walked 15,000 steps a day, with 10 percent of the population walking to work. Now the average American walks 3,000 to 4,000 steps a day, with only 2.8 percent of the country living within walking distance of their jobs.

But today I am smashing those numbers, sidewalk or no. And there is one more marker worth seeing in Leominster: the grave of—like Ro, another American war veteran—Joseph Palmer.

Palmer was a veteran of the War of 1812. His gravestone reads "Persecuted for Wearing the Beard," and includes the carving of a face (presumably Palmer's) sporting a giant, resplendent, full beard. The type of beard you would see on a modern-day lead singer in a death metal band, or perhaps a lumberjack-inspired bartender, or, hell, simply a lumberjack. The grave can be found in Evergreen Cemetery in downtown Leominster right off of Palmer Drive, which is a lane in the cemetery that runs parallel to Main Street. It is easily one of my favorite graves in America.

Legend has it that Joseph Palmer, at that time a farmer, began wearing a beard in the 1820s. Now, I for one wouldn't think that would be an issue, but I'm not a historian. Apparently beards were very much *out* of fashion during that time period, so people in the area viewed Palmer as disheveled and unpresentable at best and unhygienic to the point of ungodliness at worst. There is even a story of the local preacher accosting our bearded hero, saying, "Palmer, why don't you shave and not go around looking like the devil?" To which our boy JP supposedly responded, "Are you not mistaken in your comparison of personages? I have never seen a picture of the ruler of the sulfurous regions with much of a beard, but if I remember correctly, Jesus wore a beard not unlike mine."

But the story doesn't end there. In May of 1830 Palmer was apparently attacked by four men in neighboring Fitchburg. The men were armed with razors and scissors—and one hopes some kind of shaving cream, or at least a bit of water—and attempted to forcibly shave Joseph Palmer. But Palmer, apparently, was not a man to be fucked with, and he stabbed two of his attackers with his pocketknife. Now would be a good time to remind you that this is all over *facial hair*. Nobody died, thankfully, but Palmer was put in prison for fifteen months, during which he spent time in solitary confinement and was attacked by jailers and fellow prisoners alike who wanted to, you guessed it, shave off his beard.

Now, the length of time Palmer spent in prison was somewhat his own fault, as his captors—including the initial judge who decreed him guilty in the first place—ended up begging Palmer to *leave* the prison, which he eventually did, but not before publishing letters from jail that were widely read and often mocked (these letters are why I use the word "supposedly" so much in this section, as a New England storyteller such as Palmer has been known to embellish a tale or two).

Upon leaving prison, Palmer eventually made his way to Boston, where he met philosophers and transcendentalists like Amos Bronson Alcott, William Lloyd Garrison, and Ralph Waldo Emerson. He joined the short-lived Fruitlands utopian experiment in 1843, earning him a place as a character named Moses White in a book about the commune that was written by Amos Bronson Alcott's daughter, one Louisa May Alcott. *Transcendental Wild Oats* was originally serially published in a newspaper in 1873, and is best described as a satirical look at male arrogance and female exploitation, and a sharp-tongued critique of, well, utopian communes.

Still, Palmer ended up buying the Fruitland farm himself, and attempted a couple of other communes that also didn't pan out. He died in 1873, the same year *Transcendental Wild Oats* was published. The man was a transcendentalist and an abolitionist—very much a New Englander of that era. Yet, perhaps most importantly, given his gravestone, it is worth noting that by the time of Palmer's death, beards had widely come back into fashion.

Almost exactly one hundred years before Joseph Palmer's death, John Chapman was born. Yes, both men have intriguing markers commemorating their lives in Leominster, Massachusetts, but that is not all that unites them. Chapman also didn't believe in slavery, and found himself drawn to philosophy and theology, much like Palmer. Unlike Palmer, though, Chapman was not a writer. A reader? Yes. A proselytizer? Absolutely. But the stories we have of John Chapman were written by others, not the man himself.

That said, Chapman, like Palmer, did indeed "wear the beard."

6

AFTER AN HOUR of heavy rain, the water falling from the sky does what water falling from the sky does when it's cold and evolves into snow. I take a knit cap out of my bag—glad I at least thought to pack a hat, while still cursing myself for forgetting gloves. It's an odd feeling, being so hot as to sweat, having walked miles and miles at this point, yet incredibly cold at the same time. A chilly clamminess sets in on my skin.

Between Leominster and Fitchburg I find the Twin Cities Rail Trail. Now, for most of the United States, "Twin Cities" means Minneapolis and St. Paul, but here in north central Massachusetts . . . okay, it still means Minneapolis and St. Paul, but it's a nice name for a trail linking the two neighboring, and in many ways similar, cities of Leominster and Fitchburg.

In 2004 the Twin Cities Rail Trail Association started the long, arduous journey of turning 4.7 miles of abandoned rail corridor from the Fitchburg and Worcester Railroad into a well-paved path for the area's walkers, runners, bike riders, and others. The trail opened to the public eighteen years later, in June of 2022. It was worth the wait, or at least that's how I'm feeling after miles and miles of walking along the sides of maintenance roads, highways, railroad tracks, and through people's backyards. A few other folks are out here, strolling in the light snow.

God, the flat, smooth pavement below my feet feels so good. Projects like the Twin Cities Rail Trail are happening all across America at the moment, and I say a quick prayer for more of them.

Our country should be a walkable country. I'm a big believer in what fellow son of Massachusetts Jack Kerouac calls the "great rucksack revolution" in his book *Dharma Bums,* though the quote actually comes from the character Japhy Ryder, who is a known stand-in for American poet, essayist, and environmental activist Gary Snyder. In the book, Japhy says:

> . . . A world full of rucksack wanderers, Dharma Bums refusing to subscribe to the general demand that they consume production and therefore have to work for the privilege of consuming, all that crap they didn't really want anyway . . . all of them imprisoned in a system of work, produce, consume, work, produce, consume, I see a vision of a great rucksack revolution thousands or even millions of young Americans wandering around with rucksacks, going up to mountains to pray, making children laugh and old men glad, making young girls happy and old girls happier, all of 'em Zen Lunatics who go about writing poems that happen to appear in their heads for no reason and also by being kind and also by strange unexpected acts keep giving visions of eternal freedom to everybody and to all living creatures . . .

It's a way of being that very much reminds me of John Chapman, and one I relate to as well. I call it "being a party monk," a term I use to describe anyone living a monastic life, who is almost maniacally dedicated to something—art, culture, writing, Zen Buddhism, planting trees—making life beautifully meaningful through that dedication. Through devotion. That devotion perhaps as a way of making the tedious parts of one's life bearable. Chapman spent so much time alone, roaming and planting, yet he clearly sought out community with others. Staying at people's homes. Proselytizing and preaching.

A mix of two seemingly antithetical viewpoints, or even lifestyles, brought together. The party monk.

Japhy Ryder's dream is a good dream. One that might have come to pass, if it hadn't been followed by the serial killer–fueled fear of the 1970s and the satanic panic of the 1980s. Ours is a country of private property now, of Warning: Keep Out signs. Fences and walls. Highways that turn previously walkable areas into self-contained neighborhoods, inescapable and impenetrable, often planned purposely along lines of race and class topography.

But think of it, every town with proper sidewalks—like Iceland, where there are walking paths alongside even the highways. I visited that country and was so taken by how walking was at the forefront of that country's transportation architecture. Imagine walking in safety alongside a four-lane thoroughfare. Or hell, let's dream bigger. An Appalachian Trail, but many of them, north to south across the country, but also east to west. We build throughways for wolves and deer so that they can migrate—what if we did it for ourselves?

An entire country built around walking. Citizens' step counts rising again, perhaps even surpassing those of the average American during Kerouac's era.

I dream of visiting my cousin, who lives out in San Francisco. No plane. No trains. No car or motorcycle. Just me, a pack, some time, and a very long walk to see my family.

Time would, of course, be key.

A friend recently reminded me that when I quit my previously mentioned well-paying job a few years ago—throwing myself into a rather impoverished lifestyle—I kept mentioning how excited I was to have more time for myself. "You kept saying you were going to be broke, but that you were going to be a 'time millionaire,'" he said.

I had forgotten the phrase "time millionaire," but it sounds like the type of dumb shit I'd say, along with "party monk," and it's become a loose philosophy in my life. I'd even played around with the idea of printing little business cards that read "Isaac Fitzgerald, Time Millionaire.™"

How good for this country might it be if we had more people with more time, and large trailways for those people to use as they walk this great country of ours, learning about other areas and other people along the way.

That said, there's also the cautionary tale of hitchBOT, a "robot" (more of a plastic bucket with a computer screen attached to it, no offense to the bot's creators) that successfully "hitchhiked" (technically it couldn't walk and had to be picked up by well-meaning travelers and then driven from place to place) across Canada, Germany, and the Netherlands in 2014—only to be stripped for parts and "decapitated" the next year in Philadelphia, three hundred miles into its cross-America trip from Boston to San Francisco.

To be fair, who hasn't been roughed up in Philadelphia? One robot's failure shouldn't crush a dream as beautiful as Japhy's rucksack revolution. Nor mine of walkways all across the United States.

For now, though, I'll take the Twin Cities Rail Trail and am thankful for it.

7

THE SNOW BEGINS to accumulate more than I expected earlier. The sweat from walking—especially between my pack and my back—goes from being chilly to actually freezing. My clothes become crunchy, and I realize that what I thought was going to be a light dusting is turning into a proper spring snowstorm. I've never been good at thinking ahead when packing, or thinking ahead at all. I was definitely going to need more layers.

If we do become a country of walkers, we should probably do some training—what gear to bring, how to dress properly, how to, you know, maybe check the weather before going for a 34.2-mile walk. The importance of gloves. Just a thought.

Up ahead, I see that the trailway swings by an accumulation of shops—I have made it to Fitchburg. Luckily for me, one of those shops is a Salvation Army.

I head in.

Founded in London in 1865—roughly twenty years after the death of John Chapman—the Salvation Army grew out of William Booth and his wife Catherine's East London Christian Mission. Legend has it that they changed the name in 1878 when Booth was dictating a letter to a secretary and said, "We are a volunteer army." William's son, Bramwell, cried out from the other room, "Volunteer! I'm no volunteer, I'm a regular!" Booth had the secretary replace the word "volunteer" with "salvation," and soon the organization became known as the Salvation Army, with its own flag, uniforms, and ranks—

which they still use today. What started as an attempt to get alcoholics, gamblers, and other ne'er-do-wells in London to convert to Christianity (while Catherine wooed socialites and benefactors for lavish funding) became a powerful organization that presently operates charity shops, shelters, disaster relief, and humanitarian aid in 133 countries.

Above a rack of pants in this particular Salvation Army store is a mural of William Booth next to giant letters that read "I'll Fight!" below which is a poem:

> While women weep, as they do now, I'll fight
> While little children go hungry, as they do now, I'll fight
> While men go to prison, In and out, In and out, as they do now,
>   I'll fight
> While there is a drunkard left,
> While there is a poor lost girl upon the streets,
> While there remains one dark soul without the light of God.
> I'll fight—
> I'll fight to the very end!
>
> —General William Booth

The beard Booth sports in his painted portrait would make Joseph Palmer proud.

Below the artwork a group of teenage girls pick through the bargain-basement-priced clothing, figuring out outfits and looking for those articles of apparel that feel like finding diamonds in the rough. I remember being a child and coming to this store with my ma, who would similarly go through each rack, looking for little treasures that would make me seem like someone who could afford new (to me at least) clothes for the first day of school. No matter the time period, I guess some things just stay the same.

I wait for the gaggle of girls to move on to another rack, then grab a red plaid sweatshirt that seems to fit, pay a few bucks for it, and walk back out into the cold—forgetting to buy gloves.

I am grateful for the sweatshirt as I walk out of Fitchburg and through the northern tip of the Leominster State Forest—far now from the highways, and even people's homes—a quiet stillness surrounding me. The snow is less threatening out here in the woods. More serene. Peaceful. I'm still wet and cold, of course, but at least the world around me looks comfortable wearing its new white blanket. Like something out of a Robert Frost poem, but one that lasts for hours as I cover the distance to the neighboring town.

Westminster, Massachusetts, has an idyllic downtown. Before I get there, though, I have to hike up a hill past a rundown roadside motel that gives off the feeling of an old worn-out couch. One found in a friend's basement, where you don't ask too many questions about stains or the dust that rises when you sit down. But even a questionable couch seems appealing to me now. A questionable motel even more appealing.

The snow is now accumulating into full-on drifts at a depth that makes it hard for me to walk. In the distance I spy a big, red building that has large letters on its front reading "Westminster Crackers." Before I can laugh at how well that sign describes the town's racial demographics, a snowplow drives by, and I realize that the side of the road probably isn't the safest place to be.

As I slow down to take in my surroundings, the freeze catches up with me—I notice that there are bits of crystallized ice in my beard. I stick my hands in the front pocket of my new, used flannel sweatshirt, courtesy of the Salvation Army. My hand plays with the wad of tissues my fingers find there for a second, before it registers.

I didn't bring any tissues.

Which is how I come to be outside the Westminster Crackers building (a historic one, as the actual Westminster Cracker Company is now based in Vermont) googling "Does Salvation Army wash their clothes before putting them on the rack," prayers of industrial-sized washing machines spinning in my head. My prayers are cut down by a memory of my ma, taking the clothes I had picked out at that same local Salvation Army all those years ago and demanding to wash them before I put them on.

One guess who was right.

I see lights ahead across a parking lot. As I walk toward them, I notice a clothes donation bin—probably serving the very Salvation Army I have just walked from. So far I have covered almost twenty miles. My body is frozen and aching. The snow continues to fall as the sun slowly crawls out of the sky. As I walk past snow-covered cars and trucks, the lights come into focus. One is the sign for a straightforward-looking roadside bar called the Blueprint. The other is for a fish-shack-style restaurant called the Angler Fish Market. A message on a small A-frame chalkboard advertises warm clam chowder, and all of a sudden warm clam chowder is the only thing I want in the entire world. I take a moment to really try and recall the last thing I have wanted as badly as I want a bowl of warm clam chowder at this very moment—but the desire for warm clam chowder is so strong that I can't even do that.

I struggle a bit while taking off my Salvation Army sweatshirt—but not before throwing out the tissues from the front pocket in a nearby trash can. Once I have the used, unwashed article of clothing off my ice-and-sweat-covered body, I toss it in the donation bin, hoping that the next person who buys it has better sense than I do and knows to wash it before wearing it. I pick my pack back up off the ground and head toward the one thing I desire in the entire universe: a warm bowl of clam chowder.

The restaurant is busier than I would've thought, given the weather, but I guess that the number of vehicles in the parking lot should have been a clue. It's certainly easier to drive in the snow than it is to walk.

Three things become apparent to me the moment I enter the restaurant:

First, this isn't some simple fish tavern. The place is upscale, or at least fancier than I had anticipated. Fathers are dressed in a way that—if it weren't snowing and they weren't eating lemoned salmon with their families—would fit right in at a country club bar called the 19th Hole adjacent to some stuffy golf course.

Second, now clear to you as well thanks to my use of the words "fathers" and "families," this restaurant is definitely a family establishment—at least at the early-bird-special hour of 5:30 p.m.

Lastly, I am making the clientele uncomfortable. The reason here could clearly be multifaceted. The hostess certainly gave me a once-over when I walked in. Her face winced for a moment, although whether that was simply my disheveled appearance, the large pack that I dropped a bit too loudly on the floor beside me, or something worse—an odor perhaps. *Do I smell,* I think to myself, momentarily feeling mortified.

But the warmth is too much to turn away from. The exultation that my body feels simply by being inside. I say a quick prayer, "Praise be to roofs." Not to mention the smell that fills the air—a smell that isn't me. I swear I can pinpoint it, somewhere in the back.

The smell of warm clam chowder.

"Can I help you?" The woman who first greets me is straightforward, in a New England–style way that feels familiar—not welcoming, but familiar. She is *not* the hostess, to be clear, whom she nods at as if to say, "Don't worry, this is above your pay grade, kid. I'll handle it." I watch as the young hostess disappears into the back, but not before checking in with a few tables along the way. It's all happy smiles and niceties, intermingled with quick, curious glances aimed in my direction.

The older woman in front of me looks over my shoulder for a minute, and I follow her gaze. There's a large window at the front of the room where we're standing, out of which the entire parking lot is visible. Snow is falling—you can see my bootprints leading up to the restaurant illuminated by the streetlights. I catch the people sitting at the front table staring at me, and then looking away. I turn and glance back out the window.

Which is when I see it. The donation bin at the other end of the lot. I now realize that everyone—at least everyone at the *front* of the restaurant—would have seen me walk off the main road, take my pack off, struggle to take off my Salvation Army sweatshirt, my belly almost certainly exposing itself for all to see as I tried to pull it off. They then watched as I tossed the sweatshirt in the bin, for what reason? They have no idea, knowing nothing of newly discovered tissues, only knowing that I took the time to drop *something* in the nearby garbage can first. Then they watched as I, like something out of a slow-moving, low-stakes (or perhaps *not* low-stakes, who can say) horror movie, paused in the middle of the parking lot to weigh the two options of potential eateries, then shuffled my way ever closer, until I entered the one that they were in, dropping my bag—which holds God knows what—at my feet as I now stand before them.

"Well? *Can I help you?*"

"Uh, yeah. I was hoping to warm up with some clam chowder."

I look at the families eating, many of them still glancing over at me—it's almost certainly simple curiosity. A harmless interest: "What's going on here?" But it's also not too difficult for me to imagine higher anxieties. It's normal to want to protect your family. We live in a country where shootings and attacks in public places have become commonplace, almost always perpetrated by men. Here I stand, covered in tattoos, dressed in bulky clothing, a large pack at my feet.

Or maybe my frozen beard just looks funny.

"But listen," I go on. "This place is a li'l nicer than I assumed when I was out front—not that there's anything wrong with the front!"

The woman's scowl grows.

"It's no trouble. Maybe I'll try the bar a few doors down."

I start to leave.

"Doubt they're gonna have chowder, honey. Certainly not chowder as good as ours. If you're willing, we've got a room in the back where you can stow your gear. We've also got a single stool seat back there. The table is more of a shelf that's screwed into the wall—and it's between our two bathrooms—but if it works for you, I'll happily seat you there."

Soon I am sitting exactly where the woman described—no better, no worse. It feels so good to have my bag off, and to know that I won't have to put it back on again in mere moments. A few minutes after I sit, the most perfect bowl of clam chowder I have ever had is resting in front of me. I can't be sure, but the way the woman brought it to me, without me asking—was that her way of offering the bowl for free? Or was she wary of whether my next move was going to be offering to wash dishes for an hour instead of paying my bill? To be honest, I'll never know, because soon the contents of the bowl were warming my belly, and I had called a waitress over and ordered a second bowl, along with a couple of bottles of hard cider—the first of which I demolished in one gigantic, continuous gulp—and then asked to see a menu.

I notice that the oyster crackers I put in my chowder are from the Westminster Cracker Company. Nice touch.

People waiting to use the restrooms make conversation with me, at first making jokes about me being the bouncer for the toilets—"Are you charging to let folks in?"—but soon it turns into comments about how many bowls, plates, and bottles I am accumulating as I stuff myself with chowder, cider, salmon, and halibut.

"Not sure that shelf can hold all that, big fella," a man—almost certainly a father—says while clapping me on the back. It's an odd feeling to register, but my body does register it. After a day of walking by myself, that is the first human touch I have received. It feels good. Both the clap on the back, but also the clearness that this room, at first hesitant, has now accepted me.

Growing up, a child in the Catholic Church, I took the stories of the Bible quite literally, as children tend to do. My favorite stories—after the usual hits, of course, such as David and Goliath, Jonah and the Whale, Jesus and the Fish—always involved angels. Angels battling demons, angels trumpeting good news, angels at the Battle of Jericho, angels saving Isaac from Abraham's knife (in what can only be described as God's best troll in the entire Bible).

But it was always the simpler tales that I truly loved. A traveler knocks on a door. The traveler is road-weary and dirty. "Can you spare some bread? Maybe water? Perhaps a place to spend the night?" Much like Joseph and Mary on the night of Jesus's birth. "Is there room at the inn?"

"Perhaps a bowl of warm clam chowder?"

Of course, then the angel would reveal their true identity—a heavenly creature sent to test the kindness of mortals. The lesson was clear: Be hospitable, tenderhearted, and generous to strangers. You never know who might be an angel in disguise.

In my young brain, this translated into giving money—money my struggling parents didn't have—to any panhandler we met on the streets of Boston. So much so that my parents, themselves members of the Catholic Worker, would often know the person asking for spare change and give them a nod, with the person saying, "I'm okay today, Isaac," so as not to hit my poor parents up so often on account of their overly-generous-and-extremely-bad-with-money son.

As for John Chapman, well, he often put himself on the "*Am* I an angel?" receiving end of the charity, never having a home and relying on strangers for food and a place to sleep the night. As a Swedenborgian, Chapman very much believed in angels—Swedenborg himself claimed to have been visited by angels, and told that God on high had selected him, Emanuel Swedenborg, to convey new understandings of the Scriptures to humanity.

Now, here in Westminster, I look around the room. I too need a place to crash, but this early in my journey I don't yet have John Chapman's level of confidence: I'm hesitant to ask a stranger if they have room by their fireplace, or radiator, or, you know, home air central heating vent. That said, walking down the hill to a dingy motel I saw earlier seems a mighty cop-out, no matter the weather. Like any good procrastinator, I decide to delay my decision and swing by the bar I saw earlier to plan my next move.

Before I go, though—I'm no heavenly creature, far from it, but I can at least prove to the staff that I can afford all the food I ate and the ciders I drank and leave them with a hefty tip on top of that. I do so, thanking the staff profusely as I leave. The first woman I spoke with—a smile now on her face—hands me my pack and says, "Good luck out there," as she swings open the restaurant's front door and lets me out into the night.

8

THE BLUEPRINT HAS a large, long rectangular bar smack-dab in the middle of the room. Nobody looks twice at me, and when I sit down a friendly couple canoodling over their drinks take a quick break from their belly-to-the-bar cuddling to make room for me and my heaving bag. I nod in appreciation.

After the comfort of my fish-filled feast, the shock of being outdoors again depressed me almost immediately. Exposed to the cold night air, I was reassured that my decision to go to the bar a few doors down was a good one.

There's a band playing in the corner, on a small makeshift stage, and I sit and listen to them churn out what seems to be a mix of covers and original music. Every other song or so, the couple to my right, or other folks around the bar, stand up and dance. Nothing wild or chaotic—simply head-on-shoulder two-steps with a few quiet twists and twirls thrown in for good measure. With the snow falling outside catching in the lights of the parking lot, it makes for a charming scene. A community of people coming together to listen to live music, dance a little, and maybe find a warm body to push up against and fend off the chilly night for a bit. I order myself a hard cider and settle in.

Sadly, though, I have no time for dancing. My feast at the Angler took up a bit of time, and somehow I'm already on my second cider here at the Blueprint, which—when paired with the ciders I had over dinner—well, it's safe to say these beverages are no longer simply warming my bones, but beginning to affect my decision-making skills. I think about the basement-couch of the motel at the bottom of the hill. How easy it would be to sling my backpack over my shoulders and tipsily spill down to the motel's front desk and order a room. I could lay out my sleeping bag on top of the covers and drift off to sleep—and awaken in the morning, warm, and make myself some terrible-but-at-least-hot coffee in the room's cheap, plastic, tiny one-cup coffeemaker.

The band kicks into a more upbeat song, which snaps me out of my meandering, wishful dreams of a cheap-but-still-cozy bed. I'm beginning to realize that this Johnny Appleseed walk is going to be the first of many. There's no way in hell I can sleep inside. John Chapman wouldn't have slept inside, often electing to sleep under the stars, or in hollowed-out tree stumps. Well, okay—that's of course not the whole story. Chapman did sometimes sleep indoors, though after childhood he never had a home of his own, matching his nomadic lifestyle. But he did make many friends in his travels, who would often put him up. Or, in certain cases, he would proselytize—reading from his religious literature in exchange for some bread and a warm fire to sleep by.

In his biography, *Johnny Appleseed: Man and Myth,* Dr. Robert Price cites many primary sources from the time period who reported that Chapman would knock on doors and cry out his "famous greeting, 'Fresh news from heaven,'" before coming in, laying down his knapsack, and reading from the Emanuel Swedenborg writings that he carried with him—reportedly in his cap, which may be the origin of the oft-quoted but almost certainly wrong assertion that his hat was a tin pot.

So if Chapman had friends in the area, he probably *would* have slept indoors; but I don't have any friends in the area—nor any writings to read from—and that's beside the point. I can't throw in the towel so easily. I said I am going to sleep outside, not in a sleeping bag on top of a stain-covered bed in a cheap motel. I take out my phone and look at a map of the surrounding area.

Luckily, aside from the small downtown where I'm currently sitting, Westminster looks like it is surrounded by a lot of woods. I figure I would leave the Blueprint (after a few glasses of water, which seemed like a smart idea—and maybe one or two more ciders for the road, which at this point was certainly a *dumb* idea, but to be honest this whole walk was starting to seem like a dumb idea, so what harm could a couple more dumb ideas possibly do?) and hike down Main Street until Route 2A splits off, which I would then follow. There looked to be a big patch of undeveloped green space along 2A on either side of the road not far outside of town, which is where I figured I'd jump a guardrail, walk a bit into the woods, and set up camp.

Which is exactly what I do—after the aforementioned glasses of water and what turned out to be three ciders aka dumb ideas as I told myself the last one would help gird me against the cold, but truly it was just me killing time as I listened to the band play, watched the people dance, and did my damnedest to stay out of the snow for as long as possible.

Though, perhaps those three dumb ideas weren't all that dumb, as by the time I left the Blueprint the snow was finally stopping.

I stumble down Main Street, humming a tune the band had played—to keep warm, I tell myself—but more likely because of the drinks. Soon the quaint lights of downtown Westminster are behind me and I am entering into the darkness. The roads have been cleared by plows, but the sidewalks are still covered. I crunch through the snow until the sidewalks halt and continue on, merely sticking to the side of the road, but I needn't worry. No cars are out.

The sky is no longer dumping snow on me, but it is still covered with clouds, so there are no moon or stars to speak of.

I jump a guardrail, just as I had pictured, and cut through the underbrush and into the forest. I am happy to see that there are no signs of any houses nearby, so I walk deeper into the woods—being sure to keep the road on my left—and feel confident that, while I almost certainly am not supposed to camp here, I am not trespassing on any private citizen's property. I pay my taxes, surely some state forest could stand to let me crash for the night.

Walking through the snow-encrusted trees, I get the eerie sense that I am not alone. I keep looking over my shoulder, but all I see is darkness. The ciders probably don't help, but my brain starts remembering that mountain lions had returned to the area in the last few decades.

When I was a kid, my friend Ryan King had told his parents—and then the police—that he had seen one of the sleek, hay-colored animals in his backyard. Everyone dismissed him. Mountain lions had not been seen in Massachusetts since colonial times, when settlers killed the majestic creatures *en masse* to protect their livestock. Man had driven them out.

But Ryan hadn't been wrong, and he hadn't been lying.

Not two years after Ryan was told that he'd probably only seen a large house cat—in April of 1998—a tracker named John McCarter found scat near a beaver carcass at the Quabbin Reservoir, not far from Ryan's house. McCarter sent samples to the Wildlife Conservation Society in New York and the University of Maryland. Both samples were confirmed to be the scat of a mountain lion. A decade and a half later, in March of 2011, forester Steve Ward photographed an animal track left in the snow, again by the Quabbin Reservoir. Three tracking experts examined the photograph and confirmed the track was indeed that of a mountain lion.

The government of Massachusetts—while acknowledging these two cases—maintains that "there is no evidence of a reproducing mountain lion population" in the state.

Still.

As I walk out of town and deeper into the forest, I swear I hear the crunch of padded paws on the snow. I shake my head and tell myself that it is just my imagination, much as people had once told Ryan.

I too had a run-in with a wild animal in my youth. When my parents fought, our shabby house stuffed with the cacophony of their anger—fury toward one another and what their lives had become—I would escape the caterwauling and go for long walks in the surrounding wilderness. Less charming than the White Mountain stories, but another way I learned the importance of walking from my parents.

On one of those lonely rambles, in a mess of pine trees on the side of a hill about a mile away from the yelling and violence, I came face-to-face with what I thought was a wolf, but would later learn from a library encyclopedia was a coyote.

If the animal was surprised by my presence, it didn't let on. It lowered its head in a threatening manner. My body froze, even as every cell that made up my being told me—on a molecular level—to flee. I looked into the wild animal's eyes and it looked back into mine. My parents' unhappiness and rage suddenly felt so insignificant. Nothing mattered except what happened next.

I refused to look away, which may have seemed like some form of bravery to an outsider, but was simply a deep-seated fear of making any movement at all.

Maybe it was the eye contact, but after a few painstaking moments, the not-yet-identified-as-a-coyote coyote relaxed its head and sniffed the air. It came to the conclusion that a nine-year-old was not a threat, I guess, and simply trotted off into the wooded darkness.

Again my body cried out to run, but I worried it might cause the animal to give chase. I walked back to my house, convinced that the mass of muscle, fur, and teeth followed behind me, just out of sight.

Which is how I feel through the night I spend outside of Westminster—hunted, haunted, or both.

There is a break in the trees—and not just a break, but a giant space opens up ahead. With no natural light to help I can still tell where the trees stop. I decide to set up camp just a few trees' distance from the wide-open expanse in front of me. On the horizon I see headlights cutting through the swath of night, and thus am able to make out the road I have just left.

I am tempted, for a moment, to walk into the field. The forest isn't without its frightful, mountain-lion-shaped shadows, and sleeping in a field seemed more romantic than at the edge of the woods. From what I can make out, before me is a perfect blanket of untouched snow stretching into the darkness. But I am tired, and if it starts snowing again I will be grateful for the tree cover. I turn on my iPhone flashlight, wary about using up my battery, and make camp.

Although "make camp" makes it sound like I am doing it easily. Not so. When my father had shown me how to set up the small bivouac tent in his living room, he had encouraged me to do so over and over again, until I could unfold the lightweight metal poles, extend them out, and thread them through the small nylon holes of the bivvy with my eyes closed. But I didn't listen.

"Do you want to try again?" my father asked, but I assured him I had it. An assurance I now regretted as my freezing fingers tried again and again to find the right hole for the right pole, like some teenager unable to make heads nor tails of their first sexual experience.

For a brief moment I worry I'd ripped the tent, and I think about retracing my steps in the snow back to the road, then back to the light of town, and then down the hill and to the now, and still to this day, shittiest hotel I have ever coveted. But right as I am going to give up is, of course, when the poles start gliding into the proper parts of the tent—fully constructed it's only centimeters bigger than my sleeping bag, and just as low to the earth.

I half-heartedly dig out some snow and do my best to at least set the bivouac tent on even ground. Then I unfurl my sleeping bag, place it in the tent along with my pack (which I use as a pillow), kick off my shoes (which I use to hold my pack-pillow in place), crawl inside, and zip the tent closed. I sit there, not especially cold, but certainly not warm either, and miss the sweatshirt that I had tossed back in the donation bin, while at the same time worrying it could have given me a rash or perhaps have some small mites that, at this very moment, may be feasting on my skin the way I feasted on so much seafood back at the Angler.

In my head, the mites begin to dance, and then some fish and clams join them, along with apples and a large mountain lion leading a pack of waltzing coyotes. Soon the band is playing and before I can even realize it—because how can one really realize such a thing—I have drifted off to sleep.

9

I WAKE UP to the sound of dripping. It takes me a minute to realize what is happening: the snow is melting, and water is falling from the branches of the trees, large drops of which are bouncing off the top of my extremely small tent—and threatening to force their way inside.

In the middle of the night, I had woken up—or at least I thought I had—hearing something that sounded a lot like sniffing around my tent. I remembered the feeling I'd had earlier, as if a creature was following me. But what animal—other than myself—would be dumb enough to be out in this snow? The only answer my addled brain could come up with was "a very hungry one."

Come morning I half expect to find paw prints in the snow, but there are none.

One of the most enduring John Chapman legends is one where he befriends a wolf.

The tale goes that Johnny Appleseed came upon the wild beast—which was caught in a steel trap—while walking through the forests of Ohio. The wolf was badly hurt and snarling in fear. Instead of walking away or deciding to mercifully end the creature's life, Chapman carefully freed the wolf and treated its wounded leg. Over time, the animal healed, and—amazingly—it didn't run off. Instead, it started following John wherever he went, and became his companion, like a loyal dog.

In the legend, the wolf served as both protector and friend, walking with Chapman through the wilderness and sometimes guarding him as he slept.

Historically, there's no verified evidence that John Chapman had a pet wolf—but the story likely grew from his well-documented kindness to animals and love of nature.

While we're on Chapman and animals, there's also a rumor that he heard of a horse that was going to be put down, so he purchased the animal, bought a few grassy acres for it to live on, and eventually gave the horse to somebody else after they swore that they would treat it humanely.

Chapman's love of animals went so far as to extend to all living creatures—even mosquitos. In a dishy, if perhaps not entirely accurate, 1800s history of Ohio, there's a story of John extinguishing his fire when he realized the pesky bloodsuckers were lured to their own demise by the flames' light. Chapman is quoted as saying, "God forbid that I should build a fire for my comfort, that should be the means of destroying any of His creatures."

Some even argue that Chapman was a vegetarian. And, while there's no way of verifying that claim for sure, it *is* worth noting that in the early 1820s—when John Chapman was in his midforties—what was perhaps the first vegetarian community in America was established in Philadelphia by Reverend William Metcalfe and his followers, all of whom were influenced by the teachings of Emanuel Swedenborg.

Back in the forest on the edge of Westminster's downtown, I can see my breath, but the sun outside is promising. It hadn't snowed much more overnight, and when I unzip the front of the tent I am greeted by a bright, white, winter-in-spring wonderland, sunlight bouncing every which way and a giant blue sky above me. Realizing that I am relatively dry and have made it through the night makes me smile, and I climb out of my tent.

But what looked like a field to me in the moonless, starless night is very much *not* a field in the cold light of day. The snow is still there, but I realize what I thought was a field was actually a marsh. A very large, cold, wet marsh.

I walk up to the marsh's edge, not ten feet or so from where I set up my tent, and grab a nearby sturdy stick and thrust it into the snow in front of me—remembering all the while my plan to perhaps walk out into the "field" the night before. The stick goes through the snow, a thin layer of ice, on into surprisingly deep water, and down into a stifling muck. I let go of the stick—now most of it in the freezing water and mud—and what little pokes above snow stands on its own.

"Fuck," I mutter to nobody other than myself, thankful that I decided to stay close to the forest's edge—almost certain that I would have made a different decision if I'd had one more hard cider in me. It's those little mistakes you hear about that lead to someone losing a toe or two to frostbite—or maybe something even more dire.

I say a quick prayer of thanks that my cold night had at least been a dry one, but right then a flit of movement catches my eye. I look up from the mostly submerged stick and adjust to the sunlight bouncing off the ice and snow. Out in the middle of the . . . swamp? marsh? pond? I see a large black dog. Not the not-wolf coyote of my childhood, nor an actual wolf, nor Ryan's mountain lion or any other fearsome predator. This is a large black *dog*. Its hair is shaggy—almost matted, as if it has lived outside for a long time. It is too far away to know for sure, but it looks like a large Irish wolfhound. I get the feeling that the dog, unmoving, is looking right back at me , and had been waiting on its haunches for me to wake up.

For a moment I think it might be Susie Q, the dog from yesterday, but of course it isn't possible.

The hair on my neck rises, partially out of nervousness, or embarrassment—or maybe it's a weird form of reverence. . . . I break what feels like eye contact between us and turn my glance back down to the stick that is still protruding out of the muck, water, and ice.

But wait, I think. *How was the dog—*

I whip my head back up, wondering how the dog could possibly be out there in the first place. But when I look back, it is gone. Vanished.

The hair on my neck lies flat again, but an uneasy feeling stays with me.

I decide to follow my footsteps back through the woods and to the road. As I walk, I am grateful for my father's broken-in leather boots, thinking of the much-heralded legends of John Chapman walking through blizzards and over frozen rivers wearing nary a shoe, sandal, nor sock. A barefoot wanderer. That said, there are in fact records of Chapman buying shoes and moccasins—although there are also many first-person accounts of him being shoeless. And to be fair, who can prove he wore the footwear he purchased? Perhaps they were for trade. But, much more likely is that the man went barefoot from time to time, but wore shoes as well—that the legends of him walking through snowdrifts without protective footwear are blown out of proportion.

For a moment, I think of taking my foot out of my tightly tied boot, pulling off my sock, and dipping my bare skin into the snow just to see how it would feel. But knowing how many miles I still have in front of me, I realize that doing so would be idiotic, even for me, and keep on walking.

I continue along Route 2A. The day is sublime, and most drivers give me room when they pass me on the road—hell, some of them even wave. I divert off for a bit, hoping for a break from all the traffic, friendly or not, and walk along Livermore Hill Road, past rusted-out trucks with trees growing through them, and one house that seems to be home to a stock car racer, gorgeous beat-up vehicles in different states of disrepair, as well as repair, scattered across the house's lawn. The snow is melting fast now, and today feels like what I was hoping yesterday would be: the first true day of spring.

Not far past the scrapyard is a field of solar panels, as far as the eye can see. Of course they look black and still, as solar power panels always look—but in my mind they are thirstily drinking up the sunlight after yesterday's storm.

This is the story of a lot of New England—and really, America—the remnants of the past (old trucks discarded long enough for large trees to grow through them) mixed with the present (a young person's dreams of racing stock cars, nary a single sapling touching the undercarriage of a vehicle) with a brush of the future cresting on the horizon (a field of solar panels that surely weren't there ten or maybe even five years before). Giant white wind turbines can be seen throughout the area, while some people still get around in the summer by horse and buggy. New technologies are discovered quicker than old technologies die out or fall out of favor. Something about living in this era feels . . . like you can be a bit of a time traveler, depending on where you go, or what you seek out, or—unfairly—how much money you have in your bank account.

Maybe it was always like this, I can only speak to the time I'm in now, but I take a rest while I look at the old trucks with trees through them, then swivel my head toward the bright new panels that can harness the power of the sun. A juxtaposition that, to be honest, I don't hate. Industrial beauty.

Funnily enough, that juxtaposition seems to be the theme of my entire day walking through the outskirts of Westminster and into

Gardner, Massachusetts. I pass Greenwood Pond, and more abandoned vehicles can be seen past the tree line. There's Kay's Dairy Bar, which serves seafood and burgers as well as ice cream—closed for the season, it would seem, but I wonder a bit at how much fresh seafood Westminster can boast, here in the hills so far from the Atlantic. But Kay's Dairy Bar, like the cars in the woods across the street, gives off a 1950s or '60s vibe. It's easy to picture waiters and waitresses on roller skates as patrons eat in their vehicles and place orders for more fries through two-way radios connected to the kitchen.

The thought of fries makes me hungry, but I do my best to ignore the slowly building ache in my stomach, reminding myself of the feast I had the night before.

A great blue heron flies overhead and shakes me back into the present moment. I am crossing over the town line into Gardner, Massachusetts. Walking along the side of the road I see bits of trash, including a curious number of discarded Monster energy drinks, as well as empty nips of Smirnoff vodka. But in front of me, one of my favorite sights: a sidewalk.

"Siiidewalk. Siiidewalk. I love when I see a siiidewalk," I sing out loud to myself, which I then immediately stop doing. It seems a bit too early in my journey to start talking aloud to oneself, let alone singing.

To my left is a boatyard, with numerous dry-docked vessels up in ship cradles. At first my tired brain is confused. The scene is something you'd see in Gloucester, New Bedford, or Rockport—any seaside town. Gardner is about sixty miles from the ocean. But then I remember the existence of lakes.

It's becoming clearer and clearer to me that my brain is tired.

Gardner—much like the town I grew up in, and Leominster, and Fitchburg, and numerous others in the area—is an industrial town, but one where much of the industry has left, first moving down south, and then overseas. With that said, there seems to have been a resurgence of sorts, catering more to families and workers who want a bit more bang for their buck and don't mind commuting into Boston, which is about an hour's drive away (without traffic, it should be noted).

I've seen this happening in places all over America—again, my hometown included. In the '80s and '90s chains and strip malls moved in, creating new cathedrals to commerce that destroyed the small, independently owned businesses that made up Main Street. Soon Main Streets were shuttered, and everyone was driving to the outskirts of town—where the land was cheapest, so the corporate developers could buy it right up. This brought a convenience, not to mention more affordable prices, and options that you previously had to drive to other areas to experience. But, on the other hand, it turned much of this country into the same recurring strip malls and businesses over and over again. Have you tried the Applebee's in Hadley? How about in Chicopee? What about in Portsmouth, New Hampshire?

Much in the same way broadcast television started the slow decline of regional accents across the country, so did the strip malls and chain stores bring about an American monotony, with all the money going to a few large companies instead of staying in local communities.

But now, as often happens throughout history, the pendulum is beginning to swing back. The malls and corporate chain stores are no longer shiny and new. Often they are understaffed, and those low, low costs seem to be less low every year. The previously mentioned families and workers who are looking for more space and to save some money by not living in the city aren't going to move to a place simply because it has the best-rated TGI Fridays in the area, but they very well might be charmed by a cozy little main street filled with unique, delightful shops.

I am thinking all of this as I walk through the southern end of Gardner on East Broadway, which eventually turns into West Broadway—an area that was mostly shuttered when I was growing up, but now has new, locally owned businesses filling the once empty windows. Past the small shops and residential area there are fitness centers and auto-body shops, and a drug and alcohol rehab center as well. Keeping things tuned up—a focus on maintenance and upkeep. I take it as a sign that the area is improving, bit by bit.

Two long blocks later, though, I'd be lying if I didn't say there was a Verizon store, and a Starbucks, and a Papa Gino's, and a 99 Restaurant (the last two of which are at least local to Massachusetts, the original 99 opening up on 99 State Street in Boston in the 1950s and the original Papa Gino's opening up in East Boston in 1961), amongst a smattering of other chain stores. All of these are there to service the commuters on Route 2 more than the residential community, and, while they are an eyesore, I shouldn't complain too much.

I take a rest on a concrete step outside of the Starbucks. If I took a car, I could be home in twenty-one minutes. Walking will take me five and a half hours—and that's without breaks. I stand up and keep putting one foot in front of the other.

10

When you walk long enough, your pack—which has in reality been growing heavier by the hour all day long—suddenly starts to feel lighter. Your sweat—up until then sticky and uncomfortable or cold and freezing—begins to feel different, almost refreshing. You stop feeling your feet, which is a blessing. Because up until that moment, *all* you've felt is your feet.

Walking becomes euphoric, and that euphoria carries me out of Gardner and into East Templeton. But there the euphoria stops. Suddenly, my pack is a refrigerator strapped to my back. My sweat makes me cold again, wet clothes clinging to my skin. My feet are a bundle of raw, exposed nerves and my boots—which up until this moment had served me *perfectly*—feel like they are practically bolted to the ground.

I sit on a guardrail at the side of the road, my pack at my feet, and think about hiking up the hill behind me. I could sit in a diner I passed and have a coffee, maybe eat some food—get my energy back up. But the hill seems daunting, and I'd have to recross the waterway I'd just traversed, the East Templeton Pond, something that I barely would have noticed if I'd been driving in a car, but walking the length of it not once but twice lacks a certain appeal.

I turn and look in front of me. Farther down the road is an old New England graveyard. I have passed so many of them on this walk.

But across the street from the cemetery, a place of peace, community, family values, and warmth.

The name on its sign hasn't been changed yet, so it still reads Dunkin' Donuts, the way God intended—not the abstract, lonely Dunkin' that is now favored by the company. I think for a moment about the McDonald's in my hometown of Athol, Massachusetts: the first big chain to arrive in the area, before the Subway and the Wal-Mart and the recently added Hobby Lobby. That McDonald's was the tip of the spear for all the chains that came after it—sucking what little money there was out of the area and sending it back to some corporate headquarters, instead of allowing it to circulate within the community. Which was maybe why somebody started the rumor, all those years ago, that—as the new McDonald's was *also* across from a cemetery—they made their hamburger patties from the decaying bodies of past residents.

The legends we write in small towns.

Still, I figure you don't need corpses to make coffee, so I promise myself a long rest at the Dunkin' Donuts, despite the fact that by doing so I am falling victim to the very thing that let these corporate vacuum cleaners suck money out of small, rural communities in the first place: sacrificing my ideals at the altar of convenience.

A string of cars wraps around the building, early morning motorists hungry for their daily liquid stimulant. But inside there is no line, only an elderly couple holding hands across the melamine tabletop between them. They're talking about this morning's church service, which makes me realize that it's a Sunday.

"What can I get you?"

The woman behind the counter is as old as the couple holding hands—maybe older. Behind her, a troupe of teenagers execute service industry choreography: hash browns microwaved, breakfast sandwiches assembled, sugar dumped into unseasonably iced coffees.

"Uhhhh," I look up at the menu, never having ordered anything other than an "iced coffee, regular" at a Dunkin' Donuts in my entire life and say, "A large iced matcha latte, please."

The woman's eyebrows go up, and mine do, too. My exhaustion has ordered for me. Never before in my life have I ordered a matcha, and certainly not a matcha at Dunkin' Donuts.

"To each their own. One large iced matcha latte coming right up."

Soon I'm holding a tall, iced-filled bright green drink. I nod hello at the old churchgoers as I sit down in a booth on the other side of the room. By the time my ass hits the chair, the plastic cup in front of me is empty. A delicious, addictive flavor is already escaping my tongue. My tired body—a lightning bolt of sugar and whole milk flying through it—cries out for more. I stand back up and order another, extra large this time. And then another. When all is said and done, four massive plastic Dunkin' cups sit on the table in front of me. The old couple flash me a quizzical look.

"It's good," I say, and they laugh. The woman behind the counter laughs, too. I feel . . . not refreshed. Not reenergized. But as if I can endure.

And endure I do, through Templeton—a town I went to for ice cream as a child and once, only once, got into a fight with half-a-stand full of football fans while watching my best friend, Conner, play for our local high school. There was a bad call, and I was drunk from parking-lot Jim Beam. Soon I was swinging wildly and, mere moments later, getting my head rightfully stomped on. That was probably the last time I had set foot in Templeton, instead of simply driving through. As I walk by the town center I decide not to linger.

Near where Route 202, Route 2, and Route 2A—the road I'm currently walking—all intersect, there is a sign for the King Phillip Restaurant & Lounge. I've never eaten there, nor will I stop now. I'm slightly over seven miles from my destination. My feet are on fire. My brain can barely hold a thought. But at least I'm starting to recognize my surroundings. I could walk home from here without a map.

The King Phillip Restaurant sign shoots a memory through my weary mind—a King Philip bowling alley where I used to attend friends' birthday parties when I was growing up. In fact, King Philip is a phrase you'll find throughout north central Massachusetts and beyond (sometimes spelled correctly, with one "L," or other times colloquially and incorrectly, with two "L"s). The road I'm heading to—the end of this particular journey, even—is my parents' house on Philip Road.

I first learned about King Philip's War as an elementary student, that ever-important moment when one finds out that the story of Thanksgiving and peaceful relationships between English colonizers and the Indigenous peoples had been, up until that moment, rather glossed over. It is a war with many other names: the First Indian War, the Great Narragansett War, or the clearly one-sided Metacom's Rebellion. The conflict took place between 1675 and 1676—although its aftershocks continued to rock New England, especially in what is now Maine, until 1677. As with any conflict of such magnitude during a historic time, it is a hard story to map.

But, to summarize, the Wampanoag tribe (along with the Nipmuck, Podunk, Narragansett, Nashaway, and Wabanaki) banded together in a final attempt to stop unrelenting colonization by what would come to be known as the New England Confederation. The colonists had native allies as well (mainly the Mohegan, Pequot, and Mohawk), much like what would happen again during the French and Indian War—itself a part of the Seven Years' War—some seventy or so years later.

Other than land theft—and really, what further justification do you need for a war?—what other issues were there? Well, the white colonists wanted to limit the Native Americans' access to guns—the question of "who has the right to own a gun" being one that would be argued until the ratification of the Second Amendment on December 15, 1791 (and then, luckily, never cause any issues ever again). There was also, you know, the persistence of these foreigners who kept promising not to move inland and then kept doing exactly that—expecting the Native population not just to peacefully give up their lands, but also to follow the colonists' laws and ways of life instead of the way they had been living happily enough for the previous, oh, fourteen thousand years or so.

Metacom was the son of Massasoit, who had strong relations with the colonists of the early 1600s, especially those at Plymouth, Massachusetts, aka the location of the first Thanksgiving. At the time, Massasoit was trying to protect his tribe from the Narragansett, and so made a lasting peace with the newly arrived white people. Upon Massasoit's death in 1661, Metacom—along with his brother Wamsutta—went to Plymouth and asked the pilgrims for English names. Metacom received the name Philip, and his brother the name Alexander. Wamsutta would die within the year, leaving Metacom the leader of the Wampanoag. While we're on the subject of Massasoit's children, he had five—only his daughter Amie would survive the coming war.

Metacom became the leader of the Wampanoag in 1662, and soon after realized that the peace alliance that his father had made with the Pilgrims had, shall we say, diminishing returns. In a 1671 peace treaty, the white folks demanded—as previously mentioned—that the Native Americans surrender their guns. Not an easy genie to get back into the bottle. Then, three Wampanoag were hanged in Plymouth. The execution was punishment for those three murdering *another* Wampanoag—John Sassamon, who was an early-Harvard-educated Native American who had converted to Christianity, and was at times referred to as the "praying Indian." Sassamon was apparently trying to keep the peace. His murder and the ensuing trial led to quite the opposite.

But, again, nobody likes another culture's rules forced upon them. Soon colonial towns, villages, settlements, and homesteads were under attack throughout what would come to be known as the states of Rhode Island, Massachusetts, Connecticut, and Maine—and the self-proclaimed peaceful Pilgrims were raising militias to fight back. A time of wary coexistence had collapsed into violence—although an argument could be made that the violence began when the colonizers showed up on the country's rocky shores to begin with.

In the end, an estimated thousand colonists and three thousand Native Americans had died—the latter's population already greatly diminished because of epidemics brought by the colonizers from Europe (often spread intentionally). Skirmishes continued in the north and throughout the white-pushed frontier. The Wampanoag and Narragansett—two former enemies coming together to fight the English colonists—were almost wiped out.

That's one hell of an epilogue to put on the first Thanksgiving. And, let's be honest, that was simply the beginning of the epilogue—what would become an all-out genocide against an entire people that would continue for generations.

But what about Metacom, or King Philip, as he became known to the white people of the time? Slowly he began losing his allies—at one point he even took refuge at Assawompset Pond, where John Sassamon had been found dead at the beginning of the war. Eventually he crossed over into what would become Rhode Island, where he was shot and killed on August 12, 1676, by a Native American named John Alderman, a member of a militia led by Captain Josiah Standish—son of famed English colonist and English military officer Myles Standish, who had once helped broker a peace with Metacom's father, Massasoit, and the Plymouth Colony's then governor, John Carver.

Metacom's corpse was decapitated, drawn and quartered, and his head placed on a pike and displayed at the entrance of Plymouth for *multiple* decades—a rather brutal act of performative revenge that is not forgotten to history. In fact, a 2019 play by Daniel Glenn humorously mocks, amongst other things, bureaucracy, as the play's colonists decide the right time to take Metacom's skull down in the perfectly titled *King Philip's Head Is Still on That Pike Just Down the Road*.

King Philip's War locked in the concept of needing a militia ready to muster quickly for these new English colonies—ensuring further conflicts with regional Indigenous people as well as the French and, eventually, their own parental government, the British. Over the course of the next three centuries, King Philip's name went on to be used for roads, bowling alleys, and the restaurant I'm passing right now advertising Steaks • Seafood • Italian Specialties.

New England, and eventually America, is filled with stories like this one: gruesome histories of conflict and violence, turned into logos and slogans to help sell Tuesday dinner specials and living room sets. Hell, even the name of the commonwealth itself, Massachusetts, came from an Indigenous tribe, the Massachusett—or Muhsachuweesut—which means "near the great hill," or "by the blue hills," referencing the Blue Hills south of Boston. The tribe was hit with an outbreak of leptospirosis in 1619, with mortality rates as high as 90 percent. Not long after, the arrival of European colonists brought other devastating epidemics—smallpox, influenza, scarlet fever. The tribe was almost completely wiped out.

Those blue hills, by the way, are now an expansive park that covers seven thousand acres in Quincy, Dedham, Milton, Randolph, and Canton, boasting "scenic views, varied terrain, and 125 miles of trails for year-round enjoyment by outdoor enthusiasts."

Capitalism seems especially adept at taking a complex issue—often one with underlying brutality—and turning it into a T-shirt. Or a park. Taking a rambling religious zealot with a penchant for claiming land through planting seeds and turning him into the logo for a savings account at a local bank with 0.10 percent APY.

To live in America is to live inside a legend.

The colonists are brave revolutionaries (well, save the loyalist Tories), throwing off the yoke of tyrannical England. Yet they are also settlers, whose westward expansion through the coming generations will be a genocide against the Indigenous people who were already living here, resulting in a 96 percent population drop between 1492 and 1900 (when the Native American population in the US reached its lowest point, at 237,000 people), and a 98 percent loss of ancestral homelands.

Even John Chapman had his role to play in this sad saga. Appleseed—the legend—was very much a tool of westward expansion. Sometimes our actions have an outsized impact, and our very existence can be warped by history. An article in *Harper's Magazine* titled "Johnny Appleseed. A pioneer hero," written by William D'Arcy Haley—published roughly twenty-five years after Chapman's death—is largely credited with being one of the earliest pieces to lionize the man, turning his life into myth. Yet it also turned his life into a tool of revisionist history, offering a more peaceful and far less bloody version of white settlers' push across America and the genocide of the Indigenous people for whom this continent was their birthright.

11

BY MILE TWENTY-EIGHT of my two-day walk I am defeated. My feet feel like bloody bits of hamburger covered in blisters. My brain is constantly fixating upon grandiose thoughts about King Philip and Joseph Palmer, and, of course, John Chapman—born into all of this chaos in 1774. A child of the Revolutionary War and its often-forgotten aftermath, though his legacy is one of nonviolence, he found his own way of epitomizing the rebellious spirit of his day.

When it comes to why Chapman led such a socially rebellious, meandering life, there is no shortage of theories. Some say that he was kicked in the head by a horse in his early twenties, and the injury resulted in having a section of his skull removed. Surely traumatic brain damage—and the, shall we say, unsophisticated medical care of the time—could lead to an individual not being in their right mind. Problem is, there isn't really any documentation to back up the horse-hoof-to-the-head theory. Other folks say a young woman (or, perhaps, according to some scholars, *girl*) broke Chapman's heart, and this was somehow the cause of his eccentricity—rocked by rejection, he took to wandering the land like Caine in *Kung Fu*. Others claim that he survived a long, horrible bout of malaria and was never the same, even after his fever came down. Some folks claim all three are true; just as many say none of them are.

What we do know for sure is that in the 1790s, Chapman—then a young adult—convinced his half brother, Nathaniel Cooley Chapman, to come adventuring with him to Western Pennsylvania, beginning his nomadic lifestyle (he would part ways with Nathaniel soon thereafter) that would bring him all the way to Ohio and eventually end in Indiana—a state that didn't yet exist—in 1845.

I'm jealous that Chapman had the company of his half sibling. I hadn't asked anyone to accompany me on my initial long walk—not my own half siblings, nor my very new girlfriend, Kelly, nor any friends who might have been up for the adventure. As far back as I can remember I've had a hunger to be alone, free, making choices only for myself—a hunger that bumped up against something just as powerful but contradictory: another craving, an inner drive to go out and meet any stranger who will talk to me. When I was young out on the farm, never living with my half siblings, I spent copious time alone. Yet when I was living at the Catholic Worker, I was often surrounded by adults, who I would constantly pepper with questions. "Who are you? How did you come to be here?" Some took to it more kindly than others.

The result of those two opposite longings has been a life of making many, many friends—while also keeping most of them at arm's length. I want to get to know you, and let you know me, but something often overrides that desire to be known and I withdraw without warning. But after such a long stretch alone, I am the worst company for myself to keep, especially with my itchy brain, an inheritance from my mother. Often filled with negative self-talk, and an ability to take a happy memory and criticize myself until it becomes something else entirely. I yearn to be around other people to counteract too much introspection, but I also yearn to be by myself before the point when I, often in my own mind, become a burden or hindrance.

I'm twenty-eight miles in and I am falling apart. I decide I need a break that involves more than four iced matcha lattes and an hour inside at a Dunkin' Donuts. Near Philipston, I see a large billboard on the side of the road beckoning travelers to turn down a small country lane and visit Red Apple Farm.

Does the orchard have any relation to John Chapman? I mean,

other than, you know, "apples" as a general theme? No. But I desperately need a place to rest my head (and back . . . and legs . . . and shoulders . . . and, most importantly, feet). I want hot food and a cold cider in front of me. I want to be around people. And if a mile walk out of my way—two, considering I'd have to walk back—is the price, well, it is a price I am willing to pay.

As I walk down Highland Avenue toward Red Apple Farm, I think I see it again: that black dog sitting right at the entrance for the orchard, as if it is waiting for me. The road dips down a bit, and I lose sight of the creature. As I crest out of the dip—where I can see the apple trees covered in melting snow and the surrounding fields again—I look toward the entrance once more, but the dog is nowhere to be seen.

When I was a kid, Red Apple Farm was a place where you would pay some money and get a brown bag or basket to go collect apples in the fall. They had a store that sold pies, jams, and nonalcoholic cider. It was a quaint, pretty, and extremely New England experience. But times change. I hear the music before I see the apple trees.

Red Apple Farm is jumping on a Sunday afternoon, even this early in the spring. The place now has bands and food trucks on the weekends, plus cider slushies for sale at the Cidery, as well as the Brew Barn—a barn converted into a simple but fantastic restaurant and bar that they opened by partnering with Moon Hill Brewing Company out of Gardner. What was once a wholesale apple farm with a bit of apple picking on the side for the locals and seasonal leaf peepers has become a tourist destination year round that—on top of everything else already mentioned—also has room for a wood-fired Neapolitan pizza oven. A long way from five-dollar paper bags for picking apples.

As for me, one hard cider has turned into two hard ciders and is slowly creeping up on—okay, it is more like four at this point. I demolish a giant plate of macaroni and cheese with BBQed brisket mixed in, grateful for the delicious abundance. The sun would still be in the sky by the time I got home if I left soon, but I'm now debating a fifth cider, and whether it would be all that bad to arrive home after sundown.

The fire is going in the Brew Barn, despite the sunny day, and I appreciate its warmth—my clothes going from wet with sweat to somewhat stiff but at least relatively dry. Outside, the snow is already melting, turning into spring mud. I read some literature that was out by the register, learning that Red Apple Farm was founded in 1912, "the same year as Oreo, Fenway Park, LL Bean, and the Girl Scouts!" In that year, their first commercial McIntosh apple tree was planted, which still produces fruit to this day. The farmhouse and barn date back to the 1700s, before the Revolutionary War—meaning that these buildings were here when John Chapman was born just down the road. I also learned that the first cider they produced came about because of a freak hailstorm that decimated over half the orchard's apples on Sunday, June 30, 2019. They'd been thinking about making alcoholic cider for some time, apparently, but that's when they partnered with Moon Hill Brewing to make "Hailstorm Hard Cider."

Most importantly—and exactly the type of information that makes me feel like I deserved to stay for one more drink, and perhaps a second order of food—Red Apple Farm is the highest orchard in all of New England, with more than fifty varieties of apple being grown at 1,250 feet elevation. In hindsight, it *had* felt like a steep climb.

I get up to grab cider number five, and run right into a beaming, familiar face.

"Ma?"

She gestures at a table near the door where my father is sitting. He gives a little half wave, half salute. They must have snuck in without me noticing, not that I am noticing much of anything at the moment. I hug her, and then apologize for how disheveled I am.

"It's okay. We just hadn't heard from you, but I figured with this being a Johnny Appleseed walk and all you might stop by here." She winks at the new cider I am now holding in my hands. "Worst case scenario, we'd get some food and find you at home. Care to join us?"

"Would you mind joining me over here, actually? I want to stay close to the fire."

"We wouldn't mind at all."

I help them bring over their food. My father looks a little smug as we all sit down. "How'd the trail work out?"

"Did you know there wasn't one?" I ask, one eyebrow cocked, but he just gives a smirk and pretends to pay attention to his meal.

We talk about everything I'd seen, and I show my da how I'd cared for his camping equipment. My ma is clearly proud that Red Apple Farm has become such a large operation, often hosting festivals and having annual events. I share my limited knowledge of Joseph Palmer, King Philip, and John Chapman, and my parents help me fill in some details and gaps—my father especially, being a lover of the area's history.

"They kept his head on a pike for a generation, ya know."

My father went on to tell me the Athol Regional High School's planning committee had recently voted to replace the school's racist mascot, the Red Raiders, with the much more acceptable—and metal as hell—"Bears."

"The Mohicans referred to the Mohawks as 'Maw Unk Lin,' which means 'bear people.' And 'Maw Unk' is where white people came up with the term 'Mohawk.' Did you know that?"

"You don't say, Da."

My parents have a few bears living near their house, which I found out when, after one particularly hot night when I was visiting, I decided to sleep on a couch out on their porch. In the morning, my father asked if I'd do it again that night, and I said most likely, which is when my father said, "Well, we should probably move this, then" and proceeded to move a fifty-pound bag of birdseed that had apparently been under the very couch I was sleeping on. "You wouldn't taste so good," he quipped, "but the bears would suffer through you to get to these tasty seeds." When I went inside, my ma was holding a decimated bird feeder from their front yard—bears had been through the night before and destroyed it. I've slept indoors every visit since.

What I'll learn later is that my ma, so proud of the high school for getting rid of its racist mascot and replacing it with the area's most powerful animal, got in touch with a local printer—a recovering addict who had started a business that my ma wanted to support—and ordered four hundred black T-shirts with Athol High and a fierce bear face plastered in red on the front. The T-shirts fucking ripped. The students loved them; hell, I loved them when I finally saw one. But she never told anyone about the donation—not even my father and me. She did it anonymously.

That's the way it was with Ma. You only got a part of the story—often after it was already done.

I have a memory from childhood. I was eight, maybe nine years old. It was February, always a hard month, especially in New England. My mother and I were living alone at the time, out on that dreary, dreaded family farm where my ma—ever the realist, never one for wild emotion—began to change. To crack.

She had been sad a long time, or what felt like a long time to a child. My father was living in the city, for work, they told me, and we didn't see him much. The house was full of gaps, and the cold air would seep in. My mother and I did our best to keep a fire going in the cast-iron stove that heated the home, while also taking care not to burn through too many logs at too quick a rate: a delicate balance of staying warm and saving money.

I was sitting in front of the stove, trying to get the chill out of my bones, when my ma burst into the living room. She was wearing a bright green swimsuit, despite there being snow on the ground outside. In each of her hands she held two glass containers, one a jug that we usually put lemonade or iced tea in during the summer months, the other a vase of some kind. Each was filled with water.

"Spring will come!"

My ma started to bellow as she skipped around the room, tossing water from each of the glass containers she carried. The water landed on the cast-iron stove, almost immediately turning into steam as a sizzling sound filled the room. I remember watching the water droplets dance upon the hot metal before disappearing into the air completely.

"Spring will come! Spring will come!"

She continued chanting as she circled me, until all the water was gone—some spilled on the stove and the floor, some being absorbed into the rug. It was a promise. A reminder. She was trying to pull herself out of a dark hole, but I didn't know that at the time. I was a child, scared and also confused. My mother often wouldn't get out of bed, and tended to cry almost at random throughout the day. But she had never before presented such a display of mania. I didn't know it at the time, but it would be the first of many.

"Spring will come!"

Her voice began to waver, then crack. Her cries of defiance turned into cries of sadness and then she was simply just crying. Then sobbing. She collapsed to the ground and draped her arms around me. I held her, gently running my fingers through her hair, making sounds similar to those you use when trying to calm a baby.

Together, on the floor, we started to recite the Lord's Prayer. When we finished, we started again. Over and over, we said the prayer. A calming ritual. Eventually, my mother got up and walked back upstairs. I never saw that bathing suit again.

My ma has struggled with mental illness her entire adulthood. I don't know why I was so surprised when I started showing similar signs. Overwhelmed by life, sometimes to the point of becoming immobile. Social anxiety, then plain old anxiety, too. A lack of interest in getting out of bed, or of returning correspondence. A frozen feeling—so much to do, yet no willingness, or ability, to do it.

But I also knew that I desperately wanted to function. I built a world of levers and pulleys—tricks and sleights of hand—hundreds of ways to hold my chafing brain at bay. I learned how to read people, becoming atrociously good at inventing something that I *thought* they might need from me, and then doing my damnedest to give it to them. If I could be of value to someone, surely they wouldn't leave me alone with only me and my mind, filled with intrusive thoughts, like memories of my mother yelling, "Spring will come!"

Sitting here at Red Apple Farm, it occurs to me that there's a reason my parents are worried about my mental state—I'm the same age now as my ma was when she lost her mind when I was a child.

"So, I don't want to tempt you, but the sun's getting low in the sky. Would it be too motherly of me to offer you a ride home?"

My ma looks over at me, and it feels warm to be cared for. Also, if I'm being honest, I would've taken a ride from a stranger at this point. My legs have locked up while resting—a fierce ache fills my body.

I take a moment to admire her, absorbing more fully that I am now nearly the same age as she was on that day with the jugs. My childhood was a rough one because of her sudden instability, but over time she learned to manage her mental illness, to live with it. My da and ma never even got divorced, though whether the Catholic Church deserves credit for that, or plain New England stubbornness, I'm not sure. All I know is that she seems to be doing better, now in her golden years. Hell, my da does, too.

"Sure. Not because I'm tired, but for your peace of mind," I reply.

"So, what's next?" my da asks as we settle our bill.

"I think I might just keep going. After his childhood in Massachusetts, Chapman and his half brother headed west, eventually making their way to the Allegheny River and Western Pennsylvania. From there it was Ohio, and eventually Fort Wayne, Indiana. There's gotta be some good walking out that way."

"Given how this went—"

For a moment I'm a teenager again and I shoot him a look.

He backs off.

"Hey, it went good. You made it. You didn't get shot, remarkably. But, you know, your mother can't drive you around for the rest of the year is all I'm saying. We'll give you a lift back home tonight, sure. But, you know, for the rest of it . . . you're going to need a car, don't you think?"

12

THERE'S A CORVETTE on the dealership lot out by the main strip. Do you want to go take a look?"

I try to hear if my girlfriend, Kelly, is being sardonic, but if she is, she doesn't show it.

I could understand her being frustrated, though. We have been looking for a car for me for a few weeks. Ever since I returned from my long walk—plus a short drive, thanks to my parents—in Massachusetts.

Kelly owns a house on the North Fork of Long Island. When we first started dating—both of us coming out of long relationships, guarded against starting anything *too* serious *too* quickly—I explained to her that I hadn't spent much time on LI, save for a few visits to a pal who had a boat docked out that way, and that I didn't foresee spending much time there in the future.

"You're on Long Island right now," she said, matter-of-factly.

"I'm sorry?" We were sitting in my Brooklyn apartment.

"Manhattan is its own island. Staten Island clearly is as well. The Bronx is on the mainland. But Queens and Brooklyn? They're on Long Island. You've already lived on Long Island for most of a decade. My place out there just has a yard, instead of . . ."

She waved her hand at the small room we were lying in. Good point. Since that moment, I've been spending a lot more time farther out on—her section of—Long Island.

The reason I didn't know Brooklyn was on Long Island was,

weirdly enough, very much linked to my not having a car. A subway rider and a walker, when I thought of New York City I thought only of the subway map—never really contemplating what landmasses the boroughs were linked to.

Growing up, I'd never had my own car, though I was driving friends' trucks through the hills of Massachusetts well before I had a license, and after I *did* have a license I treated my ma's ancient Plymouth Colt—three different colors of blue—like the beater it was, often making my own half-assed repairs. After I split town for good, I remember a call from my ma asking, "Hey, have you ever fixed the Colt with . . . zip ties?"

Indeed I had—a fact that was discovered when she finally brought the junker to a mechanic to see if they might want to buy the surprisingly long-lasting vehicle for parts. The mechanic informed her that most of the undercarriage was held together with, well, plastic ties of varying sizes. Years of me bottoming out on friends' steep dirt driveways and backing into snowbanks while driving like only a Massachusetts teen asshole can—anytime something underneath started hanging loose, I got under there and strapped it back up with a zip tie. Apparently the undercarriage was almost more plastic than metal.

It might very well have been my own surprise at surviving my hellion youth filled with maniacal driving that made me stick to cities in my early adulthood, never having a need for a car. But the poverty probably didn't help. I don't even have insurance for myself, and you're telling me I need it for a vehicle?

One exception: an old beat-to-shit motorcycle I owned in San Francisco in my twenties. But after one weekend bender during which I rode while blacked out, I wandered into my favorite bar and gave it away for free to a friend who was hard up for cash, figuring she could sell it.

This was a pattern throughout my life, perhaps linked to my staccato brain and its anxieties. You can't lose anything—nothing can be taken from you—if you don't have anything in the first place.

When you're raised with nothing, you're used to having nothing. I was years into adulthood before I got a bank account, and even more years along when I got my first credit card. My first cell phone was a hand-me-down sent to me by my half sister—an old clam-shaped Motorola flip phone with a yellow Post-it note on it, upon which was written a single sentence: "Call your parents."

Not having many belongings also meant I could bounce around a lot: another habit I picked up from my parents, although their version was a trip that started in Dr. Holladay's apartment, then a homeless shelter, then a halfway house, then eventually the family farm, and then—when they were both in their fifties—to the first small home they finally owned themselves. They bounced around Boston and then the state of Massachusetts. I, instead, used the entire country to try to assuage my rambling feet. Washington, DC. Philadelphia. San Francisco. New York City. Usually with nothing more than a bag over my shoulder. An obsession with moving. Or, better said, an obsession with impermanence.

But now here I was years later—ten years after moving to New York City, to be exact. My new girlfriend living on a different section of Long Island. And I'm telling her how I'm going to spend the rest of the year walking in Pennsylvania, Ohio, and Indiana—following in the footsteps of some wild-eyed legend who was born near the town where I grew up.

"Well, you're going to need a car," she tells me.

"That's what my dad said."

"Because you can't borrow mine."

"I know."

"On account of how I have a real job, and don't get to just live like a leaf on the wind."

Kelly's pointed note was understandable. A self-made small-business owner, Kel is a very independent woman—rarely accepting help from close friends or family, let alone somewhat newish dating partners or strangers. I, conversely, have no qualms with handouts, having relied upon them at many different junctures throughout my life.

Even the beginning of my and Kelly's relationship could be viewed as an elaborate favor to me, if you look at it in a certain light. Two close friends introduced us (a few times, actually; our awareness that we were being match-made growing with each "chance" meeting), but on paper it was clear who they were hoping would rub off on whom. One of us stable, the other a person pushing forty whose only current vehicle was a skateboard.

"I understand that."

"Have you ever even bought a car before?"

I hadn't. Even the motorcycle had been a trade to pay off some long-forgotten debt or favor owed, which is probably why I was so comfortable simply giving it away when the time came. Easy come, easy go.

So my girlfriend, who has purchased and owned multiple vehicles like a normal adult, who owns the house we now spent most of our time in, and who was suspicious of me in general even before I told her I wanted to go chase the ghost of John Chapman across the Midwest—took it upon herself to help me. She went about searching Craigslist and used-car sites for a reasonable, respectable, dependable vehicle.

Problem was, on the North Fork, a lot of unreasonable cars were available, too. Old Porsches owned by coked-out bankers who moved out to the Hamptons to retire, or 1970s Buick LeSabres—fantastical cars owned by old rich people who had never even driven the vehicle on the mainland. Every time she sent me something reasonable, I responded with something that—well, let's call it what it was—smacked of a midlife crisis.

"What does a sports car have to do with Johnny Appleseed?" Kelly rightfully inquired.

I didn't have an answer. She sent me links to trucks, and cars with good gas mileage, saying things like, "Look! This is sexy—but practical," while I kept sending back Camaros, Mustangs, and one time—just one time—a DeLorean (okay, even I knew that one was a bad idea).

Which is how we got to "There's a Corvette."

I hear the defeat in her voice.

"It's apple red," she added. "American."

I recently discovered a Swedenborgian church in Bryn Athyn, Pennsylvania, and I want to head down there for Easter service. The Bryn Athyn Cathedral is the episcopal seat of the General Church of the New Jerusalem, which is the fancy modern name for Swedenborgianism, the religion of John Chapman. I was pleased to discover there were still active members.

Easter is a week away. The clock is ticking.

"Okay. Let's go take a look."

The inside of the vehicle is incredible. It's a 2002, so in a way the controls feel familiar. Antiquated, but pleasantly so—the radio could have been in one of my friends' cars growing up. Comfortable.

It is also *incredibly* low to the ground. I feel like I am in the cockpit of a fighter jet. A 2002 fighter jet with an AM/FM radio plus CD player.

"Whoa, this is so low."

Kelly slides into the passenger seat.

"Just don't get run over by any eighteen-wheelers, okay?"

"This bad boy would go right *under* an eighteen-wheeler."

A Cheshire cat grin creeps across my face as I feel the leather wheel in my hand. I am already picturing myself cruising up to the trailheads of Pennsylvania, Ohio, and Indiana in an apple-red 2002 Corvette. Sure, the car will get some dents and scrapes, but what a chariot to ride into the heartland of America.

The car feels like freedom.

"I'll take it."

Kelly nods, not exactly happy, but resigned—relieved simply to have the car situation handled, seeing as I would be hitting the road in only a few days.

"Let's talk to them, then."

We get out of the Corvette and walk over to the salesman's desk. When I first ask to look at the car, the man doesn't even look up from his computer. He just keeps typing as he says, "Fine, take a look."

I can understand—I'm sure I don't look like a serious buyer. But now I am going to let him know my intentions to go home with the vehicle. Surely his tune will change once he realizes hard cash is on the line.

"So I'm seriously considering purchasing the red 2002 'Vette," I say, trying to sound familiar. "Any chance I can take it for a test drive?"

The man continues to type. He does not look up.

"No."

"Excuse me?"

"I said *no*."

The salesman takes a pause—a breath, to be clear; he does not take a pause from typing. When I simply keep standing there, he goes on.

"We don't do test drives on Sundays."

"Look, I get it," I reply, trying to turn on the charm, "I'm young, maybe you think I'm trying to take a Sunday joyride. But I assure you, I'm going to buy this car."

The man finally—thankfully—stops typing and turns to me. We make eye contact for the first time and he gives me a once-over before saying, "Firstly, you don't look *that* young. Second, it's policy—no test drives on Sundays. Especially not showroom-floor cars. But seeing as you're a 'serious' buyer, can I ask where you'd be keeping the car?"

I don't like his tone overall, but the way he says "serious" really throws me.

"Uh, my girlfriend's house."

"In the house?"

"The driveway."

"The driveway. The previous owner, you should know, kept the car in a private garage. The garage was heated. He only drove it during the summer months. Hence its spotless condition."

"Was . . . the previous owner a family member . . . or . . . ?" I was becoming more confused by the minute.

"No. Just a loyal customer. I promised to do right by his car."

"But . . . but . . . I have money," though I am new to it—and in the grand scheme of things, I don't have *all* that much—but I think, *having money is supposed to handle most problems.*

"Money, and a paved, uncovered driveway. Yes? Will you use a car cover during inclement weather?"

I open my mouth, but no words come out, as I don't know what to say. We stand there staring at each other. My girlfriend's driveway is actually gravel. But I certainly am not going to let him know that. I picture the Corvette scraping its low undercarriage in my own driveway—which isn't technically mine.

My mother's zip-tied muffler pops into my mind. But how can this man tell I am so hard on my things?

"There's a white two-door Jeep on the lot. Could we look at that?" Kelly cuts the tension, and a tight—not smile, but something less stern than what had been happening mere moments ago—immediately crosses the salesman's face.

"The 2017 Wrangler? Sure, let me get the keys, and you can take it for a spin."

"What happened to no test drives on Sundays?" I ask, incredulous.

"Still the rule, but you can take the Jeep for a spin in the parking lot out back"—his nonsmile somehow widens to show teeth—"young man."

I still don't know what that was all about, but I do know the man's instincts were correct. I would buy the white Jeep and name the vehicle Rabbit. I would spend the next year in Rabbit's driver's seat, putting over forty thousand miles on the beast in under 365 days. The Jeep would be dented, banged up, and mistreated all across New England and into Pennsylvania, Ohio, and Indiana—but it only died on me once, out on the border between PA and OH.

Every time I came across a Corvette in my travels, I thanked my lucky stars I hadn't bought the 2002 apple-red beauty. I wasn't ready for it. I would have been biting off more than I could chew.

But I do still sometimes wonder if Kelly called ahead—tired of all my dreams of impractical sports cars. Wanting to put her new beau in a vehicle that might keep him safe, despite his maniacal, almost obsessive interest in doing the opposite. But the closest I've come to getting her to admit it is her saying, "I *had* noticed the Jeep on the lot when I saw the Corvette. It looked nice. And it's also American."

13

EXCUSE ME. We're having a service this morning. There's more parking farther down if you'd like to walk the grounds."

I'm getting out of my new used Jeep, Rabbit, in a small skinny parking lot next to a giant intimidating cathedral in Bryn Athyn, just north of Philadelphia. It's a gorgeous spring morning, the trees that cover the previously mentioned "grounds" are in full bloom, with the wind carrying cherry blossoms through the air, creating the illusion that it's snowing despite the temperature being in the sixties, or that we are standing in the opening credits of some lushly animated Studio Ghibli film, not a church parking lot.

"I'm actually here for the service." I put on my best I'm-going-to-church face as I lock up my vehicle and turn to the woman, who is now walking up to me.

"Oh? I don't recognize you." The woman looks exactly like the peaceable yet formidable type you would send to guard a church parking lot. I regret not dressing up—I'm simply in jeans and a beat-up chore coat. It is Easter, after all.

I've always felt at peace in a church. The smell of incense in the air reminds me of my time as a child in Boston, when my mother worked at the Cathedral of the Holy Cross. I would stare up at the stories told in the stained-glass windows. Vain child that I was, the story of Abraham and Isaac was my favorite. The way the light shone through the knife in Abraham's hand, the angel holding him back, the ram hiding in the bushes. What an odd story to name your child after, I would think.

My mother would say, "Your name means 'God's laughter.'" But it means more than that. A display of devotion. An edge of violence. A story, where the lesson is . . . what? Prove your faith to a devastating degree and you won't actually have to sacrifice? Or maybe that Yahweh was a fan of prank shows almost four thousand years before *Punk'd*? And that's not even getting into the scholars who believe, originally, that Abraham *did* sacrifice Isaac. But when, ya know, human sacrifice fell out of favor, the story slowly changed over time—bent to fit the ideals of the day. Oh, would you look at that! Over there in the bushes! A ram.

But as a child I just liked that there was a story in the Bible that had my name in it. I would stare up at the stained-glass window—which I, in some way, considered mine—then, my child-mind racing, my body and brain itchy with distractions, my attention would turn to something else. Church as a child always felt like that: a battle, not between good and evil but between my ability to sit still and my desire to move.

Once, as a toddler, my parents brought me to a Shaker community. Officially known as the United Society of Believers in Christ's Second Appearing, the Shakers split from the Quakers—who founded Pennsylvania—and their nickname came from what was originally an insult, being called "Shaking Quakers" because of their, shall we say, frenetic body movements during worship.

My parents were always Catholic but had an abundance of interest in any and all religions. My father often meditated, his interest in Buddhism and Eastern philosophy sparked by his love of the Beats. As a family it was common for us to celebrate Passover and to light a menorah during Hanukkah, despite nobody in our family being Jewish. More even than Catholicism, my parents loved ritual. Their interest in spirituality was cavernous in its depth. My mother, raised on that farm in the hills of Massachusetts, in buildings as old as the many religions that started in the eighteenth century—like the Shakers and the Swedenborgians—always leaned a little more pagan. The woods were her true church. The mix of it all—a love of nature combined with a deep interest in the many different traditions of giving thanks and praise—is how you become a family that visits a Shaker community as a fun day-trip idea.

The story goes that my parents brought me to the Shaker village where we went on a tour, during which I was very well behaved. In the meetinghouse we attended a traditional service, where the Shakers moved and danced as a form of prayer. The dance was choreographed—although early Shakers simply moved their bodies, with no steps to concern themselves with—and there was a string down the middle of the room: men on one side of the string, women on the other. My father noticed that I, too, started to dance. My parents, their love of faith and God being what bound them together, must have felt a certain level of pride. Their child, filled with the spirit, was moved to dance with the Shakers. Sure, I crossed the line and began dancing with the women, but everyone was laughing. How cute, this li'l toddler, joining in the service of physical prayer.

That is until, as my father puts it, "You moved faster than you ever had up until that point in your short life." Surrounded by the dancing Shaker women I proceeded to rip my clothes off as quick as a magician might pull the tablecloth out from under a table's settings. "You were clothed one second, and naked the next," my mother chimes in, as they tell the story together. What happened then, according to legend, was a Benny Hill–esque chase as my mother and father—deeply embarrassed—tried to catch their naked son, and I did my best to lose them among the Shaker women's deeply pleated, spinning skirts.

What's funny is, I would have made a great Shaker. Using the body as a form of worship, instead of sitting still. So much more freeing than the uncomfortable pews and long bouts of sitting in Catholic

Mass—sitting so long that you find yourself desperately anticipating those moments when the congregation kneels, or even stands. All I had to do was stay on my side of the string, and, you know, keep my clothes on.

Today, most Shaker villages are museums. The last active community is Sabbathday Lake, in Maine near New Gloucester—because it's tough to keep your numbers up when, as a religion, you don't do much evangelizing, and also hold celibacy up as the purest ideal. The Shakers believe that Adam's original sin was sex, and thus sex is an act of impurity. Dance for God? Yes. Bang for God? No. The four virtues Shakers held in the highest esteem were virgin purity, confession of sin, communalism, and separation from the world. Again, not exactly putting up numbers in terms of making new members. Established in England in 1747 and organized in the United States by the 1780s, by 1900 there were less than a thousand practicing Shakers. As of 2022 there were two surviving members, named Arnold and June. They sleep in separate beds, but hope that new members might join the community before their passing.

So, on second thought, maybe I wouldn't make such a good Shaker after all.

The 1800s saw a boom of religions in America. Starting a new Christian religion during this era was the equivalent to creating a website in the 1990s or a social media platform in the 2000s. If you threw a rock in the 1800s—especially in the newly formed and still expanding start-up known as the United States of America—you'd be hard pressed not to hit a new religious movement, including those inspired by the Second Great Awakening, new interpretations of the Bible, and the many new social, scientific, and philosophical forms of thought. Along comes Adventism and Dispensationalism—the Latter Day Saint movement, alongside Christian Scientists and Jehovah's Witnesses.

The Swedenborgians are currently doing better numberswise than the Shakers, but still not all that great. Not Mormon numbers, to be sure. As I sit in their empty cathedral, I wonder how many would show up for service that day.

There are some ten thousand Swedenborgians practicing worldwide, with most living in North America. The religion is based on the teachings of Emanuel Swedenborg—a, yes, Swedish philosopher, scientist, and theologian who, uh—listen. It's a lot.

Born into a well-to-do family of scholars and government officials, Swedenborg fit right in with his relatives and was a bit of a Renaissance man, often described as the "Swedish Leonardo da Vinci." Early in his life he made contributions to a number of scientific disciplines, including but not limited to mathematics, astronomy, physics, and engineering. In his fifties he was inducted into the Royal Swedish Academy of Sciences, which is also around the time he had his spiritual awakening. You see, while he was doing all that science, Swedenborg was also exploring philosophy, and what started out as an interest in nature quickly snowballed into questions about the existence of God and the relationship between the physical and spiritual realms. This is where it gets really fun. Before his fifties were over, Swedenborg claimed to have experienced visions of—and not just visions of, but interactions *with*—angels, demons, and other spirits. Quite the party. These, uh . . . observations . . . led Swedenborg to believe that he was called by God to interpret certain spiritual truths and reveal them to the general public.

Emanuel Swedenborg spent the rest of his rather lengthy life—he lived to the ripe old age of eighty-four—writing theological books and essays describing his interactions with the spiritual world as well as his thoughts on the existence of an afterlife, the Bible, spiritual fortitude and upkeep, and the very nature of God. While his writings were heralded—as well as besmirched, but hey, so long as people are talking—during his lifetime, it wasn't until after his death (albeit shortly after) that Swedenborgianism, also known as the New Church or the General Church of the New Jerusalem, was formed.

Swedenborg has gone on to influence generations of theologians, philosophers, writers, and artists. Helen Keller, a devout Swedenborgian, read his writings in braille and is quoted as saying, "For the first time immortality put on intelligibility for me, and the earth wore new curves of loveliness and significance." William Blake, while sometimes critical of Swedenborg, certainly engaged with his works. Ralph Waldo Emerson, Jorge Luis Borges, and W. B. Yeats also copped to being influenced by Swedenborgian ideas, with Emerson writing:

> There is one man of genius who has done much for this philosophy of life, whose literary value has never yet been rightly estimated;—I mean Emanuel Swedenborg. The most imaginative of men, yet writing with the precision of a mathematician, he endeavored to engraft a purely philosophical Ethics on the popular Christianity of his time. Such an attempt, of course, must have difficulty which no genius could surmount. But he saw and showed the connection between nature and the affections of the soul. He pierced the emblematic or spiritual character of the visible, audible, tangible world. Especially did his shade-loving muse hover over and interpret the lower parts of nature; he showed the mysterious bond that allies moral evil to the foul material forms, and has given in epical parables a theory of insanity, of beasts, of unclean and fearful things.

How John Chapman came to Swedenborg is unclear, but it was almost certainly after he had left Massachusetts. The New Church first attempted to set up in the New World in 1784—ten years after Chapman was born—and officially found their flagship in Philadelphia in the 1790s. Not long after John Hargrove of Baltimore went to Western Pennsylvania to preach Swedenborg's works, but there's no documentation to prove Hargrove and Chapman ever met—

but there *are* several accounts of prominent Philadelphian Swedenborgians sending letters and books to Chapman. Whether or not those books arrived is another question, since it was difficult to get things to him, according to historian Dr. Robert Price, on account of his not having a permanent address.

Kelly grew up six miles from this American Swedenborgian nexus. The day before the service I'm attending, she, her mother, and I walked the grounds. It was a resplendent spring day with a light wind lifting blossoms off the trees. Kelly's mother remembers Swedenborgians in the area growing up. "They were nice, but mostly kept to themselves." Which is true, seeing as Bryn Athyn is a borough surrounded by Lower Moreland Township—which it left for religious reasons on February 8, 1916—with a population of over a thousand people. It has no public school, as 90 percent of the children are sent to private school or are homeschooled. Bryn Athyn has its own fire department and police department, and is home to Bryn Athyn College, which was founded in 1877 and is a private liberal arts college "dedicated to a New Church approach to education." The campus is right across from the cathedral.

But for Mass I've come alone, taking a seat in the very last pew, hoping not to be a distraction or a bother. An older woman walks in with a young child, who appears to have Down syndrome. The choir is finishing practice, their voices reverberating through the large empty room while what can only be described as a truckload of flowers are being laid out in front of the altar.

The child gives me a quiet wave, and I wave back. For a moment I worry that the Easter services will be underattended, but of course that worry is unfounded. Ten minutes before the service, the place is suddenly packed with families dressed in their Sunday best, the nave close to bursting. I scoot deeper into my pew, until the wood is pressing into my hips. The old woman and the child she is with scooch closer to me to make room.

"I like your tattoos," the child says to me. He holds out his hand and at first I think I'm supposed to shake it, but then realize what he's looking for and I slap him five, fulfilling his offer.

"Thanks, buddy." We nod at each other, and the older woman greets me.

"Welcome."

The service begins.

For the most part, my Catholic upbringing serves me well. I stand when I'm supposed to stand, kneel when I'm supposed to kneel, and believably mouth along to the hymns when everyone else sings—the choir is, unsurprisingly, transcendent. I have no ear for music, so they don't need my tone-deaf attempts at harmony.

At one point during the service I say "Amen" far too loudly—by which I mean I say it with all the confidence in the world while everyone else in the entire space stays silent. The kid to my left gives me a devilish—but forgiving—grin. *Bad timing on the Amen. Got it.*

Overall, though, the service is like many Catholic Masses that I've attended throughout my life. That is, at least, until the homily. It being Easter and all, the Scripture reading was of course about Jesus rising from the dead.

"And having looked up, they see that the stone has been rolled away."

The Swedenborgians' beliefs on the afterlife are, for lack of a better word, pleasant. Your body dies, but the *essence* of who you are continues to exist. Death is a transition period—your soul moves on and comes to exist in the world of spirits—eventually ending up in either heaven or hell. Your life on earth was simply the first part of your spirit's journey.

What does this next plane of existence look like? It is Earth, but—in the case of heaven—more splendid. Think of it as *better* Earth. The colors are brighter and more vivid. The smells more delectable. The feelings of joy are stuck on the highest setting. You are still yourself, and the people who you love and care for are there to welcome you. You will set up a home in the afterlife, and your community will continue, as will your spiritual growth.

The priest describes death in his homily with this metaphor: in *this* world, we only have one eye open, but in the next, we have two. A comforting thought. Surrounded by your loved ones, continuing your growth as something of importance in this universe.

As to hell, that one surprised me a bit. Swedenborg's hell isn't one of devils and pitchforks. Hell is of one's own making. The idea is—to put it in simplistic terms—if you're evil in this life, you will go to the place where your spirit will thrive in the next, in a manner of speaking. A place where evil is part of your spirit's development. Let me quote the man himself, from his most popular book, *Heaven and Hell:*

> Picture a community made up of people all totally in love with themselves, not caring about others unless they are allies, and you will see that their love is no different from that of thieves for each other. To the extent that they are acting in concert, they embrace each other and call each other friends; but once they stop cooperating, once anyone resists their control, they attack and butcher each other. If their deeper natures—their minds—are probed, it will be clear that they are full of virulent hatred for each other, that at heart they ridicule anything fair and honest and even ridicule the Deity, tossing it aside as worthless.

Hell is nothing more than the shittiest people you know spending their eternity trying to gladhand each other in order to enact control—to manipulate each other in order to gain power and esteem. I sort of loved the idea that hell wasn't a punishment—or it was, but only because you allowed your life on earth to be a living hell already. In my head, I picture a violent biker who loves drinking and raising, well, you know, hell—then their afterlife being filled with simply the same, for all time. That wasn't quite right—and the priest only touches on this concept for a moment—but I find it fascinating, and make a note to myself to study Swedenborg's writings further.

It feels good to be in church again, connected to a room full of strangers. Do I hold their beliefs? No. Or maybe that's not even right. I hold . . . some of them? But instead of scorekeeping, dissecting what I do and don't agree with—my own beliefs being something I'm never fully sure of, if I'm being honest—I know that I feel more at peace.

Here in the United States, roughly three in ten adults—or 30 percent of the population—attend religious services regularly (that same number, three in ten adults, say they have no religious affiliation). In the early 2000s, an average of 42 percent of American adults attended some form of religious ceremony around once a week, and in the 1990s it was 50 percent. US adults who were members of a church, synagogue, or mosque made up somewhere around 70 percent of the population from the 1940s to the 1990s, but so far in this century that number has fallen to 47 percent.

These days I don't attend service regularly, when I talk to God it's more of a one-on-one conversation. But I feel joy in having sung with these strangers, and praying with these strangers, and—maybe most importantly—being in the same space as these strangers. In general, getting everyone together once a week to sing and be grateful together doesn't seem like a terrible idea. As we exit our pews, I offer my hand to the kid who has been sitting next to me throughout the entire service. We now feel like quiet confidants. He slaps my low five, and we make our way to the large doors that now stand wide open, the grounds outside blooming like God's majesty spread out before us.

I watch as the stations of the cross—along with the resurrection of Jesus Christ—are acted out in meticulous detail by full grown adults in costumes. How snarky it would be for me to try and mock these people and their practices, but I walk the stations and see only devotion—something I will never ridicule. Devotion to love? To community? To a wish for spiritual fulfillment? If anything, I'm jealous that my belief is not as strong, even as it grows. That devotion is something that still perplexes me—unless it's a devotion to art, or my friends, or walking. But in a way, as I grow older, I'm beginning to realize that it may all be the same thing, and that's enough.

That said, there are—as with all self-appointed prophets—some dubious tales about Emanuel Swedenborg as well.

There is a story about Swedenborg being at a party in Gothenburg during which he became upset, and began describing a fire in Stockholm, more than two hundred miles away. He claimed that the fire was threatening his home, but after a few hours had passed, he said that the fire had been stopped merely a few doors down from his own abode. Two days later, so the story goes, messengers from Stockholm relayed news of a large fire that *had* indeed been stopped not far from Swedenborg's house.

There are other stories like this, not to mention claims that Swedenborg had an IQ ranging anywhere from 165 to 210—in spite of the fact that IQ testing didn't really begin until the early 1900s. But *The New York Times* reported, "A Stanford University study estimated that Swedenborg, along with Johann Wolfgang von Goethe and John Stuart Mill, had the highest IQ in history."

Do I believe this? No. I am suspicious of things like reports of IQ scores before the test was even invented, and stories about having clairvoyant knowledge about fires two hundred miles away. More legends and stories—we want nothing more from this monotonous human life than to be astounded and filled with hope. With love. That part I do believe, and would come to understand more thoroughly as my own journey went on.

Swedenborg writes of heaven:

> They who dwell in heaven are continually advancing to the springtime of life and to a spring more and more delightful and happy the more thousands of years they live; and this to eternity, with increase according to the progress and degrees of love, charity, and faith. . . . In a word, to grow old in heaven is to grow young. Those who have lived in love to the Lord and in charity towards the neighbor become of such beautiful form in the other life.

In Swedenborgianism, spring is associated with sacred rebirth and the dawning of a new spiritual understanding. I speak aloud to myself as I walk amongst the true believers, enacting the death and rising of their savior. The son of God, a messiah to many, but whom the Swedenborgians believe they more truly understand.

The cherry blossoms on the cathedral grounds seem even more fully in bloom now than they did before the service. Spring is fully here, and then some. Soon it would be summer. But whichever the season, that belief in spring, rooted so deeply in Swedenborgianism, was also my ma's repeated prayer all those years ago, as she tried to survive her own mind during a long, difficult winter, raising a child on her own on a farm she had sworn to escape:

"Spring will come. Spring will come. Spring will come."

· SUMMER ·

14

I WASN'T SUPPOSED to be alone for my trip down the Allegheny River.

Remembering the lonesome walk I'd had in Massachusetts, I had spoken to several friends about making the expedition with me, friends who are better in boats than I am—who have spent meaningful time on lakes and rivers, or sailing out on the ocean. Friends who could gauge rapids and eddies, and know how to execute a proper J-stroke. Friends who had, in short, done this sort of thing before.

At the very least, better to have someone else there, in case the boat capsizes, I figured.

Walking alone brings on a unique sort of calm. A meditative state that I deeply relish. You turn inwards, and are left alone with your thoughts. *Maybe boating alone can be similar,* I thought. I'd read many books about people out on the water, all by themselves. Books like *Dove* by Robin Lee Graham, or the aptly named *Sailing Alone Around the World* by Joshua Slocum. People circumnavigate the *world* in boats by themselves, surely I could handle the Allegheny River. Boating, another way of moving through the world at human pace. But then I remembered there is a significantly greater chance of drowning when you're out on the water than while walking on dry land. A greater chance of going under and never coming back up, so another set of hands couldn't hurt. Especially hands that knew what they were doing.

I reached out to some of those friends when there was still snow on the ground, and a few of them were interested in my proposal—hell, some even agreed. But it's easy to go along with some foolish, imaginative outdoor adventure in the distant summer while you're sitting in a bar in New York City in the dead of January.

To be fair to those friends, though, that initial request on my part was the last they ever heard of the trip. Until the early weeks of June, that is, when I called, asking if they'd made proper preparations.

"I have a job, Isaac. I can't drop everything to go boating down some river in Western Pennsylvania just because I seemed interested over a few beers six months ago."

Warranted.

It's another one of my weird, personal peccadilloes. I'm bad with time. A conversation that took place months ago often seems far more recent to me. It sometimes feels like time moves around me in a unique way—much like water is sometimes changed when moving past a rock, speaking of rapids and eddies.

I tried other friends. Ones with less boating experience, but perhaps more flexible schedules. The answers I got were the same. Nobody wanted to summer in Western Pennsylvania eighty miles shy of the Ohio border.

"Look, I can send you a list of supplies you might want to bring. But I can't make the trip."

One of my more knowledgeable boating friends, who spends his days taking tourists out to sea on a sailboat off the coast of Maine, sent me a list of items that might be helpful on my now-solo river excursion. A wet bag. Rain gear. Sunscreen. Insect repellent. A first aid kit. A life preserver. That last one bolded and in all caps.

But in the days leading up to my trip, I got distracted, which is how I now find myself driving Rabbit across the great state of Pennsylvania—always a longer trip than you imagine when you're traveling longitudinally—with nothing but a few old clothes in a backpack, a list of things I can hopefully find in Warren, PA, and a lime-green, donut-shaped pool floatie that I picked up the previous summer at a Wal-Mart and had in my basement.

The reason I am headed to Warren—about 100 miles north and slightly east of Pittsburgh and 330 miles northwest of Philadelphia, in the middle of the Allegheny National Forest—is that John Chapman supposedly planted his first apple nursery on the bank of Brokenstraw Creek, a tributary of the Allegheny River a bit south of town.

How Chapman, and his younger half brother Nathaniel, came all the way to Warren from their home in Longmeadow, Massachusetts, is a bit of a mystery, as there are no permanent records about their journey. But the consensus is that they traveled along Native American trails the 420 or so miles between the two locations, eventually taking shelter in the Warren area during the winter of 1797.

"I probably should have planned this better."

It's what I'm muttering to myself as I pull into town. The summer sun has set already, but there is still light in the sky despite its being well past 9 p.m. A small benefit of being farther west yet still in the Eastern Time Zone. I have driven Rabbit straight across the state of Pennsylvania without stopping. God, the Keystone State truly goes on for miles and miles.

Warren boasts a population of around ten thousand people, and is not as rural as I was expecting. I pass an industrial plant as I drive over a bridge and cross the Allegheny River—the United Refining Company is one of the main employers in the area, providing gas for Kwik Fill, Keystone Gasoline, and the ubiquitous Red Apple Food Mart gas stations. I drive by one of these as I head for the center of the town.

This area was originally inhabited by Native Americans of the Seneca Nation, with French colonizers planting plaques claiming rights to the land in the mid-1700s. Ultimately, control of the region—at least as seen by the invading Europeans—was transferred from the French to the British after the French and Indian War. Years later, after the Revolutionary War, General William Irvine and Andrew Ellicott were sent to the area to establish a settlement in 1795. They chose to name it after founding father, patriot, and war hero Joseph Warren of Massachusetts, whose death at the Battle of Bunker Hill was immortalized in John Trumbull's famous—and appropriately named—painting *The Death of General Warren at the Battle of Bunker's Hill, June 17, 1775*.

Daniel McQuay of Ireland was the area's first permanent non–Native American resident, and history claims he and John Chapman crossed paths in the region at that time. Lumber was the main industry, until David Beaty discovered oil in Warren in 1875 while drilling for natural gas in his wife's flower garden. Warren's boom era thus began about a hundred years after Chapman was planting apple seeds on the banks of the Allegheny, with oil dominating the city's economy and paying for many Victorian mansions which were built in the area and that you can still see to this day. At the height of Warren's growth, the town reached a population of over fifteen thousand people, but it's since been in a steady economic—and population—decline. Yet there are ongoing efforts to bring tourists to the area, capitalizing on the surrounding national forest's beauty, with local businesses lining the main street.

Most of the shops and restaurants are closed for the night when I arrive, and eventually I find myself parking in an empty lot across the street from a large echoing parking garage along the river. At the far end of the lot I see public restrooms. Before I even have a chance to wonder if they're open, a man opens the bathroom door and exits. The light behind him creates a silhouette, and I can see that he wears a big beard but is skinny in stature. The man holds the door open, reaches behind him, and pulls a giant pack onto his slight shoulders. It's clear the weight doesn't bother him in the least.

I have become so used to "public" restrooms—and parks, and so many other supposedly "free" spaces—being closed, or locked, or charging money for access, that I am quite thrilled, perhaps even delighted by this seemingly minor convenience. What a relief to use a bathroom, maybe even wash my face and brush my teeth. The surveillance-obsessed world we live in seems more and more privatized every day, everything behind a proverbial paywall, that it's a wonderful moment when something is not. A public restroom in the center of a small town, when did that become a luxury?

With relief on my face, I hold my hand up and wave. The man returns the gesture—a wild, toothy smirk filling his face, and then abruptly trots into the shadows of a nearby forest, his huge pack bouncing on his back.

For a brief moment I want to follow him—he's a near spitting image of the Johnny Appleseed logo that I saw back in Massachusetts. It's as if I've caught up to the historical figure himself, out here on the road, or caught a glimpse of his spirit, or perhaps even the ghost of America, one that happily haunts public areas that haven't been hidden behind lock and key. The specter of "This Land Is Your Land, This Land Is My Land" or "Big Rock Candy Mountain."

The lyrics of the latter play in my head.

In the Big Rock Candy Mountains
You never change your socks
And the little streams of alcohol
Come a-trickling down the rocks
The brakemen have to tip their hats
And the railroad bulls are blind
There's a lake of stew and of whiskey, too
You can paddle all around 'em in a big canoe
In the Big Rock Candy Mountains.

I begin singing to myself, and realize that I haven't eaten all day. After using the thankfully unlocked restroom, I look on my phone to see if there's anything in town that might be open. One single location comes up.

Cronie's Pub.

15

ARE YOU A COP?"

Cronie's is only a few blocks away from the empty lot where I parked Rabbit, so I walk over. The old rundown building has some faded geometric shapes painted on its exterior, along with portraits of regulars from the early 2000s on wooden window covers that look as if they never came down, which gives the inside a cavelike feel, perfect for a river town dive bar. The music is playing loud enough as I approach that you can hear it from the street, and when I open the door and walk in, I'm surprised to find a rather full room.

There is a pool game going on, most of the tables have couples or groups of people sitting at them, and at the bar there are only a few empty stools, one of which I take. The fridge behind the bar—which I later learn is over a hundred years old—is a giant metal and glass cooler with a spinning display showing off a variety of chilly bottles of American beer.

I do my best not to notice how many people are glancing in my direction. It's clear the place is filled with locals and that I stick out like a turd in a fruit bowl.

"What can I get ya?"

I hadn't noticed up until this moment, but the bartender—who is my age or perhaps a li'l younger—only has one eye, and is not wearing an eyepatch. I glance twice before making eye contact with his one good eye, which he rolls slightly as if to say, "Yes, I have one eye. Now that we've gotten that out of the way, can we proceed?"

"Uh, can I get a cold bottle of Bud?" I stammer.

"Wouldn't make much money if they were warm, would we?"

The bartender laughs at his own joke as he opens the antique beer fridge and grabs me a bottle. I sit and drink while I take in the mildly raucous room around me. The barkeep chats with other regulars while folks make conversation at their tables. Classic rock ranging from AC/DC to the Smashing Pumpkins with a sprinkling of Willie Nelson and Lil Wayne plays on the 2000s-era internet jukebox.

About halfway through my beer a man comes over and asks me if I want to play pool. I do my best to decline but he insists, and at the urging of the bartender, I eventually relent.

"How much do you want to bet?"

I immediately realize that I'm about to be a little bit poorer than I was when I walked in. A light hustle of the new guy, me, by the local pool shark (with help from the bartender) is taking place. We settle on five dollars a game, much less than the man was hoping for, and we talk while he brutalizes me on the felt in an almost playful manner—the way a cat might play roughly with a mouse, always leaving me a little room for hope, but ultimately crushing me. Thirty dollars later I manage to talk him into letting me recover for a bit.

I ask the pool shark if he'd grown up in the area, and he responds, "Of course."

"What do you like about living here?"

"The location."

He answers so quickly that it takes me a moment even to be surprised. Location? We are in the depths of the Allegheny National Forest in—I'm hesitant to use the phrase "the middle of nowhere," but having grown up in the middle of nowhere myself I feel like I know it when I see it.

"So you enjoy the outdoors? The river? Hiking and such?"

It is my best guess—and it is wrong.

"Fuck no. But I love rock and roll."

The man has been feeding the jukebox all night, but I still am not following.

"You know. Concerts."

"Do, uh, do a lot of bands come through Warren?"

"No the shit they do not. But like I said, location."

I just stand there, holding my pool cue, looking at him. He lets out a little sigh of exasperation and explains.

"Let's say there's a band playing—what band would you want to see?"

"I don't know. The Grateful Dead?"

It is the first band that pops into my head, probably prompted by a song that had played on the radio during my drive out.

"Well, Jerry died over twenty-five years ago, so that might be hard, but fine. Dead & Company, right? The band as they tour now. Let's say Dead & Co. are going on tour, and you want to see 'em, okay?"

"Sure."

"Now, you might think the best place to be is New York City. Or maybe Chicago. Or somewhere out on the West Coast. But I say the best place to be is Warren."

"Warren, Pennsylvania?" I finally just blurt it out, "Why is being in the middle of nowhere the best place to be?"

"I'm fucking happy you put it that way. Because that's right. The *middle* of nowhere. The middle is the key part of your, if you'll excuse me, dumb-as-shit ignorant comment. Because being in the middle of *nowhere* means you're not a far drive to *somewhere*."

"I meant no offense, just—"

"Five hours."

"Excuse me?"

"Five hours. That's how long it takes me to get to Philly. Maybe less if I'm really moving. Two and half hours or less to get to Pittsburgh. What about New York?"

"What about wh—"

"New York City's only six hours. Buffalo? Less than two. Syracuse? Four hours, easy."

"So you can get to other places from here?"

"You're starting to get it, but we haven't even talked about heading west yet."

"West?"

"Cleveland is less than three hours. You know what's in Cleveland?"

"Uh, *The Drew Carey Show*?"

"Close—given the 'Cleveland Rocks' theme song—but I'm talking about the Rock and Roll Hall of Fame. Columbus, Ohio, is less than five hours away, and you can get to Cincinnati in six. But hell, if you're going to go all the way to Cincinnati, might as well do Detroit."

"Michigan?"

"Detroit's only five hours away. But if the band you wanna see isn't playing Detroit, don't worry, because you can get to Indianapolis in seven. Or Chicago in eight."

"Okay, eight hours seems like a lot."

"Depends. How much do you love the band? Because . . . me? I love live music. So from here, if one of my favorite bands goes on tour, I can see 'em three, maybe four times depending on where they're playing. I can afford to live out here and save money for tickets and hotels. A dollar goes a lot farther in the woods."

"Pretty good scheme," I say, and I mean it. The man had made me see the area in a different way. As with most things, it really is all about perspective. "What are some of your favorite bands?"

"Oh, I have *a lot*. Another game?"

As we're playing he lists a few of his favorite bands—Dio, Rush, and Van Halen, the logo of which is tattooed on his arm. He turns and lifts up his long, stringy hair, and shows me another tattoo. The back of his neck reads "Life's a gamble," and he laughs as he takes another five dollars from me after I lose our final game, same as all the others.

It'd be easy to see the tattoo as hokey, except deep down, I know I agree with the sentiment. Gambling has never been my thing. I often tell friends that I have every vice, save that one. But as I've gotten older, I've come to understand that isn't quite true: I gamble with my pursuits. With the way I live my life. What I really am is someone who gambles with time. How I choose to spend it. Hell, we all do.

Life's a gamble.

"Can I get another Bud?"

"You got any money left?"

The one-eyed bartender, whose name is Clay, is joking, but I put some cash down on the bar just to prove that the rock-and-roll-loving hustler didn't totally clean me out.

Clay goes on to tell me that he's from the area, too. Born and raised. He'd been selling cars south of here, but came back after he got in a fight with his boss—"He was ripping me off, trying to skim off the top of my commissions"—and got his old job back at Cronie's, where he'd worked off and on for twenty years.

"This place is a house of misfits, but we all take care of each other."

It's a story I'm familiar with, and one that warms my heart as I think of it playing out in all the dives across America. Communities of people brought together to drink, talk, maybe smoke a cigarette or two, and listen to music. Dance. Hustle a little pool. Take thirty bucks off the newest patron.

Which is when the woman sitting next to me at the bar asks, "Are you a cop?"

She's wearing a Domino's uniform—visor and all—and nursing a large mixed drink. Coca-Cola and something strong. I look across the street and see a Domino's location, closed for the evening.

"Do you work there?" I gesture in the direction of the store, trying to change the subject.

"No shit, Sherlock. Like to solve mysteries, do ya?"

I shrug.

"A detective. I'll ask you again. Are you a cop?"

"No, I'm not a cop."

The woman looks me up and down, suspiciously. I press, "Do you not like cops?"

"I don't like cops I don't know. And I don't know you."

I let out a grunt. "Look," I say. "If I was a cop, I'd have to tell you, right? Like on TV."

The woman nods, slowly. "Entrapment."

"Exactly! Entrapment. So I'm telling you, I'm not a cop."

I'm not sure if the woman buys it or not, but she stops asking. It would only be later, when telling this story to two friends who both happen to be FBI agents, that I learned what I had told the woman was *completely incorrect*. A police officer is under no obligation to identify themselves as a police officer unless they are in uniform and on the job.

"How do you think I do undercover work?" one of my friends would scoff.

"Yeah, they've been saying that on television for years. It's a real help for us, to be honest," her wife would continue. "I get asked, 'Are you a cop?' or 'Are you a Fed?' all the time, because people think we have to identify ourselves. We don't."

Good to know.

Still, I am neither a cop nor a Fed—although the woman's insistance does make me wonder what I would be there to bust. I've seen a few folks going to the bathroom in groups every once in a while, but other than some mundane bar drug use nothing seems out of sorts.

"Do you know what time this place closes?"

The woman in the Domino's uniform shakes her head. "Always with the questions. That's why I think you're a cop."

"Place stays open until the party's over," Clay says while walking over to us, and gives the woman a look that seems to say, "Cut the guy some slack, would ya?"

It is clear that Cronie's is the spot in town that stays open late—hell, they might even stay open past closing. An after-hours bar, or a lock-in, where the place locks the front door at 2 a.m. but lets patrons and staff continue drinking so long as there are no "in and outs," people coming and going that might raise suspicion. All of a sudden the Domino's woman's interest in whether I was a cop or not makes a bit more sense.

Clay and the Domino's woman, whose name was Mary, start chatting, and I take the break in our conversation to text a friend of mine who's worked in Pennsylvania politics for over twenty years.

"Hey, I'm in Warren, PA. Any tips about the area? Anything I should know?"

"If you're out there, know that you're far from anything else."

"Sounds accurate. Is that all?"

"Stay white. Stay polite. You'll be alright."

"God damn."

I put my phone down. The room *is* very white.

"What are you in town for, though? If you don't mind me asking." The bartender is grabbing me another Bud. It is a fair question, and one I'm starting to ask myself.

16

As I mentioned before, after Massachusetts, the next actual *proof* we have of Johnny Appleseed's existence comes from a trading post ledger rediscovered right here in Western Pennsylvania—John Daniel's Ledger, to be exact.

The early days of John Chapman going west, much like his childhood days in Massachusetts—and mine—are hazy. Nobody is exactly sure how he and his younger half brother, Nathaniel (remember, Chapman's mother had died when he was two and his father went on to remarry), made their way from Longmeadow, Massachusetts, to the area now known as Warren County in Western Pennsylvania. They almost certainly crossed the Allegheny Mountains, though, following other Europeans who trod footpaths forged by Native Americans, who were in turn following ancient animal trails created by deer, bears, and other creatures of the land as they roamed looking for food or places to hunker down for the winter.

Why go west? John and Nathaniel headed out of New England sometime around 1795, putting Chapman in his early twenties and his brother somewhere around sixteen. The two young men lived off the land while traveling until a treacherous winter storm forced them to take shelter in what is now Warren County, Pennsylvania. The weather would not allow for further travel, so in 1797, they settled near the Allegheny River in the Brokenstraw Valley.

In his definitive-for-the-time biography, *Johnny Appleseed: Man and Myth* (published in 1954, right after the discovery of the aforementioned John Daniel's Ledger), historian Dr. Robert Price points out that there is a tale from the brothers' time on the Allegheny—but perhaps before they settled near Brokenstraw Creek—in which Nathaniel fell ill and was starving. The story goes that a traveling tribe of Munsee or Seneca Native Americans stopped to help young Nathaniel, nursing him back to health and teaching him how to use a bow and arrow to hunt small game, while his brother was away searching for provisions for them. The anecdote comes from William M. Glines's *Johnny Appleseed by One Who Knew Him,* originally published in 1875—so there is no way of fact-checking—but many reference this maybe-myth as the point when Chapman's positive relations with Native Americans may have started.

What we do know with certainty is that John Chapman and Nathaniel were in the area in 1797. John Daniel's Ledger was unearthed in the archives of the Warren County Courthouse in 1953 by Warren County Commissioner George Seavy, providing the earliest documentation of Warren County's settler citizens from 1795 to 1799. The ledger provided the receipts and accounts of each purchaser, and their payment method. Among the accounts was Chapman's, which was opened in 1797. Following his birth and baptismal records discovered in Leominster, these are the next chronological documentations we have of John Chapman's life.

According to the ledger, Chapman purchased a carpentry tool—a spike gimlet, which is T-shaped, with a wooden handle for turning, attached to the top of a forged spike, very popular at the time for making clothes out of animal hides, or even building a primitive shelter. According to the ledger, he also came away with three pairs of "mockasins," some cheese, and "sundries." There's no guessing what these sundries were, but the post also sold whiskey, sugar, chocolate, tobacco, gunpowder, pork, and even books.

Warren had its beginning on April 18, 1795, when the Pennsylvania legislature established three new towns in the northwest part of the state "to facilitate and promote the progress of settlements within the Commonwealth, and to afford additional security to the frontiers."

It's here that Chapman would develop into the man he would become—somewhat obsessed with living on the border between American settler "society" and the very-much-already-populated wilds to the west. That kind of life means there aren't a lot of documents with his name on them—and there are plenty of stories of him losing the ones he *did* have—but the business model he developed, of planting apple orchards as a way of halfhearted land speculation, was born here, on the banks of Brokenstraw Creek where it meets the Allegheny River, between what would come to be Warren and Youngstown, PA. It was on that Pennsylvania riverbank that the legend of Johnny Appleseed, the nurseryman and the nomad, was really born.

But back at Cronie's on my first night in Warren, I of course don't tell the patrons any of this. I also don't say what might be even a little closer to the truth. I'd felt stuck in my life recently, and wanted to spend time outside, away from people, or at least around people I didn't yet know: very possibly the same thing that may have brought Chapman here two hundred and twenty something years ago. Either way, I am chasing the trail of some long-lost hermitlike American saint and settler. A probing interest in the ways facts and fictions get mixed up in American mythology. To take it one step further, that grand tradition: trying to figure myself out while traveling this great big country of ours, out on the road. You know, by myself. Because none of my buddies could make it.

Instead, trying desperately to seem like a normal tourist, not someone maybe having a smidge of a mental breakdown, I tell anyone who asks what I am doing in town that "I'm gonna raft down the Allegheny River for a couple of days and see what happens."

"Huh." Clay the bartender sorta shrugs, and leaves it at that. Which is exactly when the jukebox switches from '80s rock and roll to Jay-Z and Kanye West's "Ni**as In Paris." The whole bar—entirely white—starts singing along, and when they get to the chorus . . . or, well, throughout the entire song, really, I listen as almost all the patrons, and certainly the one-eyed bartender, recites it word for word. Without the asterisks. I watch as Clay glances over at me as if to say, "This bothering you, out-of-towner?"

I look down at my drink. It is getting late. I had planned on asking Clay where I might be able to find a campsite, but now figure I am overstaying my welcome, or more plainly put, I no longer want to be here. I settle my tab, and all Clay says is, "Kanye means the party's about to really get going. Shift three over at the plant just ended, and the late-night crew love to have a good time. You'll meet my best friend—hell, I'll pour you a shot. You sure you want to leave?"

"Gotta find a place to crash for the night," I offer, and hope it is enough.

"Suit yourself. Maybe ya come back when you finish on the river."

I step out into the night, just as a few cars pull up. Shift three, I assume. I hold the door open for the influx of new patrons, another Kanye song blasting out into the night. I watch as every car empties into the place, almost all of the passengers Black men, still in uniforms. They nod and say hello as I hold the door open for them. My friend's text rattling in my mind, but seen differently now. Mary in her Domino's outfit leaps from her barstool and starts dancing. Soon everybody is—even my Van Halen pool hustler, a cigarette between his lips. Clay starts pouring shots, but not before he catches me looking through the front window as I let the door close. One of the men—I'm assuming his best friend—has jumped behind the bar and has thrown his arms around Clay's neck. They are singing together. Every word.

The bartender's face seems to say, "Judge not, lest ye be judged." Not sure I agree with him, I'm not really sure what I think at all. I just know what had happened, and what I'd seen, and that it all feels *uniquely* American.

17

THE NEXT MORNING, I brush my teeth in my beloved public restroom. I had pitched my tent down on the bank of the river—in the middle of the night it seemed as safe a place as any—but luckily I was up with the sun, because in the day's warm morning light the town of Warren is bustling. I walk to a nearby coffee shop, the Arbor, and try to chase Cronie's cobwebs out of my skull with a large black iced coffee.

By the time I drink my coffee and walk through Warren's beautiful brick-laden town center, Allegheny Outfitters is open. The shop, I would learn, is run by Piper VanOrd, who moved back home in 2006 after a stint in Alaska to open the Allegheny-oriented store, helping "10,000 people connect with the outdoors each summer." Piper was an air traffic controller for the US Navy for almost a decade, but she had grown up on the Allegheny River, and wanted to help others discover its natural beauty. The store is filled with life jackets and camping gear for sale, along with Yeti mugs and T-shirts that say things like "Life Is Better on the River," "I'd Hike That," "Small Towns Not Small Minds," and "Floats Well with Others."

I learned about Piper while talking to Kyle, who is the one opening the shop that morning. When he asks if he can assist me, I tell him about my plans to raft down the river. At first, I was worried he might not want to help, given that I'm not renting a boat from the shop, but he has a generous attitude, kindly showing me a map and immediately marking it up for me—pointing out places to camp, and where the more scenic spots to stop might be.

"You got a life jacket?"

"Uh, no, I don't."

"Okay, well you should definitely have one."

I gaze out at the water. It looks so peaceful. I'm a damn good swimmer. Still, safety first. I buy a life jacket—neon green, to match my floatie.

"How much for the map?"

"Ah, don't worry about that. We're here to encourage people to enjoy the river. Safely, of course. The map's free. As is the advice. Just be sure to look us up if you ever need to rent a canoe or kayak, or want a guided tour next time."

I promise him I will. It's funny, by trying to pay for the map I am, by extension, trying to buy his advice—it feels very New York City of me, assuming everything costs something. "Encourage people to enjoy the river," and they've been doing it for almost twenty years. A calling, almost something holy in it.

I say goodbye to Kyle as I leave, grateful for his guidance.

Grabbing my gear out of Rabbit—which Kyle graciously tells me I can leave parked in their parking lot for as long as I want—I walk back through downtown Warren wearing swim trunks and a life preserver, and carrying my lime-green mini-tube along with camping gear stuffed in a supposedly floatable wet bag that I also bought at the shop. A few people watch from the bridge as I slide down an embankment and decide that here is as good a place as any to enter the river (I would later learn that Allegheny Outfitters of course had a lovely place right by their shop to launch from, but I hadn't thought to ask).

Immediately I find myself up to my shins in river muck. My floatie slips out from under my ass time and time again, and at one point my wet bag, which *did* thankfully float, starts to drift downriver.

"You need a hand?" a man from the bridge calls.

"No, I've got it. Thanks!" I cry out, the green life jacket accentuating how red my embarrassed face has become.

Eventually I figure it out. I stick the floating wet bag under my legs, and my now-obviously-too-small floatie under my ass. I awkwardly try to paddle with my hands, making my way to the middle of the river, and wait for the current to take me.

And wait.

And wait.

And wait.

About fifteen minutes pass as I float under the bridge. The other people watching have gone on with their days, but not my helpful friend. When I pass through to the other side of the bridge, I look up—to be honest, because of my positioning, up is pretty much the only direction I *can* look—and the man is looking down on me. He actually crossed the street and waited for me there.

"You sure?"

"Gorgeous day to be out on the water!" I retort, doing my best to seem like everything is going according to plan.

Half an hour passes before I look back and see that the man has finally abandoned his post. But that means that a half an hour has passed and I am still in view of the bridge—I haven't even made it to a bend in the river yet. To my left is a hospital, and to the right a row of lovely old mansions from the oil-moneyed days of the late 1800s that are still regal, if a little rough for wear. But my movement is more like floating in a swimming pool than rafting down a river. The lack of a paddle doesn't help.

After over an hour passes—I know by the long chiming of the town's church bells—I am able to get past my stubbornness and admit that the man on the bridge had been right. I need assistance. Some help. I slowly hand-paddle my way to a concrete boat landing near the hospital, and—covered in water and mud—exit the river, and endure the short, but very public, hike back into town.

When I enter the outfitter shop, I feel like a child. Foolish. A fool.

"How'd that work out for you?"

Kyle is smiling behind the desk, but he doesn't mock me, and I am grateful for that.

"When you said 'raft,'" he added, "I figured you had something that involved paddles, not . . ."

He drifts off as he gestures at the floatie that still hangs off my shoulder. Why I haven't yet thrown it out—or even deflated it—I have no idea.

"You said something about rentals?"

Which is how I found myself, a half-hour later, in a bright orange kayak, coasting down the Allegheny. Happily assisted by a double-bladed paddle, no longer at the whims of the river's slow current.

When I was young, my father and mother would take me on long canoe trips. We'd often camp on the riverbanks, making small fires to warm our food. During the days we would ride the water, often going over Class 3, 4, and 5 rapids. My father would steer the canoe from the stern and my mother would sit in the bow, pushing her paddle against the water with all her might. The gear and I usually sat in the middle of the boat. I would grip the thwart—the wooden crossbar in the middle of the boat that strengthened the hull—for dear life, yelling out, "I can't believe this is happening to me!" as we were swept over the rocks by the rushing water.

"I can't believe this is happening to me" became a bit of a mantra in my family in those early years, before we moved out to the farm and our luck took a change: the phrase lost its shine once it matched reality.

There are no such rapids on the Allegheny, though. I swiftly pass the spot where I pulled out earlier in the day, covered in mud and cursing my lime-green floatie. Before, it took almost two hours to get to this point. Now a mere five minutes had passed.

The water is still slow and smooth, but my kayak cuts down the river swiftly.

I begin to see deer on the banks of the Allegheny and, at one point, a bald eagle floating above me, on the hunt for its midday meal. What a bad deal for the fish, I think. Simply swimming in cool, dark water, only to be snatched by claws and dragged into the sky. Your view of the world forever changed. The equivalent of some alien ship flying down through the clouds, plucking me up off the Allegheny and out into space.

You think weird thoughts when you're alone on a river.

But there are also the deer, and the bald eagle, and the great blue heron I find standing in the water of an inlet I turn into. It doesn't fly away. I still my paddle and we just sit there. Two creatures on a river in America, watching each other.

A trail of ducks follow me, and without thinking I use a J-stroke to straighten the path of my kayak. I remember my father teaching me the stroke when I was a child, my paddle just a small piece of wood he had carved. It's funny the things your muscles remember. I hadn't paddled a J-stroke in thirty years.

Chapman and his brother had no family in the area, but they did find a father figure when they lived here, out past the edge of colonial civilization.

When John and Nathaniel arrived in Pennsylvania they would

have found a single blockhouse, in which lived one sole permanent resident—the aforementioned Dan McQuay. McQuay worked for the Holland Land Company. Lumber and land speculation was a booming business at the time, and certain companies would hire robust frontiersmen like Dan to stake claim to a region and its natural resources.

An 1887 history of Warren County edited by J. S. Schenck, assisted by W. S. Rann, describes McQuay as "a genuine son of Erin, full of recklessness and adventure, fond of fun, fight and whiskey," which is to say that I liked him the moment I read about him. What's more is that he—like Chapman—was one helluva walker.

McQuay made as many as ten trips from the Warren area to New Orleans in command of virtual floating islands—small rafts lashed together to make huge barges—piled high with lumber and steered with a long pole that would push against the bottom of the riverbed. Water from the Allegheny eventually flows into the Gulf of Mexico via the Ohio and Mississippi Rivers, so McQuay followed the highway of flowing water all the way down.

He would surely have laughed at the image of me, earlier in the day, trying to float down the river on my back.

Since the rafts went only with the current, not against it, McQuay traveled the 1,200 miles back home by foot. This, according to Schenck, was "a perilous undertaking. . . . The few towns along the Ohio and Mississippi Rivers were then but insignificant villages, and all else between them tangled thickets, swamps and dense forests infested by Indians, wild animals, and frequently by worse foes—white desperadoes and highwaymen."

According to Howard Means's *Johnny Appleseed: The Man, the Myth, the American Story,* "Whatever John Chapman and Nathaniel might have made of Dan McQuay on first meeting, they must have been somewhat enchanted because for the next year, they seem to have tied their fortune and future pretty much to his own. John and

Nathaniel bunked with McQuay in the Holland Land Company blockhouse during the very early part of their time in Warren."

Is there also contemporary erotica based on Chapman and McQuay? Weird question, but I'm so glad you asked. *Man & Beast,* by Michael Jensen, was published in 2016, and while it is absolutely not based on any historical evidence, the *Advocate* praised the book as "equal parts romance novel and history lesson, heaped with sex and violence." Certainly one of the more idiosyncratic examples of the way John Chapman shows up in American culture these days.

But all pioneer paranormal shifter sexual fantasy fictions aside, there is a clear and *historically accurate* friendship between McQuay and Chapman. When you meet a hero in your early twenties, it's easy to fall under their spell: to mimic them, essentially, while you find your own voice. One can imagine John Chapman hearing about Dan McQuay's adventures, and thinking he might travel the wilderness by foot one day himself.

18

KYLE AT Allegheny Outfitters had told me to watch out for islands. For one thing, there were certain islands that—if you passed them on the wrong side—might end up getting you stuck in shallow waters. But, more importantly, some had people on them.

"You can camp on some if you want, but some islands have residents, and they don't like visitors."

"How will I know the difference?"

"Oh, you'll know."

I remember that conversation as I float by my first island covered in No Trespassing signs. Not long after a more clearly communicated STAY THE FUCK OFF OUR ISLAND message is painted in large block letters on a square of plywood. All these years later, people still making land claims. And wanting nothing more than to be left alone.

Out here on the river with few belongings, looking at signs claiming private property, I am struck by a fact about myself: I've never signed a lease in my entire life, despite constantly searching for a place to call home. As I've mentioned, I grew up in the Catholic Worker, my parents down on their luck while trying to figure out their lives: a baby, no real jobs, and still married to other people, each with their own kid—my half siblings—before I even showed up on the scene. After the halfway house and the gray house out on the farm, I got a scholarship for boarding school, then college—where I spent one semester living off campus in a rich woman's basement. An acquaintance from boarding school who was partially being charitable, and partially trying to get her conservative parents off her back (they were from outside St. Louis and worried about their daughter living in Washington, DC, all by her lonesome, never mind that she lived on Swann Street in Dupont Circle, one of the swankiest streets in the whole city at the time). Eventually I moved back onto campus and was replaced by a big brown pit bull, its wire crate in the basement where my bed used to be.

After that it was a half-renovated townhouse in Philadelphia that was more flophouse than home, then I threw myself across the country and landed in a cramped, thin-walled apartment in San Francisco that wasn't much of a step up. Still no lease, just monthly payments of around $650 that I pieced together working at a nearby bar. The man whose name was on the lease almost certainly was pooling the rest of our rents to cover his own, and he had no job to speak of, it seemed, other than taking his homemade puppets downtown to protest against male circumcision.

A few years later, another rich acquaintance let me sublet his one-room studio apartment. It was in a huge building with an Art Deco elevator that had a pull-close door and metal sliding gate. There was roof access and a view of downtown and the Oakland Bay Bridge. The acquaintance was getting married but wanted to hold on to the lease "just in case." Luckily for both of us, the marriage worked out and I lived in that beautiful apartment alone for four glorious years before moving to New York City, where a friend of a friend gave me a good deal on the basement apartment of his Brooklyn brownstone. A handshake agreement, no paperwork involved. I have now lived there for eleven years, the longest I've had the same address in my entire life.

Mix in with all that leaseless living: an affinity for sleeping outdoors.

A feeling that outside can also be a kind of home, an idea almost certainly planted in me by my father and our time, when I was very young, spent sleeping in tents in the forests of New Hampshire and Maine. Or later, in north central Massachusetts, sleeping in the woods near my best friend Conner's house when a party went too late or got too out of hand. The outside not meaningfully different from the inside when it came to Conner's plywood box of a home.

In college I would sleep on a bench from time to time, even developed a habit of breaking into worksites and scaling half-built buildings, the entirety of the city laid out before me—sometimes falling asleep in yet-to-be-finished offices, waking with the dawn and leaving quickly, hungover and hoping to avoid the construction crew.

California was much the same. Sleeping down on Ocean Beach after watching a sunset, or on the roof of a friend's house, a jacket pulled tight around me against the night's damp cold fog.

Was this adventure seeking? Sure. But it was also something deeper, that I carried steadfastly in my heart. Having grown up in a homeless shelter, there was a fear that I might be in that same position again—with no options. Here was a way of testing myself, pushing myself to an edge, almost to say to myself, "Even if the worst happens to you, you can handle it." A way of keeping that fear in check. Rough sleeping being both a reaction to my past, but also my way of facing it—both disease and prescription.

But also, I like sleeping outside, almost as if I'm proud of my ability to do it.

When I first moved to New York City in December of 2013, the apartment I was moving into was still being renovated—but I had nowhere else to go, so I made a habit of sleeping there once the workers left for the day, rolling myself up in tarps on the worksite. One night I found work gloves and wore them, only to oversleep the next morning. I awoke to a Jamaican man named Junior—who would later become a friend—walking into the apartment. I leapt to my feet so I was standing, fully dressed, while he set down his tool belt.

"Are you the carpenter?" he asked. I was still groggy, and ever since childhood I have always been afraid of—well, of many things, but one of them was being caught. So, not knowing what else to do, I just nodded in agreement.

"I have to get a few more things out of the truck. I'll be right back."

When he left I panicked and ran out the back, into a yard covered in snow. But the walls were high and there was nowhere to go but back inside, where Junior was waiting for me.

"You aren't the carpenter, are you?"

"No," I admitted.

"Okay, then. Why don't you take off my gloves."

Ten years later, locked out of that same apartment—now very much finished, thanks to Junior's fine craftsmanship—not wanting to bother my upstairs neighbor after having lost my keys, I chose to sleep under the stoop.

As my bright orange kayak floats down the river the sky turns bright orange, too. The sun is setting. I've enjoyed my day on the water. Well, eventually I did. But there isn't much light left, so I pull the kayak up onto an island and make camp for the night. I bought a few beers at the brewery right next to Allegheny Outfitters—Bent Run—and, not wanting to make a fire in case I missed a No Trespassing sign, decide that they'll make do for dinner.

I look out across the river as I crack a beer and settle in, a fallen log at my back. But soon I'm sitting upright again. Out on the other bank, outlined by the quickly fading orange light, that same large black dog. I stand up, but the dog doesn't move. It just sits there stoically across the water as the orange sky transitions to a dark blue.

"What the fuck," I say to absolutely nobody. It can't be the same dog, some 350 miles away from where I last saw it. But there it is, looking exactly like the dog I saw in the marsh outside of Westminster, and then again at the entrance of Red Apple Farm. I want to yell out to the dog—to what end? Maybe see if I can call it over? Can the dog swim? But I'm worried I might be an unwelcome guest on somebody's island, and don't want to draw attention to myself. The sun has fallen out of the sky at this point. The sitting dog moves, but only to lie down and then curl up, like a large cat. It rests its massive head on its hindquarters and continues watching me.

I stare back until night engulfs us both. With no fire to read by—and realizing that I'm being eaten alive by bugs, as I've forgotten one of the few things from my friend's list that I actually purchased, bug spray—I wrap myself up in my sleeping bag and slip into an uneasy sleep.

The next morning, the first thing I do is look out across the river to see if the dog is still there, but all I see is dawn reflected in the water. The woods on the other bank are empty save for a few birds. The second thing I do is realize I've overshot my pickup spot. After traveling so slowly during my first attempt, I've traveled too quickly on my second. Still, *how hard can it be to paddle upstream?*

Turns out the answer is *quite.*

It's like my first foray on the river in my lime-green floatie, but in reverse. I paddle hard against, well, the current, I guess. Which is frustrating, as the water itself seems almost still. There is no visible current, but it is in there somewhere. Like fighting an imaginary foe, one that is still kicking your ass.

After an hour or so of arduous paddling, I give up the meager progress I've made to steer closer to the bank of the river, the invisible undercurrent pushing me back while I do. When I can see the bottom of the river, I jump—or, more accurately, roll—out of my kayak, miscalculating the depth. I find myself up to my chest, doing my best to escape my life jacket, which keeps trying to pull my feet off the river floor, while not letting my kayak float away.

For the next hour I walk back upstream, my kayak in tow. If this was two hundred or so years ago, I might be part of a party heading west, with some help carrying my boat over dry land. Or if I were as skilled as Dan McQuay, I'd be having no difficulties at all, even if my boat was a barge and not a kayak. Or, if you want to believe some of the legends about John Chapman—which he himself may have perpetuated—I could navigate the Allegheny even during the winter. The story goes that Chapman, realizing that ice floes moved faster downstream than he could paddle, would pull his canoe up onto them and rest while he traveled, one yarn saying he fell asleep and ended up a hundred miles past his destination.

But instead I struggle, even in the warm summer weather, my ankles rolling as I walk the uneven, rock-lined river bottom, embarrassed—despite there being no one there to see me—by how ridiculous I must look to the birds circling high above. The current is barely perceivable, my struggle very much so.

Only once do I lose hold of my bright orange kayak, and am forced to jump in on purpose to swim after it.

An hour later and about half a mile upstream I drag my kayak onto the shore at the Buckaloons Boat Ramp, and then collapse. I'm covered in muck—even more so than the day before when I first entered the Allegheny with my dinky tube. I smell like shit, am exhausted, and most of my gear is wet. I enjoyed my time on the river, but have proven myself to be not so good at navigating it.

I lie down in the grass, bone-tired. Crumpled up. I am right where Brokenstraw Creek joins the Allegheny. For all I know Chapman himself once rested on this very shore—his first nursery planted right up the road, er, river—along with his brother, or maybe even Dan McQuay.

—

“Terrific day, isn’t it?”

I must have fallen asleep in the grass—I didn’t even notice the man pull his kayak from the river, but as I cup my hand over my eyes to block out the sun and get a better look at him I can see that he’s a lot less muddy than I am. Not to mention better rested, and just, well, more refreshed.

Peter has come east from Ohio to do some adventuring and is also awaiting pickup by Allegheny Outfitters. I do my best to wipe the mud off me and look a little more presentable as we get to talking.

“I love to do little trips like this,” Peter says. “Traveling internationally is great, of course, but looking up some spot not too far away and just *heading there* . . . finding a good local motel to stay at. Some good restaurants in the area. There is so much America to explore.”

Peter has a point. Not just about international travel, either. There are a couple landmarks everyone keeps on their bucket lists—the Statue of Liberty, the Grand Canyon, the Golden Gate Bridge—but with a bit more research the entire country turns out to be teeming with national parks, state parks, and national forests like the one we’re in right now. So often people flock to cities or big attractions that it’s easy to forget how much wilderness there still is out here to get lost in.

Peter mentions that he’s an EMT out of Cleveland. He bemoans the need for more EMTs—both where he’s from and elsewhere.

“Usually a class size of new recruits is around fifty people, more recently there’s only been seven or eight students. It’s tough. So many areas experience brain drain—it happens all across the country. Of course you have the people that move to New York, or Los Angeles. Austin, Texas. But even when young people don’t move out of state, they usually head to the cities. That can leave areas—like this one—feeling underserved.”

I mention Piper VanOrd, who runs Allegheny Outfitters—how

she grew up in the area, moved away, and then came back. Plus the guys next door, at Bent Run brewery. How the whole town is trying to amplify the beauty of the river.

"It'd be great to see that everywhere. There's so much space, so much room in this country. It'd be interesting to see what would happen if everyone didn't always go running for the cities. Now, you of course have to have opportunity. But there's always ways to make your own."

When I think of how many people I know who wish they could afford a house—and yet there *are* houses *out there* to own. It just comes down to whether you're open to not living in a place you've come to think of (in your mind, or at society's urging) as the center of the universe.

The van pulls up, driven by a young man who isn't Kyle. We load our kayaks into the boat pull. As we drive back into town, we ask the driver if he grew up here—he did.

"Any plans on leaving?" Peter asks.

"No. Got a job. Got the river. That's all I need."

Peter smiles, and I smile, too.

19

THE NEXT MORNING I rock up to the Peppermill Restaurant, a favorite during my visit to Warren. They serve a mean breakfast, with pancakes the size of a monster truck wheel (don't order more than one if you're traveling solo). You can have the pancake plain or with blueberries, or you can get a strawberry pancake roll-up. The cream chipped beef on toast and sausage gravy and biscuits are also delectable, though they probably aren't helping my blood pressure.

While at the Peppermill I enjoy watching the elderly, mostly male patrons—right out of an old Sears catalog, wearing mesh baseball hats advertising farming supply companies, with flannel shirts and large thick glasses—getting served by the younger generation, who are dressed like mannequins in the display window of a Hot Topic: all green hair and piercings, wide jeans and nu-metal tattoos. You'd think they'd be serving Monster energy drinks instead of coffee, or flat-out beginning some generational warfare right there in the diner. But instead, the patrons and waitstaff get along splendidly, asking about family, or school, or work, or thoughts on the upcoming weather. It is like some kind of Norman Rockwell painting, if Norman Rockwell had gone through a goth phase.

This morning I've ordered the Breakfast Skillet—an iron skillet stuffed with two eggs, home fries, sausage, ham, cheddar cheese, grilled peppers, onions, and a side of deli toast. After I finish my abundant breakfast and tip my skate-video-ready server, I walk out of town toward the Kinzua Dam, one of the largest dams east of the Mississippi.

The dam is about a seven-mile walk out of town along Hemlock Road. It takes me about two and a half hours or so to get out there on foot, and the same to come back, passing rustic huts and houses along the way—but you can take Route 59 in a car if you want to get there quicker. The structure is giant, a massive man-made marvel in an otherwise natural setting. The dam created the Allegheny Reservoir, also known as Kinzua Lake, the second deepest lake in the entire state, which extends twenty-five miles to the north—just south of Salamanca, New York, which is within the Allegheny Reservation of the Seneca Nation. Looking at the lake on a map, though, it looks less like your traditional lake and more like an extremely fat river, snaking north over the Pennsylvania–New York border.

The reason the dam was built all the way up here was a flood that occurred all the way down in Pittsburgh—on March 17 and 18, 1936—known as the Great St. Patrick's Day Flood. Local residents had been begging the federal government for help with flooding in the area for almost thirty years at that point, but now there was a death toll, with at least sixty-nine fatalities occurring in all of Western Pennsylvania, including forty-five within Pittsburgh city limits.

Not long after, Congress passed the Flood Control Acts of 1936 and 1938, but the construction of the dam—built by the US Army Corps of Engineers, who maintain the dam to this day—did not begin until 1960, with it being completed in 1965 and the filling of the reservoir lasting until 1967. Besides flood control along the Allegheny River, another benefit was hydroelectric power production, which is largely distributed to Pittsburgh.

Over those twenty-five or so years, though, opposition to the dam had grown, particularly and unsurprisingly among the Seneca Nation based in New York State, who had been having a pretty rough go of things since white people first showed up. The Seneca Nation fought the construction of the dam but ultimately lost their legal battle—unsurprisingly, given this country's track record of keeping its promises to Native Americans. The Army Corps of Engineers moved forward with the Kinzua Dam as planned, and construction began on October 22, 1960. Over ten thousand acres of Seneca land was drowned on September 16, 1966, when the dam became operational. Some six hundred Seneca were displaced—nine communities in total—as well as multiple descendants of European colonizers in the area. But it was the Seneca, many of whom had been living traditionally, with no modern conveniences, whose lives were completely uprooted. Two residential resettlement areas were constructed, both of which included modern amenities. This forced modernization rightly infuriated the displaced and their descendants.

Imagine if we forced the Amish to start using the internet.

The dam's construction violated the 1794 Treaty of Canandaigua, signed by President George Washington—but by the 1960s almost all treaties between Native Americans and the federal government had been broken. Even President John F. Kennedy, who campaigned on what he called a "sharp break" from the federal government's mistreatment of Native Americans, denied a request by the Seneca to halt construction once he was in the White House. Kennedy, in short, had fucked over the Seneca.

Peter La Farge's song "As Long as the Grass Shall Grow," which Johnny Cash recorded as the first track on his 1964 album, *Bitter Tears: Ballads of the American Indian,* covers the Seneca's failed fight against the Kinzua Dam. The second verse is filled with lines like:

> Across the Allegheny River, they're throwing up a dam
> It will flood the Indian country, a proud day for Uncle Sam
> It has broke the ancient treaty, with a politician's grin
> It will drown the Indians' graveyards, Cornplanter can you
> swim

More than five hundred years after white people showed up in this hemisphere as its first illegal immigrants, broken treaties and forced resettling are not things of the past—and their implications still have heartbreaking results. "History" is a convenient word for strife that is still ongoing.

Though, around 225 years ago, John Chapman was learning to exist in the wilderness, perhaps even being abetted by Seneca—yet his very existence and continued westward march would make him almost a peaceful, amenable mascot for American expansionism and Manifest Destiny—after his death and lionization, that role became all the more solidified. A Mickey Mouse for western expansion. Yet it is always made clear, in all the John Chapman legends and histories, that he was a "friend" to Native Americans. The problem with the real world is that two things are often true at the same time. Chapman was, in life, often a friend. But in death he becomes a legend used to help America look away from the darker aspects of its past.

John Chapman isn't the only symbol of western expansion that has its roots in Warren, Pennsylvania. St. Louis's famous Gateway Arch—the "gateway to the west," a 630-foot-tall archway that is one of America's most famous national monuments—was built from 142 triangular stainless-steel sections, each about twelve feet long. But those sections weren't made in St. Louis. The stainless steel pieces of the Gateway Arch were fabricated at a now closed Pittsburgh–Des Moines Steel plant in Warren from 1962 to 1965—the same time the Kinzua Dam was being constructed. Those pieces were then shipped more than seven hundred miles by railcar to Missouri, where iron-workers assembled the sections into the gigantic inverted catenary curve that now sits on the banks of the Mississippi River. But you wouldn't know any of that if you were at the monument itself. No mention is made of the skilled Western Pennsylvanian boilermakers who made the sections, as a historian pointed out to me while I was visiting the Warren Historical Society before leaving town the next day. Wanting their skilled laborers' contributions to history not to be forgotten, the town of Warren erected its own "Baby Arch" in 2017 at the Warren County Visitors Bureau, located about a mile west of Warren's downtown on US 6. The mini-replica stands fourteen feet tall, and is made of the same polished stainless steel as its big, older brother down in St. Louis.

The Kinzua Dam itself is huge, made of concrete, and 179 feet tall. It rises up brusquely, almost violently out of the Allegheny. A monument itself, but a functional one. Not for decoration. All dams bend the natural world to man's will. Yet again, we have complexity—the benefits the dam provides by fighting against nature, alongside the destruction it caused.

In *Zen and the Art of Motorcycle Maintenance,* Robert M. Pirsig writes, "The way to solve the conflict between human values and technological needs is not to run away from technology. That's impossible. The way to resolve the conflict is to break down the barriers of dualistic thought that prevent a real understanding of what technology is—not an exploitation of nature, but a fusion of nature and the human spirit into a new kind of creation that transcends both."

Tell that to the Seneca.

As I walk back on a windy road alongside the Allegheny, a few cars pass, a couple of people wave, but for the most part I am by myself. The surrounding woods keep me cool, despite the heat.

I cross a bridge—on the other side a young man is fishing. It's another wholesome Norman Rockwell painting with a '90s rave twist. The young fisherman is dressed as if he's the manager of a Korn cover band. I wonder if the fish appreciate all the gel that went into keeping his hair that spiky in the damp summer air.

"Anything biting?" I call out as I walk by.

The Manic-Panic-meets-Camo-Life poster child looks up from the water.

"Not yet, but they will. They always do."

And with that confidence and self-assurance, he turns back to the river and throws his line out as I continue making my way back into town.

20

YOU LOOK LIKE SHIT."

I'm at Cronie's again, and Clay the one-eyed bartender is right. I *do* look like shit. It's probably for that reason that I'm back here, and not at the aforementioned Bent Run brewery, which looks like it draws a lovely crowd of people who aren't covered in river grime and haven't camped—okay, more like half drunkenly fallen asleep on the ground—outside the night before. I've been bumming around Warren for more than three days now.

"Looks like the river treated you just about as how I would have expected. You want that shot now?"

I nod, and the bartender and I take shots of whiskey together.

"To Dan McQuay," I say. Clay flashes me a confused look, and I tell him all about the man who I believe helped inspire Johnny Appleseed. The lesser-known legend who inspired the legend we all know. Like a comedian's comedian or a writer's writer.

"Well, that tracks, at least him being Irish anyway."

"How do you mean?"

"It's how my ancestors got out here. Scotsmen, Irish. The Quakers, ya know? Pacifists. Couldn't fight the Indians—I'm sorry, Native Americans"—he gives me the same "too much for ya?" look from earlier—"but that doesn't mean they didn't want to, right? There were raiding parties and skirmishes all around here. So what do they do?"

I shrug.

"Well, the Quakers tell the immigrants—the Scots and the Irish—

'Hey, go kill the Indians out there and we'll give you parcels of land once you make it safe for us to come out and expand.' Tale as old as time. People who already got enough sending poor people to go fight for scraps so they can take the lion's share and have even more. Same reason we still go to war today."

I start to put something together in my mind. His missing eye—

"Are you a vet?"

"Oh, fuck no. What? This?" He points at his uncovered hollow. "Nah, this happened when me and Derek—remember my friend from the other night? That's Derek. He and I were fucking around with roman candles and fireworks and shit and—*boom splat!*"

He puts his hand by his face and mimics an explosion, his laughter filling the bar as he pours us both another shot.

Clay's telling of the area's history isn't wrong, but it certainly has a ring of legend to it. The facts, in a way, are even more gruesome.

The Treaty of Paris—the one in 1783, which ended the Revolutionary War and formally recognized the independence of the United States from Great Britain (not the one in 1763 that marked the end of the Seven Years' War, and the French and Indian War along with it)—established the boundaries of the newly formed country, at least in the eyes of Europe and, well, white folks. The United States claimed vast stretches of land between the Appalachian Mountains and the Mississippi River, extending from the Atlantic coast to the Mississippi and north to the Great Lakes.

The US called it the Northwest Territory, but the land had been long inhabited by Native American nations—mainly the Miami, Shawnee, and Delaware, along with other tribes. The settlers came quickly, moving into Ohio's fertile river valleys, carving farms out of forests, often under the protection of newly built forts. But the tribes of the Northwest Confederacy, a loose alliance formed to resist US expansion, would not surrender their lands without a fight.

Leading them was Little Turtle, a savvy Miami war chief, alongside Blue Jacket of the Shawnee and Buckongahelas of the Delaware. They saw clearly what the Americans' westward ambitions meant: loss of territory, culture, and sovereignty.

In 1790, President George Washington sent General Josiah Harmar to bring Native resistance to heel. But Little Turtle's warriors ambushed Harmar's troops near the Maumee River, inflicting a devastating defeat. The following year, another force under General Arthur St. Clair advanced deeper into tribal lands. On a bitter November morning in 1791, just outside present-day Fort Recovery, Ohio, Native warriors launched a massive assault. More than nine hundred American soldiers were killed or wounded—one of the worst military disasters in US history at that point.

Congress was stunned. The federal army was in shambles, and the credibility of the young republic seemed at stake. In response, Washington turned to a battle-hardened veteran of the Revolution: General "Mad Anthony" Wayne. Wayne took his time, spending nearly two years building and training a disciplined force called the Legion of the United States.

In 1794, Wayne marched north into the heart of Native territory. At the Battle of Fallen Timbers, near present-day Toledo, Ohio, his troops crushed the Native confederation. Crucially, the British, who still held nearby forts and had long encouraged Native resistance, refused to open their gates to the retreating warriors. The alliance between Native nations and their former British allies had fractured.

The war formally ended in 1795 with the Treaty of Greenville. Native leaders, recognizing their position, signed away much of present-day Ohio, along with parts of Indiana, Illinois, and Michigan. The Northwest Indian War was more than a border conflict. It was a brutal, costly struggle over competing visions of the land. For the United States, it secured a vital region and helped assert federal authority. For Native Americans, it marked the beginning of a tragic era—one of broken treaties, forced removals, and the long shadow of displacement and genocide.

It is also one of those conflicts they don't really teach you in school—unless you end up taking an American history course in college focused specifically on this time period. More likely than not, you're taught about the Revolutionary War, then some vague talk of westward expansion, and then it's time for the Civil War. But there were many other conflicts, like the Whiskey Rebellion in 1791 right here in Pennsylvania, or the Daniel Shays Rebellion in 1786, back in Massachusetts. These mini-rebellions—often led by men who had fought against the tyranny of England only to find they had new financial masters who weren't much better than the monarchs—helped strengthen the newly formed federal government.

So many people in this still-quite-young country—a new country built on land stolen from Indigenous peoples and with an economy buoyed upon slavery—still feel aggrieved to this day. A real and true problem, especially when you build a country on lofty ideals and philosophies—an experiment that has lasted 250 years, which has been showing wear and tear since the moment it was stitched.

On my way out of town, I swing by the spot where historians claim that John Chapman grew his first orchard, out past where Brokenstraw Creek meets the Allegheny. The area is suburban—save for a large empty farm field. I think about how beautiful this land must have been back before it was settled. When John and his half brother Nathaniel were trying to figure out their lives. But also, I see that the area's beauty still holds.

It was here that Johnny Appleseed came closest to settling down.

Collecting seeds from the discarded pomace—the pulpy remains of apples after the juice had been extracted for cider—given to him for free at cider mills in Western Pennsylvania, he would use those seeds to establish his first nurseries, selling apple seedlings to westward-heading colonists.

This cycle would turn a 100 percent profit, though most of Chapman's money would go to charitable acts inspired by his burgeoning Swedenborgian beliefs, not lining his own pockets. Yet, after a few years, Chapman's own wanderlust kicked back in, and he decided to take this very same show on the road, establishing orchards across what would become Ohio and eventually Indiana.

I park my Jeep by the side of the road and follow an unmarked path into the woods and down to the banks of Brokenstraw Creek. I dip my fingers into the water, feel its coolness, and then I raise my wet hand up to my forehead. I make the sign of the cross, get on my knees, and pray.

21

THE CHECK ENGINE light has been on for over a hundred miles. I've been hoping it's something simple—sometimes the light comes on because you didn't properly close your gas cap, or the hood of the vehicle is ajar. But I pull over at a scenic lookout, with lush green hills and a wide blue river on display to check both. No such luck.

I drive for another fifty more miles or so, taking my usual approach to problem solving: hoping the problem will go away on its own. Again, no such luck. Which is how I come to find myself in the middle of nowhere—like *truly* the middle of nowhere, like Warren is a cosmopolitan hub in comparison—when I finally exit the highway and decide that this problem needs fixing.

The town I pull into is by a river somewhere near the Pennsylvania-Ohio border. It could be any town in America. There's a closed-down train station—just like the one in my childhood home of Athol, Massachusetts—and a closed-down river rafting shop, and a closed-down bar with old murals of bikers painted on an exterior wall. There is an old sign highlighting some small but seemingly significant role the river played in US history, and another sign reminding passersby that some local homes were safe houses along the Underground Railroad.

It takes me longer than I'd hoped to find the town after I pulled off the highway—I had to cross and then recross the river. There were signs that I followed claiming a detour, but no indication of any actual roadwork being done. But as I drive along the sleepy, mostly boarded-up main street, I'm pleasantly surprised to find an auto shop, which has a faded mural of a wild bearded man—half the backpacker I saw in Warren and half Johnny Appleseed—in a canoe riding a raging river, and it's open.

"Hello?"

I hear fast-paced music playing—all trumpets, guitars, and rhythm—on a small radio as I enter the garage. A man maybe my age or a little older peers out from underneath the hood of a car.

"¿Qué?"

The man looks at me quizzically.

"Uh, hi. I was wondering if you could take a look at my Jeep? The check engine light is on and I want to make sure everything is okay."

"¿Qué pasó?"

I suddenly regret dropping Spanish my freshman year of high school for Latin because I'd read *The Secret History* and really liked the movie *Gladiator*.

I stutter, "No hablo español. ¿Habla inglés?"

"No."

But the man is wiping the oil from his hands with a rag and walking toward me. The only other thing I know how to say in Spanish is "Dónde está el baño" or "Dónde está la cerveza." So I'm relieved when he confidently waves me outside.

"Vamos a ver cuál es el problema."

I take him out to Rabbit, jump into the driver's seat, and start the car. I point to the check engine light, which shines a vivid orange.

"Okay, mete el coche en el taller."

I turn off the car and hop out. "Yeah, so, I don't know what's up. But can you take a look?"

The man looks at me again, a bit more bemused than quizzical now as he holds out his hand. I go to shake it and he laughs.

"Dame las llaves."

He pantomimes turning a key in an ignition.

"Oh. Yeah." I hand him my keys. "Any idea how long this will take?"

The man doesn't react, only jumps in my Jeep and drives it into the garage, but not before shouting back at me, "Vuelve en una hora."

I have no idea what he said.

I walk through the town and find an antiques shop that's open. I peruse some tchotchkes before landing on a glass that boasts sights and history of New Hampshire, figuring it would make a good gift for my half brother who lives in Portsmouth, NH, and collects old American souvenirs—but really I just want to buy something and not be a lookie-loo before asking, "Is there anywhere to grab a bite around here?"

The woman glances up from the paperback romance she is reading and says, "Sure, there's a Mexican place a few doors down. Food's good. They'll make you a sandwich if you like. Call it a 'torta.'"

I know what a torta is, having lived in San Francisco for many years. But not the way this woman just pronounced it, like it was something closer to the word "turtle."

"Where are you from?" the woman asks as she rings me up.

"Oh, New York."

"Whereabouts?"

"Brooklyn."

"Oooooh, the big city. How'd you find us out here?"

"Uh, I had engine trouble, actually."

I feel bad momentarily but she responds flatly, "Well, you don't come for the sights, that's for sure. But that mechanic is good. Do you speak Spanish?"

"Nada," I say, trying to be funny. The woman doesn't smile.

"Well, he'll give you a fair shake, but it'd be better if you spoke Spanish. Most people around here do nowadays."

The woman's voice stays flat, just stating a fact. She doesn't seem too concerned one way or the other.

"Immigration, or . . ."

"Mostly. Which I'm thankful for. Most people around here have moved away. Kids don't stick around. Want to move to Pittsburgh or Philadelphia or Ohio, or—" she smiles before finishing her sentence. ". . . New York City."

"Well, it really is lovely here," I offer.

"Sure, but lovely doesn't pay the bills."

"Business is tough?"

"The highway used to roll through here. I've had this shop for over thirty years. Used to sell antiques to folks like yourself who were traveling through. We used to have a gas station and a diner and you could rent a canoe across the street there, and tourists would play on the river. But that slowly started dying out. Then they diverted the highway a few years back. Said it was for repairs, but whatever the repairs were they never made 'em. Business dried up even quicker after that."

"How many people are in this town now?"

"Under five hundred, and like I said, mostly new faces. Land is cheap. Families who have been here for generations will sell their house and try to make it somewhere else."

"And you?"

She laughs again. A smoker's laugh. Raspy, but somehow not harsh. She holds out her hands.

"What? And leave all this? I make enough to keep my shop open, and that's all that matters to me. And like I said, I like the tortas."

I chuckle and she nods approvingly.

"Before I ring you up, did you know that this glass is part of a set?"

I exit the shop with six different state glasses—Vermont, Maine, Connecticut, Massachusetts, Rhode Island, along with New Hampshire, plus a glass pitcher inscribed "New England." There are lobsters and sailboats and green mountains and Minutemen and the Old Man of the Mountain adorning each appropriate glass. My brother will love them, but as I awkwardly carry them in a plastic bag—doing my best not to crack them—I wonder whether the woman had just been a Chatty Cathy happy for the passing company or if she could just spot an easily upsold sucker from a mile away.

Twenty minutes later, though, I no longer really care—having just eaten the most delicious Mexican meal since the last time I was actually in Mexico, right there at the ass end of Pennsylvania.

Widen the aperture enough, and you'll see that this is what we do as a species. We move around this planet, chasing resources—sometimes violently, especially when there are other people already there—or trying to avoid natural or man-made disasters. Even in this country's relatively short existence, immigration and migration have always been loaded topics.

But as I walk through this town and think of all the towns like it that I know throughout every state in America, I think again about my conversation with Peter, and the possibility of a great reshuffling. A new, far less genocidal western expansion, or eastern—or southern or northern—depending on which way you're traveling. Small towns like this one not simply crumbling into the past, but thriving with a new influx of residents, building on what came before.

According to the Census Bureau the urban population in the United States was around 80 percent of the total population in 2022. But it wasn't always this way. In the 1960s, two out of three Americans lived in cities, around 66 percent versus today's 80 percent. In the 1920s it was around one in two Americans, or 50 percent. In 1870, it was one in four Americans, a mere 25 percent. And in 1790, around when John Chapman was born? Around one in twenty Americans lived in what would have been considered urban areas at the time. That's 5 percent of the entire population.

For decades, and you can even say centuries (two of them and change, to be exact), Americans (especially young Americans) have increasingly flocked to cities. The industrial revolution—which coincided with the founding of the nation—of course played a large role in that movement. People tend to move to where the jobs are.

It's also a rite of passage. Who doesn't want to get out of their hometown, at some point in their youth, and move to the big city? You're sick of everyone knowing you, whether you want them to know you or not. Of making your own fun and driving around aimlessly for no good reason. You want to go see the world, which usually means moving to a nearby city within your home state. Or maybe even New York, after watching *Sex and the City* a few too many times.

But we live in a time of high rents, alongside technology that allows many people to work from anywhere. In my mind, I visualize all the towns across the country that have been steadily losing residents repopulated and thriving. A reverse of the last two hundred years, almost like a slowly beating heart—expanding after years and years of contraction. Or perhaps like the Big Bang, a whole universe from an initial state of high density and temperature. Young people leaving cities in droves to build communities—like the one I'm now in, rebuilt by immigrants revitalizing a dying town. Houses fixed up and reinhabited. Local business and cultural centers brought back to life, or perhaps built for the first time. It makes me think of what Piper is doing with her river rafting shop in Warren, PA, and the crew at Bent Run brewery right next door.

A new expansion, refilling the vast, mostly empty regions of this country.

"¿A qué velocidad manejas normalmente?"

I look at the mechanic and shrug. He takes me over to Rabbit, opens up the driver's side door and points to the speedometer on the dash.

"¿A qué velocidad?"

I get a sense of what he is asking. When I was a rambunctious youth, I always loved speed. Going fast: pedaling my rusty bike up the largest hill in town, sweat beading on my forehead, only to rip the bike around at the top of the hill—flying down, the wind whipping past my ears, the sweat on my forehead being wiped away, grinning so hard my cheeks would begin to hurt. This love of speed followed me as a young driver, leading to the type of reckless driving that turns my hair white just remembering it.

Now, years later, with the great roads of America stretched before me, I still find it hard to slow down. I'd only had Rabbit for a short while but I'd say I averaged 90 miles an hour or more while on the highway, the radio turned up, Outlaw Country like Waylon Jennings or Hank Williams Jr. blaring loud to drown out the wind roaring through the Jeep's interior, the Wrangler's boxy shape not approaching anything near aerodynamic.

I point to around 75/80 on the speedometer, like a patient who doesn't want to admit to their doctor the number of drinks they actually consume in a week.

"No manches, tienes que ir más despacio."

The man pushes out both hands and gestures downward.

"Slow down," I say. "Got it."

The man points at Rabbit and makes the same hand motion.

"Jeeps aren't built for speed," I agree, knowing he does not understand me. I make the slow-down hand motion back at him. He smiles.

"Falta un repuesto que debería llegar en unas horas. Si quieres, espera aquí."

I shrug, not understanding. The man goes back into the shop and returns holding a simple wooden chair. He puts it in the shade and motions for me to sit.

So I do.

After a few hours the man comes outside again. I had been reading a book, *Old Glory* by Jonathan Raban, but then must have dozed off and woken up when he approached me.

"Mi esposa maneja un Jeep. También le gusta manejar rápido."

The man laughs, so I laugh too, not knowing what we are laughing at.

He pulls out a pack of cigarettes and offers one to me. I quit smoking years back, but I also don't want to be rude. I haven't been bored in quite some time, something I notice in this moment. A stretch of time with nothing to do. A boredom born of being stuck in one place. Nowhere to go.

There's nothing quite like a cigarette when you're bored. Hell, maybe that's why I was able to quit—society hasn't allowed me to be bored since the early 2000s.

I accept the cigarette and the man lights it for me before lighting one of his own.

"El repuesto debería llegar pronto."

I've given up on trying to understand. If the man wants to sit out here and smoke with me as the sun slowly falls out of the sky, let him. Maybe we will never fix my Jeep. Maybe I'll just live here now. Welcome boredom back into my life. Pick smoking back up.

After a few hours, a large delivery truck pulls up to the garage.

"Bueno."

That one I get.

The man flicks his cigarette away, converses with the driver in Spanish, then walks back into the garage. The truck driver gives me a friendly wave and continues down the road.

Ten minutes later, the mechanic pulls Rabbit out, leaves the engine running, and beckons me over.

He doesn't even try anymore, just holds up his phone. The number 150 is typed into the calculator app. I hand the man $200 and do my best to say "gracias" in a way that doesn't sound like "grassy ass."

"Es nada. Solo recuerda a manejar despacio. No seas como mi esposa."

He hands me a piece of grease-covered machinery—the piece of my engine that had failed me. I toss the offending metal into Rabbit's middle console, thank the man again, and drive out of the small, sleepy stateline town.

That piece of machinery is still in my middle console to this day. I drove sixty-five miles per hour out of that town and have continued to do so. Rabbit hasn't needed anything other than her oil changed since.

22

THE DAY I LOST—or maybe "lost" isn't the right word: the day I spent sitting quietly, serenely, contemplatively in that town, has made me a day behind schedule. I am crossing into Ohio and the sun is setting and I don't have the faintest idea where I'm going to sleep tonight.

While much fanfare is given to how many nights Johnny Appleseed spent sleeping outdoors—often by a fire, with his feet pointed at the flames to keep warm, or in a hollowed-out stump for a few winters—the truth is he often ended up sleeping at a stranger's house, and more often than that, at a friend's. After leaving Pennsylvania and heading into Ohio, Chapman began walking in what could almost be described as seasonal circles. Hundreds of miles each year, checking in on his nurseries and planting new ones, sharing seeds and, over time, building up relationships with the farmers, settlers, and homesteaders who lived more grounded lives than he did. A rambling man, Chapman would share news from other parts of the region, and spread Swedenborg's teachings. It is said that he loved children, and would often impress young ones with feats of derring-do, such as showing off the toughness of his oft-unshoed feet—walking on hot coals, or even sticking his gruff, hardened soles with needles.

Many of the firsthand accounts we have of John Chapman come from children, who were adults by the time of his death, and were still around to be interviewed as his fame grew in the late 1800s. Rosella

Rice, an author and poet born in Perrysville, Ohio, in 1827, once described a visit from Chapman at her family's farm: "We can hear him read now, just as he did that summer day, when we were busy quilting upstairs, and he lay near the door, his voice rising denunciatory and thrilling—strong and loud as the roar of wind and waves, then soft and soothing as the balmy airs that quivered the morning-glory leaves about his gray beard. His was a strange eloquence at times, and he was undoubtedly a man of genius."

In the days before radio, television, and the internet, why not let a wandering nomad who plants apple orchards and carries messages from heaven—along with a healthy dose of mysticism and love of nature—into your home? Some Christianish entertainment in exchange for a bit of food and a warm place to sleep, not to mention a bit of good karma. Did some people, even at the time, find Chapman odd? Of course. But oddness can be a panacea for boredom. The man may have been sleeping in a hammock slung between two trees the night before. Why not let him inside and hear a few of his stories?

John Chapman never had a fixed address for his entire adult life. Not even a lean-to or shoddy cabin—only the aforementioned hollowed-out stump, and even that was only for a few seasons.

Eventually, when he was older and had followed the edge of "civilization" as it went west, out into Indiana, there are stories of people still welcoming Johnny Appleseed into their homes, or at least onto their property. One woman who remembered Chapman from her childhood days claimed that her family built an extra room just for the roving horticulturist. The catch? The room—while built off the house, to allow for heat—didn't have a single entrance *into* the house. Only a door that led to the outside. The reason, the woman stated, was that in his older years, to be quite frank, Chapman smelled a bit, and the woman's family worried about lice, bedbugs, and other critters.

Commenting on Chapman's traversing of Ohio back and forth, until at least the 1830s, the historian Howard Means writes in *Johnny Appleseed: The Man, the Myth, the American Story,* "He was welcomed in many homes along the way, as he always had been, but on more than a few occasions, reservations crept in. According to one family tradition, the proprietor of a tavern on the Muskingum River at Lowell, Ohio, recorded in his diary that Chapman would arrive annually on his migrations back and forth to Western Pennsylvania. The proprietor wrote that he would feed Chapman without charge, then point him to the barn for the night, so that his 'wee beasties'—i.e., lice—would not contaminate the other guests."

Not even saints last forever, and I for one appreciate a saint who shows the wear and tear of time. Not lofty, above reproach and suffering, but down amongst the people. Sometimes living in a shed in your backyard. Jesus himself, born in a manger.

My friend Matt Sumell is one of those mad saints of America who bounces around the country so much that it can actually make this massive expanse of dirt between the Atlantic and Pacific seem small.

When I first met him, he was holding down a small, rent-controlled apartment in LA—an exposed-brick studio in down-and-out Hollywood, half bachelor pad, half ship's cabin. He shared the small space with two dogs, both so close to death that I more than once caught myself holding a hand up to their noses to check for breath. They leaked fluids of every kind and had faces that almost made my heart hurt when I looked directly at them, but Matt loved them mightily. A large part of his day was planned around their care. Matt had a history of taking in stray dogs—sometimes birds, too, or even turtles. Animals that nobody could love except for him. Or at least that's how it seemed to me: A noble calling. Holy work. Devotion.

So it should come as no surprise that the first time I stayed at Matt's place it was only because a mutual friend told him I needed a place to crash—that same day, in fact. By that night, Matt and I were drunk, he in his bed tucked into a small alcove in the wall, reminiscent of a boat's berth, me snoring away on his couch. We were fast friends.

Other than strays and ugly dogs in need of love, Matt also collected vehicles. Or perhaps clunky toys would be a better way to put it. Vintage Jeeps and boats, Japanese minivans (the legality of which I'm still unsure of), classic motorcycles with sidecars for his pups or, occasionally, a buddy such as myself. He always drove safer with the dogs. Helmets strapped to our heads, Matt would rip me through the hills of Los Angeles at speeds that had me gripping the metal bar in front of me as he took a corner and lifted the sidecar off the ground, Matt's bike at such an angle that his knee was grazing the asphalt as I yelled out into the night, a tremendous yawp that I tried to play off as bravado but was actually an animalistic release of fear and joy and something deeper. Every living creature needs to yell at the sky, the moon, the stars. To scream at the universe—at God—"I am here."

For a brief moment, I was lifted into the dark night and everything was still—all anxiety cleansed. Just a perfect moment of high-speed serenity. When the yell faded from my mouth, I was at peace.

Which is when Matt would shift his weight, an artist of movement, and slam the sidecar back onto the pavement, himself barely breaking a sweat—silent—as I yelled out again, this time in pure terror. A high-pitched shrill, leaving me to wonder how nobody had called the cops.

Matt loved his old vehicles not just because of his obsession with analog machines (they don't beep you into seatbelt compliance), but because they allow him to travel the country, and to bring his wonderfully named pups—Lunch Money, Tink, and Seymour (aka the Night Shitter)—with him. He often found himself down in North Carolina, or visiting his sister in New Orleans. After a few of my visits in LA, Matt came out to the East Coast. His family had a large house on the water on the south shore of Long Island, where he kept his prized possession:

Old School, a twenty-eight-foot Groverbuilt lobster boat (based on the original Verity Skiff design) powered by a Ford Lehman 120 diesel.

On my first foray out to Long Island, long before Kelly came into my life, I rode the LIRR to Oakdale. The house at the corner of Woodlawn Ave. and Connetquot Drive looked like a mansion to me—something out of *The Great Gatsby,* sure, but mixed with *Grey Gardens* if *Grey Gardens* had years of hard, masculine living at its core. I don't know how else to put it. Matt's mother had died twenty years before. His sister was down south. His brother, the saner of the two boys, had moved to Ohio. Leaving Matt's father alone, with Matt visiting him in the summers. There was a suit of armor in the living room like the one I'd seen in Bruce Wayne's manor in the '60s *Batman* reruns when I was a kid. A suit of armor in the home. A sign of wealth. Class. Except . . . on this suit of armor atop the helmet rested a large, loud, festive sombrero. About an inch of dust covered the whole getup, and the rest of the house too, if I'm being honest.

In a decadent, all-wood dining room with windows looking out over the water where a long, heavy dining table had surely stood at some point, there was now a ping-pong table, the net long lost. We ate more than a few meals there during that first visit. Matt and I took acid from a small aerosol can he carried at the time: like a breath freshener, but for making the whole world shimmer. And we set sail.

This became a regular occurrence. We would ride out across the water to Fire Island, drinking at Kismet or Cherry Grove and swimming off the bow of Matt's anchored boat at sunset. This was after the disintegration of my engagement—as if Matt had made mending my bruised heart his own personal responsibility.

That summer bled into other summers. Sometimes Matt would bring friends; other times whichever wonderful woman had recently captured his attention. Sometimes we'd meet up with mutual pals on Fire Island, and a few times there were even celebrities that Matt had met back in Hollywood. Acid, mushrooms, alcohol, and salt air. Dockside bars and sunburns. Matt talking about what he calls "grief derangement"—the cornerstone of *Making Nice,* the gut-wrenching novel he wrote about his mother's death—which usually led to me talking about the importance of heartache, as if he didn't know. One of his beloved dogs dying, only for Matt to find a more desperate mutt before the month was out.

The day Matt's father came out to the boat is one that I will never forget. It started in New York City. I was blurry with a hangover when I woke up—the way almost all my mornings started in those days. My phone was ringing at an obscene volume with infuriating consistency.

"Isaac—it's Matt. I can't find my shoes."

"Okay . . ."

"And I'm in Brooklyn."

"Wait. Why did your number come up 'unknown'?"

"Lost my phone too. And my belt, it would seem."

"Your shirt? Your pants?"

"Pants are on. Shirt is TBD. This gentleman here was kind enough to loan me his phone. I'm down by the Barclays Center. Come bring me some shoes, would ya? And a belt if you've got one."

Which is what I did. The story was a familiar one: Matt had gone out with friends, pissed someone off (friend? stranger? who knows . . .), and ditched. Eventually he lost his phone, which meant he couldn't contact the person he was crashing with, or me. I had become his backup person more recently—my apartment at the time a hostel for wayward boys between the ages of thirty and fifty.

That night Matt had simply tried door handles on cars—found some rich family's large SUV unlocked, and slept for a few hours in their backseat. He awoke without his phone, belt, or shoes as previously mentioned.

"But I had your number memorized for exactly this sort of situation."

I brought Matt some sandals, a belt, and a clean shirt for good measure. I made the mistake of calling the flip-flops "flippy floppies," and to this day, every time Matt sees me, he welcomes me with a "Hey, it's Mr. Flippy Floppies."

We got Matt cleaned up and rode the LIRR out of the city toward Matt's boat. It wasn't until we were almost at his house that he told me, "The old man's gonna come out with us today. Not sure why, but he seems to like you."

Matt's father was a nineteen-year-old US Navy submariner when he lost his leg in a motorcycle accident that nearly killed him, but didn't. He eventually recovered and went to work at the VA, building the very prosthetics he himself wore, until he left to start his own company and build better ones. And then better ones. Vietnam happened, a war littered with mines, and soon missing limbs abounded. Matt's father's company flourished, the house by the water bought and paid for—his company's prosthetics eventually used in the Paralympics. What an incredible story. But even those of us with incredible stories sometimes still become cranky drunks.

The loss of Matt's mother, the onset of old age, the house falling into disrepair. Matt had undertaken the Herculean task of trying to save the Long Island family home with what little money there was left. But he couldn't be there full-time. His siblings forced the sale of the property, breaking Matt's heart, and his father moved out to Youngstown, Ohio, to be near his grandkids, eventually moving in with them and Matt's brother when his health began to fail. Other than a few rough nights in my early years, I didn't know much about Ohio back then. Only that it was far from the sea.

That day on the boat we drank whiskey and Matt's father told us tales until the sun dropped into the ocean. Eventually the old man fell asleep, and we gently laid him down and covered him with a light blanket.

That was a few summers ago now. I've heard word that Matt might be visiting his father and brother in Ohio this summer, somewhere near Youngstown. It's not on my list of Chapman sites to visit, but I need a place to stay, and I figure it's worth a shot.

"No chance you're near the PA/Ohio border at the moment, is there? Perhaps with a couch to crash on for the night?"

Matt responds to my text within minutes. Simply an address, and a follow-up text:

"No couch, but you can sleep in the backyard shed with me."

A shed, a room, a place to sleep. But kept safely separate from the house.

23

IT'S INTERESTING TO imagine Ohio not as the center of the country—its heart, as some Ohioans refer to it, given the state's placement and shape—but as it once was: the frontier. At least to the mostly white colonial immigrants/invaders who had, historically speaking, just recently arrived on the continent's shores. As Michael Pollan puts it in *The Botany of Desire* while talking about the frontier "found" west of the Alleghenies in the 1700s, "'The wild' was never quite as innocent of our influence as we like to think; the Mohawks and Delawares had left their marks on the Ohio wilderness long before John Chapman . . . showed up and began planting apple trees."

Which is true, of course. "The Mohawks and Delawares," along with the Erie, Kickapoo, Shawnee, Wyandot, Miami, Iroquois, Ottawa, and Potawatomi to name a few more. People had already lived in the lands that we now call Ohio for fourteen thousand years or so. But to the new settlers (much like when they first started visiting the "New World") the lands that became Ohio seemed fertile, lush, and bursting with promise: a literal land of milk and honey, ripe for—well, what the white expansionists seemed to be good at: the taking.

"Remember when we had to take the old man off the boat after he drank a bottle of whiskey?"

"I do."

"That's sorta my whole life for the time being."

Matt is staying in a shed behind his brother's house, but—much like his small apartment in LA, now in the middle of a suburb—he has turned it into a sort of cozy storage area where, at least for tonight, he and I are both the cargo. To put it another way: a ship's cabin, landlocked out here in the middle of Ohio.

I say hi to Matt's father, and he remembers me. He and Matt lovingly give each other shit for about an hour, and then it's time for him to go to bed. The man had drunk four alcoholic root beers just in the time that I was here. Matt sees me noticing.

"Let me show you something."

He leads me into the basement and I immediately notice that it looks like a bottling factory.

"We were never gonna get the old man to give up drinking—I mean, why would we, poor guy—so my brother and I came up with this."

I follow Matt around a corner to a fridge filled to the brim with the root beer I had seen upstairs: the old man's drink of choice, ironically named "Not Your Father's Root Beer." Matt explains that the fridge also contains liters and liters of diet, *non-boozy* root beer. They've been secretly cutting it.

"See, we even have a color-coded system and everything."

The black caps are a full, unopened bottle. The blue caps have been halved—half boozy root beer, half nonalcoholic diet. Red caps are only a quarter boozy, and white caps have no booze in them at all.

"For when he's already sauced," Matt explains.

"He doesn't notice?"

"Hasn't yet. But then again, he's noticing less and less each day."

Matt tells me stories as we sit there amidst the root beer, drinking the black caps—stories of caring for his father. The heartbreaking stories, the shit-filled ones. Wiping his own father's ass, and cleaning up after him when he pisses the bed.

There were lighthearted stories too, of course. His father stealing his brother's car and ending up on the neighbor's lawn. The time they all went to visit a nursing home, and the old guy managed to escape the building where they were simply taking a tour.

Funny stories, sure. But not without difficulty. Or perhaps it was the difficulty that begged to be cloaked in humor.

We sit in the basement, my laughter bouncing off the walls, then fading. A silence envelops us. Here is Matt, my devilish saint of the road, simply just being a saint. Caring for his father, with whom he has a complex relationship, as all fathers and sons have. Anchored in Ohio. I know more than a few people who might describe Matt, in passing, as irresponsible. Yet here he is, being more responsible than most people I know. When it really matters. Caring for his father like a baby—bottles and all—the same way his father had cared for him when he was small.

Pattering feet above us break the silence.

"My nieces are back from their mom's place. Wanna get your ass kicked in Mario Kart?"

The kids do indeed kick my ass in Mario Kart—but Matt at least wins a few rounds. It's joyful to watch Sumell refuse to lose, the way some adults might, but instead place bets based on some cookies and/or sweet treats currency that I don't completely understand. It's easy to picture Matt at some horse track, sweating as the animal he put money on thunders down the back stretch, his hopes for a better future riding on equine muscles and hard hooves pounding loose dirt, the crowd on its feet. But the reality is he's in suburban Ohio trying to figure out percentages of Laffy Taffy for "Win, Place, Show" bets on a Japanese cartoon racing game.

An American saint, charming the children in exchange for a place to rest his head.

Matt's brother watches us, grateful for a reprieve from entertaining his kids. The man clearly loves his daughters and gets a kick out of watching Matt be a good uncle. But parenting is hard. He's going through a divorce, as so many Americans do. His ex-wife loves the girls, too, of course. They're staying close to make it easier on the young ones.

I'm never having children. It's a decision I made at a very young age and have never wavered from. There are a number of things I can point to in my childhood that led me to this decision. The town I lived in when I was young had the highest teenage pregnancy rate per capita in the entire state, which means I grew up doing my damnedest to avoid procreating. My own parents were married when they had me, just to different people, meaning that my mere existence definitely . . . complicated things for the both of them. There was violence in my home, and I worry about where that violence now lives in me. The list goes on. The end result is that I'm not having kids, no matter how many people tell me—as they did when I was a teenager, in my early twenties, late twenties, thirties, and still now, approaching my forties—"Oh, you just wait. You'll be a father soon." Simply stated, for a plethora of reasons—from emotional to financial—raising another human being full-time is not for me.

But to help out with the children in my life? To be a good uncle? That is a calling that I relish. Whenever I spend some time—even a little bit of it—goofing off with a friend or family member's kid I can see the small respite it gives to the parents. Matt, I can see, feels the same with his nieces.

Now, let's be clear: obviously, community-driven child rearing is nothing new. I'm hardly the first person to come up with this, but as I grow older I become acutely aware of the ways I can be beneficial to the friends in my life who have children. That *not* having a child—

which, to be fair, in certain ways is a very selfish act on my part—allows me great financial freedom, the ability to travel more and do wild things like follow the ghost of John Chapman across the country, instead of doing my damnedest to raise a healthy little one. But the nonselfish part of not having children for me is that I can literally show up for people who need the help, especially in an era when healthcare costs and finances don't make it easy to raise a child, problems too complex for me to solve.

Come read your kid *Fox in Socks* for the hundredth time while you take a work call, though? That I can do. Or, you know, get beaten at Mario Kart ten times in a row.

I can't speak to John Chapman's views on being what I would call a good uncle, but the historical record points to the man being a friend to children—as he was, it would seem, to all living creatures. He never married, had no children, which meant he had no heirs when he died. Of course he spent many hours, days, and weeks alone, but he clearly liked the company of other people as well, save maybe for his own family (something we will also get to later).

The night is getting late. The two girls show me a Taylor Swift board game that they invented recently—made the rules, drew the board, created pieces—along with a Taylor Swift quilt they were planning on making next. Each square represents a different song. Something about being shown a quilt layout in the twenty-first century while following a hero of the 1800s moves me.

Swift herself is on the move this summer, and the girls' father seems proud to have gotten them tickets. An American rambler bringing the circus to town, the big tent entertainment of the modern day—the show a compilation of Swift's eras.

Imagine a show of America's eras, played out on a big stage, I think to myself.

Matt's brother takes the girls to bed and then has to hit the hay himself. Work in the morning. Matt and I retire to the shed in the backyard where we drink more and talk, which leads to smoking a joint and eating a small amount of mushrooms, which leads to talking and drinking more. Holding on to each other's company until eventually I close my eyes for a moment—when I open them, it's morning.

"It's something about you that has always made me jealous."

"What's that?"

Matt is packing me back into Rabbit after making me some coffee—but not before he demands to take the Jeep for a cruise around the block, his eyes wide with the excitement of playing with a new toy, even if only for a couple of minutes.

"Your ability to fall asleep. The first time you stayed at my place in LA I noticed it. You just put your head down and you're out. On Long Island you used to sleep on the boat instead of in the house. Mosquitos didn't bother you. Waves didn't bother you. Less than a minute later? Gone. Asleep."

"It's a gift."

"Sign of a guiltless man, never tossing and turning."

"Not sure about all that, but it helps out there. Been sleeping outdoors a lot."

"Well, I've never seen someone take mushrooms and then fall asleep, but I covet your peace of mind."

I laugh and Matt hands me an "extra strong" road coffee he's made me, along with a small yellow box.

"A tiny care package to keep you busy out there."

Which is how I come to be rolling out of Youngstown, Ohio, like some sort of suburban Hunter S. Thompson. No famous doctor's bag in tow, stuffed with "two bags of grass, seventy-five pellets of mescaline, five sheets of high-powered blotter acid, a saltshaker half-full of cocaine, and a whole galaxy of multi-colored uppers, downers, laughers, screamers. . . ." Just a li'l yellow box—the PG-13 version, if you will—with five small "dog walker" joints, a tiny dropper of acid meant specifically for microdosing, and a handful of mushroom gummies shaped like comical 'shrooms you might find drawn on a '90s T-shirt worn by a teenager who wished they had lived during the '60s. Thompson wrote, "Not that we needed all that for the trip, but once you get locked into a serious drug collection, the tendency is to push it as far as you can." I have a sneaking suspicion this box will do me just fine and then some for the remainder of my travels.

There are no bats, "swooping and screeching and diving around the car" as I make my way down the road, but the lines on the highway still have a little sparkle from the night before as I set out across Ohio.

24

MUCH LIKE Johnny Appleseed used the Muskingum, Walhonding, Mohican, and other rivers to move about Ohio when he wasn't walking, I am—well, I am driving. Leaving Sumell and his family, I find myself scooting onto Interstate 80, looking for a way to cut south so I can get to Columbus.

Before we were all using Google Maps, Apple Maps, or Waze, there were, of course, regular maps. Not ideal to look at while you're barreling down a highway, though. Which is why the signs you pass when driving along any given highway in America have more meaning than you may know. Much like the way Magellan and so many others throughout history used the stars to navigate, so too did our more recent ancestors—say those of the mid-1950s, '60s, '70s, '80s, and '90s. They knew how to glean knowledge from highway signs, knowledge that is in danger of being lost to the sands of time.

The Dwight D. Eisenhower National System of Interstate and Defense Highways was begun on June 29, 1956, commencing the construction of forty-one thousand miles of interstate highways, the largest public works program in the United States up to that time. Rumor has it that President Eisenhower was influenced by his experiences as a young lieutenant colonel in the 1919 Transcontinental Convoy—the first army transcontinental motor convoy, which was from Washington, DC, to San Francisco—and his observations of the ease of travel on the German autobahns during World War II. He felt that the newer multilane highways were essential to a strong national defense. They also gave us that most heavenly of places, the roadside truck stop.

There are seventy primary interstate highways in the Interstate Highway System. The major interstates all run east–west, and you know you're on one because the sign's blue shield will have an "I-" along with a double-digit number ending in zero. For example, the longest and most northern of the interstate highways is I-90, which stretches from Boston, Massachusetts, to Seattle, Washington. The southernmost is I-10, which goes all the way from Jacksonville, Florida, to Santa Monica, California. So, the bigger the number, the farther north you are. I-80 goes from Teaneck, New Jersey, to San Francisco. I-70 connects Baltimore, Maryland, with Cove Fort, Utah. I-40 takes you from Wilmington, North Carolina, out to Barstow, California, while I-30 is a li'l guy who'll whisk you from Little Rock, Arkansas, to Fort Worth, Texas. Okay, I-30 is both short and more diagonal than "east to west," technically, but nobody's perfect. I-20 gets you from Florence, South Carolina, to Kent, Texas, which brings us all the way back to the aforementioned I-10.

Now, if you're more interested in moving north to south in the United States, you should look for blue shields that have the same "I-" along with a double-digit number, but this time ending in 5. I-95, for example, goes from Miami, Florida, all the way to Houlton, Maine, where it stops at the US-Canadian border. The interstate's length, stretching the entirety of the East Coast, has led to a bit of relevance. One could argue that Route 66 is to country music what I-95 is to rap, referenced in numerous songs and even the namesake of "9 5 . s o u t h" by J. Cole.

On the West Coast you have I-5, which will take you from Blaine, Washington, all the way down to San Diego, California. Technically, I-5 should be "I-05" but, again, the DOT went for simplicity over perfect continuity. The rest of the north–south interstate majors include I-85, Petersburg, Virginia, to Montgomery, Alabama, and I-15, which is San Diego to Sweetgrass, Montana. If you want to get from the tippy-top of Michigan—say, the Upper Peninsula, in a place called Sault Ste. Marie—all the way down to Hialeah, Florida, you're going to take I-75. Las Cruces, New Mexico, to Buffalo, Wyoming? I-25. I-45 goes from Houston, Texas, to Dallas, which, again, the DOT and continuity. Not *technically* interstate, right? But c'mon. Texas is big. Finishing up the north–south majors, it's Texas again in Laredo all the way to Duluth, Minnesota, on I-35, then Chicago, Illinois, to LaPlace, Louisiana, on I-55, and finally hop over to Mobile, Alabama, up to Gary, Indiana, on I-65.

The interstates are a beautiful web crisscrossing this great country of ours, and there are even more numbers, symbols, and hidden messages in the highway system. Interstate minors, for example, split off from interstate majors, and have "I-" along with *three* numbers—the last two being the same as the interstate major they diverged from. If the first digit is even, it means it will eventually reconnect. Even-numbered minors are often called bypasses or beltways, as they take cross-country travelers around cities instead of through them. But if the first number is odd, it means the road will *not* reconnect, but they do, at times, bring you to another major interstate. There are also interstate mediums, along with loads of other exceptions to rules and outliers, but you get the idea. As I leave Matt Sumell behind in Youngstown, I am going east to west on I-80 and looking for an interstate, major or minor, that might help me move farther south.

After a couple hours of driving, even with my knowledge of highway signage, I finally admit that it's time to take a break from the road and get my bearings. I pull over at a random exit on I-76 while driving deeper into Ohio. I hadn't showered or done anything hygienic at Matt's place—wanting to split early so as to not disturb his nieces' morning routine, his brother already kind enough to let me stay the night in the first place on an hour's notice.

But it might also have been guilt from doing drugs in their backyard shed on a Tuesday night.

This exit is like any other: gas stations and fast-food restaurants serving truckers and everyday commuters who are all driving through, trying to get somewhere else.

As I slip out of Rabbit at a BP gas station, I let out a fart. Not something I'd usually share with you, but it had become a habit, a ritual. Whenever I pulled over I would rip a few to let 'em out as I exited the driver's cabin. If I'm being more honest, it was a tradition I'd begun looking forward to on my travels. I did the same when getting out of the tent.

But this time it is . . . not as pleasant.

Because this time, in an instant—in fact it may have been one of the quickest things I've ever done—I have shit my pants. In the blink of an eye. An instantaneous before and after. One moment, I am an adult who has never shit their pants. And in the next moment, and for the rest of my life, I am someone who has, and will always have, shit their pants.

I panic. I get back in my Jeep, pressing my back into the driver's seat, hard, so that my ass and shit-filled shorts hover in the air.

I freeze for a moment. And then, stiff-legged, get back out of the Jeep and walk myself inside the gas station, praying an undignified prayer that my underwear can hold the ever-shifting crap inside my shorts together, instead of letting it drip down my leg as I pass a spin rack filled with a variety of flavored peanuts.

"Uh, bathroom?" I yell.

The gas station clerk doesn't even look up, just points. Which meant he didn't watch, thank Christ, as I walked through the store in a style that could only be described as someone-who-just-shit-their-pants.

This is what gas station bathrooms are for, I tell myself. *Unfortunate road mishaps.* And indeed, this bathroom does not disappoint. It is unclean, disheveled, a mess. The exact place where a person could clean themselves off, toss their shit-filled undies out without too much shame (it's already gross in here, anyway), and figure out their next move.

If there were any toilet paper, that is.

Or even paper towels.

There are neither.

I stare at myself in the mirror for a moment. How has a search for freedom, a longing to be outdoors, an interest in one of America's most memorable—if oft-misunderstood—legends, led me to a disgusting BP gas station bathroom with a flickering light and no paper products—let alone soap—off I-76 in Ohio?

The thing is, it's tough to have soul-searching and self-reflection when there's a dump hanging off your backside, giving you the weirdly long-forgotten feeling of what it was like to be wearing a full diaper.

I panic even more than I already have. I walk out of the gas station store like my legs are stilts. This time the attendant does give me a funny look.

I haven't bought anything, or even purchased any gas, which Rabbit desperately needs. I pull out of the BP and drive—my back held straight as a plank like before, so my ass doesn't touch the seat, as I clumsily use both feet on the Jeep's pedals—across the street, docking in the middle of two spots in a McDonald's parking lot.

I do my stiff walk inside, where there's a congregation of old men clearly out together for a morning bike ride, their expensive road bikes resting on the outdoor wall of the restaurant, their bodies covered in gleaming spandex.

I can tell right away that more than a few of them recognize my walk.

"Excuse me, sir?" cries out an employee.

I am beelining it for the bathroom. Surely a McDonald's bathroom would be clean, respectable, well stocked.

"Sir? The restrooms are for customers only."

The cashier is a teenager, or maybe in her early twenties. Pretty in a way almost all young people are. Not yet scared of death. The boys and girls of America. Here is a person who had never, ever shit her pants. We lock eyes.

"Sir. The restrooms. They're for customers only."

I want to yell it right then and there. *Listen, lady, I crapped myself.* But I still have a thread of dignity left. Instead I offer, "I promise to get a McMuffin on the way out! I swear!"

"Well, sir, you have to—"

"Sally," one of the old bike riders mercifully speaks up. "Let the man go to the bathroom. I'm sure he's good for it."

I look at the elderly gentleman and nod my thanks. My roadside hero nods back.

"Fine." Sally rolls her eyes and turns back to her coworkers, her whole long life stretching out in front of her, while I stiffly power walk to the bathroom.

The bathroom is clean. A paradise. All I could have hoped for. I immediately go into the closest stall. Before I get started, though: no toilet paper. The next stall? No toilet paper. The third and last? You guessed it.

Goddamnit, Sally.

Perhaps my bicycle buddies had used it all up. This bathroom doesn't even have a paper towel dispenser. Just futuristic-looking air dryers.

I've had a lot of low points in my life, but judged on a scale of *just* dignity? Standing in that bathroom—my second of the morning—with shit in my pants for what was at this point over ten minutes. But it was its own lifetime. This was perhaps the worst I'd ever felt.

Still, what the fuck am I going to do? Go to another bathroom? Maybe to the Denny's down the road? I have to at least make some progress here. I take off my overshirt and use it to wipe my ass as best

I can, and take off my soiled underwear. I am not clean—not by a long shot—but it is a step in the right direction. I stuff the offending garments into the trash bin and hope no one will notice them. I scurry out of the bathroom, take a deep breath, and approach Sally.

"Uh, one McMuffin. And a water."

"Want a coffee?" she offers.

"No. No thank you. But could I get some napkins? Like, a lot of napkins?"

Sally silently stuffs napkins into a bag for me along with the bottle of water.

"Anything else?"

I wonder if I smell bad. Could Sally smell me? Just trying to work her minimum-wage job and some hungover maniac still coming down from last night's drugs stands in front of her with remnants of shit in his pants wearing a T-shirt, a much different shirt than what he went into the bathroom wearing. Does she notice? Do the bike riders?

"I, uh, I think the trash bag in the bathroom might be full. Someone should probably take it out."

"Okay . . ."

Sally is going from annoyed to suspicious. I almost mention the lack of toilet paper, a valiant effort to help the next person who comes in with my condition. But it is time to cut some of my losses. I could be valiant some other day.

"Thanks so much."

I take the bag and stiffly, though not as stiffly as before, walk out while waving to the bikers and head for the parking lot.

I drive Rabbit in the same style as before, my back pressing into the seat, my ass carefully touching nothing. A quarter of a mile down the road, I find a dirt turnoff, some sort of electrical generator resting behind old wire fencing. The road is a maintenance road, but all the empty beer cans and cigarette butts tells me it is more often used by teenagers—either that or the electric company employees are covering up a fairly robust drinking problem. Not that I am in any position to judge. I open Rabbit's doors and use them as some sort of attempt at modesty, not that anyone is around. I take off my shorts and quickly confirm there'd be no saving them. I use the water and the napkins and a bar of soap I have in the Jeep to properly clean myself, before putting on a clean pair of underwear and jeans. Then I put everything into the McDonald's bag—I haven't even taken the McMuffin out, hunger being the farthest thing from my mind—and huck it as far as I can, deep into the woods. Hoping no teen or beer-blurry electric worker ever has the misfortune of discovering it.

Back at the BP, I find some hand sanitizer and use it liberally and abundantly. Then, finally, I get some gas.

Pulling back onto the highway, I hope to never return to that exit again. If I ever go missing and they find my DNA in some woods near Youngstown, know that they should leave that McDonald's bag alone. A monument to nothing but my long-lasting shame, and the not so pretty parts of life on the road.

25

THE IDEA WAS to stay in Columbus for one night and then head out to the Harvey-Algeo farm in Savannah, Ohio, the next day. My reason for going to the small farm in Ashland County was that supposedly they had the last confirmed apple tree planted by John Chapman still in existence.

But after Rabbit's engine troubles and my mini-mushroom night in Matt's brother's backyard shed I am now a couple days behind, and you know how slippery time can get.

My best friend, poet and author Saeed Jones, and I have been in a constant conversation since the moment we met, fifteen years ago. Though we don't live in the same place anymore—after stints together in San Francisco and New York City—anytime one of us connects deeply with a film or is moved by a book, we are desperate to talk with the other about it. Our lives and work have been intertwined since before we even knew each other, and our bond has survived everything that's come after. It is a friendship like that of two children, born out of necessity. We read each other's work and got each other jobs—we even quit a couple together, too.

When we first became friends, still in our twenties, Saeed's ma had died the previous year. Saeed was an only child, raised mostly by a single mother. Their relationship would become the cornerstone of his memoir, *How We Fight for Our Lives*—but before that, there was just the grief. The crying in bars and drinking in bars and Saeed traveling all around the world to try and escape his sadness—eventually landing with me in the Mission District, where I lived at the time. Crashing on my couch, where I tried to distract him from his mourning by throwing knives into my cut-filled coffee table—aptly called the Knife Throwing Table™—or taking him on never-ending bar crawls through the city, before he eventually found his own apartment and decided to stay for a year. After the year was up, he returned to New York. I followed him six months later.

When Saeed moved to Columbus, Ohio, looking for a gay-friendly, diverse midwestern city to live in after he grew tired of lighting his money on fire in New York, I traveled out to visit him often. When lockdown happened, I worried about my friend in his new home, and traveled on empty planes with bandanas tied over my face to make sure he didn't go mad with loneliness, our mutual friend Teddy often making the journey with me.

I shouldn't have worried, though. Saeed makes friends as easily as he travels, as easily as he pulls up stakes. Soon a visit to Columbus to see Saeed also meant hanging out with poet Maggie Smith and photographer Maddie McGarvey, along with a slew of Columbus artists and midwestern bon vivants.

This is why I know I have a place to crash in Columbus. Our friendship is built on sleeping on each other's couches and, sometimes, floors. Crossing the country only to spend some time together. It didn't matter that I was lingering a day or two longer than I'd set out to. I could stay a month if I wanted. Wherever I was, there was always a home for Saeed. And wherever he was, I was always welcome.

Turns out I didn't stay a month, but I did stay four more nights than I meant to.

I am reminded of Jack Kerouac's book *Desolation Angels,* which chronologically takes place after *Dharma Bums*. In the first half of the book, Kerouac's stand-in, Jack Duluoz, is a fire lookout on Desolation

Peak in Washington State's North Cascade mountain range, near the Canadian border. Initially the solitude Jack experiences is transformative, a spiritual type of loneliness. But after sixty-three days in the tower, Jack describes his mind as being "in rags," and says of the two-month stint, "Many's the time I thought I'd die of boredom or jump off the mountain." Desperate for companionship, Jack makes his way down Desolation Peak and promptly hitchhikes to San Francisco to go party with his friends. An oversimplification of the second half of the novel, sure, but you get the idea. I had been driving meditatively for too long. Seeing Matt had awakened within me a need for more connection. I wanted to spend time with my best friend.

Saeed had recently gone through a devastating breakup. It involved a London trip to see a Beyoncé concert and returning to his hotel room early only to find his boyfriend . . . well, let's just say he had to tell him, "Boy, bye."

We are now partying the way one does when brokenhearted, which is to say going into the warm Ohio nights and dancing and yelling and doing anonymous drugs while smoking cigarettes that aren't yours and sitting at home watching YouTube videos together and then going out again.

One night on this leg of the trip, at a particularly charming gay bar that presented as a stiff-upper-lip Irish bar in the front, only to open up into a rainbow-fueled midwestern dream of corn-fed men in the back, there was a shooting nearby that resulted in a three-hour lock-in of intense dancing and shot-taking the likes of which I'd never seen, while helicopters circled overhead. By day four we were huddled in a movie theater matinee, crying at a Marvel sequel involving sentient animals and friendship.

After almost a week of partying, I finally get on the road and head out to Harvey-Algeo Farm in Ashland County. My body feels scooped out, but not in a particularly bad way. I am somewhat purified through my mistreatment of my corporeal form, and time with my friend always fills my heart, no matter what it does to my liver.

It's worth taking a moment in the midst of my own Dionysian jamboree in Columbus to let you know what the relationship was between Americans and alcohol in Chapman's era. Put bluntly—and to once again quote Howard Means: "Hard cider was as much a part of the dining table as meat or bread back then . . . no one thought there was any harm or danger connected with its use." This included daily consumption by children, by the way.

Chapman's scrub stock of apples may not have always made for tasty food, but they were perfect for the creation of cider, and in this booze-fueled young nation, no amount of milling was too much. Between 1800 and 1830 the average American was putting down twenty-three gallons of booze per year, and cider was the majority of that—an average of fifteen gallons per person. But this consumption wasn't just for fun and revelry, the alcohol in the cider killed off all types of bacteria and diseases commonly found in plain water at the time, making it an almost healthy poison.

The history of cider is itself the history of America. Potted seedlings and bags of apple seeds were brought over on the *Mayflower*. The Puritans were many things, but they were *not* teetotalers. A man named William Blackstone planted the first apple trees in New England nine days after the Puritans landed. The first recorded shipment of honeybees—instrumental in the pollination of apples—was to Virginia in 1622. All of this was for the creation of hard cider.

To put this in terms of consumption of pure ethanol (the chemical that makes alcohol intoxicating), by the early 1800s the average American was consuming 7 gallons per year—compared to the current average of 2.4 gallons a year. By the 1830s it was assumed that the average American would miss work on Mondays due to a hangover from their weekend binge, which, unsurprisingly, is around the same time that the temperance movement began to gain followers.

Still, I'm wishing for a bit of a small, personal temperance movement by the time Columbus is behind me. It's dawn when I leave, and Saeed is still asleep in his bed. I roll off the couch as quietly as I can. Out the window I can see the sun, bursting over the Ohio State University campus and Columbus's downtown. I do my best not to slam the door as I climb into Rabbit (although slamming a Jeep Wrangler's door is indeed one of life's little joys) and head toward I-71 North.

It's an hour and a half drive to Savannah, the small town where the farm I am looking for is located, and the time goes by quickly. Already the Midwest, where people won't bat an eye when considering a nine-hour drive, has swept me up into its navigational philosophies. An hour-and-a-half drive feels like nothing, and I push down on the gas while the wind whips through my open windows (but remembering the mechanic's warning about driving too fast).

By the time I pull off the interstate I realize that I'm offensively early. Truth be told, I haven't even bothered to call ahead to the owners of the farm—an unannounced visitor is already an annoyance, but one that shows up around breakfast time? Jail.

I cruise up to a public trail. Days of drinking, plus the night in the shed with Matt Sumell before that, has me in desperate need of physical exertion. Walking is so easy, but it's also so easy *not* to do. A day without a hike or a long walk has turned into a few, and then nearly a week. But here I am, still so early in the day, near the Ohio woods that John Chapman so dearly loved. I get out of my Jeep.

There are signs up cautioning hikers to look out for turkey hunters, which seems odd to me as it is still summer, but the seasons are listed and go well into May.

I walk into the woods, carrying my ever-encroaching hangover with me. The sun, still low and early in the sky, doesn't feel warm; it feels hot. Soon boozy sweat is sliding down my face and my shirt is sticking to my back. The fresh air—usually crisp and revitalizing—

feels oppressive instead, filled with small, pesky bugs that I swat at with little success.

As I go farther, the calmness that usually comes like a wave of peace washing over my soul when I walk eludes me. But I keep going, like an addict chasing a high. The birdsong—usually delightful, filling my heart with lightness—well, seems more like shrieks this morning.

I look up into the branches of the trees, wondering if it's possible to have an entire forest of only screeching blue jays—which is when I almost step in the scat.

Now, why we call it scat—which potentially originated from the Greek word "skōr" (σκῶρ), which means "dung" or "excrement"—instead of just animal shit I'll never know, but what I do know is that in this exact moment, I look down right before plunging my foot into a pile of fairly fresh-looking shit.

The birds seem to go quiet.

My brain does a quick inventory. It isn't human shit or deer shit or rabbit shit and certainly not turkey or blue jay. I am grateful I haven't stepped in it, but the relief is short-lived. I want to tell myself that I am really just hungover but I can't shake a nagging feeling that seems to come from deep within my very being. As if my DNA is saying to my brain, "Be alert."

I take out my phone and snap a photo of the scat, then do a reverse image search. Suddenly I'm looking at a screen full of bears.

The hair on the nape of my neck stands up. The sweat pouring down my back has turned cold.

My rationalizing brain takes over. As a child of a violent household, rationalizing is almost a superpower—or perhaps a better word for it would be "delusion." I start speaking aloud to myself.

"You were just in Columbus. Hell, you were just at a rest stop. There were about fifty signs about turkey hunting. Surely if there were bears around, there would have been signs about the bears."

A feeling as if I'm being watched cuts through my body. I stand still. Then tell myself I am silly for standing still. Then stand still again.

It's Ohio. Like, pretty suburban Ohio. I punch "are there bears in Ohio" into my pocket computer.

"Yes, black bears live in Ohio."

Okay, sure. But what about *this* part of the state?

I punch in the name of the nearest town I know and add the word "bears," along with a question mark for good measure.

"Northern Ohio Gets Nearly Twenty Black Bear Reports in Three Days" is the first story that comes up. It was published two weeks ago.

The story right below it?

One about black bears thriving in the area, returning after decades of not being active here.

Below that? A helpful reminder to never come between—or disturb in any way, really—a mother bear and her cubs.

The birds really had stopped singing. Whether or not I heard a stick crack loudly in the woods, I'll never be sure. What I do know is that I turned around, stepped over the pile of bear shit, and began to walk back the way I came.

Some walks in the woods are restorative. Others end with a quick retracing of one's steps as your walk quickens, then turns into a jog. And sure, it wasn't as if a bear was *actually* chasing me, but my brain was really leaning into a "better safe than sorry" mindset. It's good to keep in mind the brain's ability to see and feel danger where there is none. My mother was always sure that the other people in town were talking about her. Judging her. There always seemed to be one metaphorical bear or another chasing her through the woods of her mind. A mind I was increasingly convinced I'd inherited.

Plus, I *did* just party in Columbus for almost an entire week, my nerves frayed at best, hangxiety pumping through my mind, body, soul.

Still, my jog turns into a flat-out run as I flee the turkey-filled-and-perhaps-bear-containing woods at breakneck speed, jumping into Rabbit and crashing down on its gas pedal until I am ripping out of an empty parking lot via a small trail in the middle of nowhere like a getaway driver fleeing a bank robbery in the middle of Manhattan.

As I mentioned before, there are countless tales and legends about Chapman's companionship with animals, each harder to verify than the last. For instance, it was said that Johnny never rode a horse—but there is a record of him riding horseback in 1801. There's the story where Appleseed was seen wearing only one shoe, and when asked where the other one was he said he threw it away because it had stepped on a worm and thus offended him. It is said that he survived on nuts and berries while living in the woods but never meat, and let's not forget the wolf that he nurtured back to health who then supposedly followed him around for the rest of its days.

When it comes to bears, Dr. Robert Price mentions one person who claims to have seen Chapman playing in the woods with three cubs "while the mother calmly looked on." Another story has Johnny crawling into a large, upturned stump—a common place for him to camp while in the wild—only to find a bear family tucked in there; he decided they needed it more than he did and moved on. (Though one might consider that this was not so much out of kindness but simply the wise thing to do.)

John Chapman, friend to all animals, might have stayed to commune with the (perhaps imaginary) bear, along with the turkeys and the blue jays, too. But John Chapman hadn't had the week I had in Columbus.

I remember a joke that my ma used to tell, a fairly common one about two people walking in the woods, coming across a mama bear and her cubs—my ma's version was always a long, winding story. She was one of the hikers, and as the bear gave chase, she started to run. "You can't outrun a bear," the other, smarter-seeming hiker yelled out to her. "Yeah, but I can outrun you," my ma called back. Once, when I was sick and my ma had to take me to work with her, I saw her tell that joke to one of her classes. I was younger than her students. Everybody laughed when she got to the punch line. My ma was beaming—I didn't know it at the time, but when she was younger, before I came into her life, she had participated in poetry readings and open mics. Stand-up comedy, before our idea of modern stand-up comedy was really a thing. I remember how happy it had made her, to make that room of children laugh. I remember how it felt to join them.

Sadly, I have no other partner to outrun standing next to me. There are moments in life when we learn it's dangerous to be alone, often too late.

"Hey, Ma."

The memory of my mother's joke, or maybe it was the childlike fear produced by a *maybe* bear in the woods, moves me to call home. I'm speeding up the road in Rabbit—as if there's a bear still maybe chasing me—so I have my ma on speakerphone. My da told me recently that my mother was losing weight, staying indoors more than usual. Caring for her own, aging mother, still alive on that terrible farm, is really taking its toll. I'm trying to be better about checking in.

"Hey, kiddo."

I don't ask her about the weight. I don't ask her about her mother. I try to be a respite. A reprieve. I tell her about the almost-certainly-not-actually-a-bear and how it reminded me of the joke she used to tell. I do my best to try and cheer her up. But eventually, a little curiosity gets ahold of me.

"Ma, do you remember back when—you know how you had a rough go of it, when we first moved out to the farm?"

". . . Yes?"

We don't often talk about the past.

"Well, did you ever—did you ever see things?"

"See things?"

"Like, hallucinations? Or things that weren't there?"

"Kiddo . . . it was all a long time ago."

The tone in her voice makes it clear that she doesn't want to talk about it. It's so easy, not to look at history.

"No, I know. I just—"

"Are you seeing things?"

"I mean—"

What am I supposed to say? That I'm worried that either there's a dog able to cover a wildly impressive distance that somehow has a lock on me, for unknowable reasons—or that, yes, I'm a bit concerned I'm seeing things. Worried I have the same busted brain that my mother has, and want to compare and contrast notes, to see how rough this is gonna get.

"No, Ma. I'm not seeing things. Just imagining that bear got me thinking."

"You always did have an active imagination."

She sounds like she's worried about me, but we slip back into that comfortable, familiar space. Not talking about what's really on our minds.

26

I'VE STOPPED SPEEDING by the time I reach the Harvey-Algeo farm, and my heart has stopped beating out the front of my chest and returned to a somewhat normal rhythm inside my rib cage after the phone call with my ma. The farm is off County Road 658, which in turn is off Route 250—eight or so miles north of Ashland in the small village of Savannah, Ohio, which boasts a population that fluctuates between 300 and 350 people, depending on which census report you look at.

The house is white, and there is a nearby barn and shed, a wooden fence in front of fields across the street. About half a mile west, the Vermillion River—a tributary of Lake Erie—flows. In the front yard there's a small hand-carved wooden sign which reads:

1837
Centennial Farm Harvey-Algeo
Sponsored by Ashland County Historical Society

As you approach the front door of the house, there is an old gnarled tree stump, beside which two younger trees have sprouted up from the earth. Younger in that they are not as old as the stump, but they are not saplings, having grown tall and strong. I sit there and admire the small green apples produced by the trees, or so I tell myself. The truth is, I am hesitant to knock on the house's front door, conscious of how road-weary I look, how unkempt.

It occurs to me that it's been quite some time since I've simply dropped in on anyone, let alone a stranger. No call ahead of time, no email or text. Simply me, knocking on the door. "Hi, I'd like to talk with you about this tree. Rumor is that it's one of the last—if not *the* last surviving tree—planted by John Chapman, aka Johnny Appleseed, a transient religious land speculator with an alleged heart of gold who also might have been a bit touched in the head. Sorry I smell like half the bars in Columbus. Can I come in?"

I don't use that as an opener. But truth be told, Patti might've invited me in even if I had. The moment she comes to the door, midwestern hospitality is on full display. She promptly welcomes me, even as I make excuses for her not to—"I'm sure you're busy. I didn't mean to disturb you. I can simply get a way to contact you and schedule a better time to visit." But she won't have it, and soon I am sitting at her table—she and her husband are in the middle of renovating the house's kitchen, but she has some time. Would I like water? Lemonade?

I choose the lemonade. It is that perfect balance of sweet and tart, and I drink it while Patti gives me her full name—Patricia Algeo Young—and tells me her family history. Great-great-grandparents, or was it great-great-*great*-grandparents, came over from Scotland in the early 1800s, making their way west through Pennsylvania, much like Chapman's early movements across the land. They purchased the property in 1837—the barn was older than the house, and there was an original farmhouse that used to sit farther back in the pines, away from the road. The buildings that still stand from that time are held together with wooden pegs. The old-fashioned way.

"Built to last," Patti says. "The only thing we've lost—the doors both blew off during a bad storm, but that's it. The barn stayed standing. Now we *have* done maintenance and repairs, added some aluminum siding and such, but the bones have never changed."

I think of my grandparents' farm, where my grandmother still clings to life in that hulking red former tollhouse built sometime in the 1700s. Built to last, indeed. Now you can't inhabit roughly a quarter of the place because it's been taken over by bats and their copious amounts of shit—I worry about my ma, breathing in that air. Patti and her family have done a better job taking care of their inherited homestead.

"Do you know what your family was farming back then?"

"They had sheep. You can still see some of the old fences over on the other side of the road. There's about twenty acres on this side and thirty acres or so on that. Or maybe it's vice versa, but fifty acres altogether. But they always kept the sheep on the other side of the road."

"That's funny, my grandparents on my ma's side are also Scottish—bit of Scandinavian, too—and also started a sheep farm, though theirs is in Massachusetts," I share, so it doesn't seem like I have just shown up to grill this poor woman on a random weekday before noon.

"What's your other side?"

"Irish."

"Me too. Who knows, maybe we're related."

I glance outside and see the tree again, remembering why I'm here.

"So did you grow up on the farm, as a little girl? Do you remember Chapman's tree as a kid?"

"My aunt always said, 'Protect the tree. You've got to take care of the tree.' Then she would tell me the stories her grandmother—my great-grandmother—would tell to *her* about the times John Chapman came to visit. He was, his religion is hard to pronounce—"

"Swedenborgian."

"Yes, thank you. So he had a minister—a Swedenborgian minister—that he would visit right here in this part of Ohio. Chapman would come up and worship with him, visit with him, have Bible studies with him. Plus, Chapman had several orchards here because, well, he did that. Planted all over, but especially places he visited annually or semiannually."

Patti knows her stuff. By the 1810s, Chapman had orchards in easily more than twenty different townships across Ohio, and then, later in his life, in Indiana. If the late 1790s found a young Chapman in Western Pennsylvania with his half brother, the early 1800s—and up until his death, as he used to return to the state even after migrating west to Indiana—found Chapman in Ohio, often using two canoes lashed together to transport himself and his seeds up and down the Muskingum, Walhonding, and Ohio Rivers.

Chapman's father even came west, with his large new family in 1805, and settled around Dexter City, Ohio, where many of the Chapmans are still buried. It's around this time that historians believe Nathaniel parted ways with his older, wandering half brother, opting instead to stay and help his father and siblings farm the land.

Here we find another common myth about Johnny Appleseed, that he simply rambled aimlessly all over. In actuality—especially during his early Ohio years—he lived a somewhat more settled life.

Well, settled for him.

Chapman had no permanent address to speak of, but he did have repetitive routes. Walking in large circles around the state, coming back to an area once or twice a year to check on the apple trees he had planted, often partnering with a local farmer. By planting the land, he was laying claim to it—in accordance with the laws of the day—and by maintaining those trees, that claim remained secure. John was savvy, often more savvy than his legends give him credit for, and was always looking for the edge of westward-expanding civilization and the wilderness, where he felt most comfortable. Picking up real estate along the way.

Patti goes on to tell me that she believes Chapman might have had a full orchard on the property, but either way he certainly planted trees here. Eventually time and storms took almost all of them, saving one old monster that continued to thrive. That tree had offshoots, but then—

"Then this other one popped up more recently. We thought it was an offshoot of the original, but when it started bearing fruit, the apples were red—"

"A different color than the Chapman tree? So a whole different tree, from roots that were under the ground?"

"Right. Someone or other eventually came and took a DNA test."

"A DNA test for a tree?"

"Yes. Took DNA tests from both trees and sent the samples off to someone in Washington State who does apple tree DNA tests."

"So what happened?"

"Turns out both trees are from that time period. So—yeah, it's still a mystery. Not sure where that tree came from."

"So there's the Chapman tree, which has the younger offshoots, and then this *other* tree that popped up—it only showed up like ten or so years ago, but the DNA testing—"

"Yeah. The theory is that those trees got taken out—maybe a storm years ago—but the roots were still in the ground and eventually it fought back to life."

There's a glacial deposit in rural Ashland County. The soil is rich—scientists and botanists who examined the tree say this is the reason for its ripe old age: a steady supply of water and mineral-rich nutrients runs deep underground, nourishing the tree's root system for well over 150 years.

While your average apple tree lives between fifty and eighty years, there are many that have lasted over one hundred years when well cared for. On my grandmother's farm, there was an old crab apple tree between the dreary gray house I lived in as a child and the bright red house where my ma's parents lived. The last time I visited the farm, the tree was still there, bearing small, rock-sized apples that were almost as hard as stone.

In Henry David Thoreau's essay "Wild Apples," first published in *The Atlantic Monthly* in 1862, he talks about how certain apples can seem edible while out in nature, but once brought home, well: "When I take one out of my desk and taste it in my chamber, I find it unexpectedly crude,—sour enough to set a squirrel's teeth on edge and make a jay scream."

And while we're talking tree care, it's worth noting that the oldest known tree in the world is Methuselah—a Great Basin bristlecone pine in the White Mountains of eastern California. Methuselah's age—based on tree ring data—is estimated to be between 4,800 and 5,000 years old, and its actual location is kept a secret to make sure nobody comes to vandalize it, or chop it down and claim it as their own. Or come knock on your door before noon and start asking you questions about it.

Patti tells me that I'm not the only person who has stopped by to ask about the tree—hell, even local politicians will occasionally swing by to take photos for promotional purposes, though she does her best not to play favorites.

"I have my politics—of course—but I don't want anything looking like an endorsement. The tree is a part of history. The tree is for everyone."

That said, the number of people who show up now has nothing on what the farm saw a few decades back.

"I wasn't here then, but they used to get busloads of people. Tourists used to really make a trip of it."

"Did your family ever charge admission or anything like that? Like a *Field of Dreams* situation?"

"Absolutely not. Again, the tree is for everyone."

Patti goes on, passing down the stories from her great-grandmother as told to her by her aunt, giving me an impromptu oral history.

"So Chapman had a bunch of trees and orchards in the area, and he would come down to the farm and check on them. He would usually stay for supper—there's a rumor that he would sleep in the barn, not in the house. But I don't know where that rumor comes from, and we can't confirm it one way or the other."

"Well, in a way, that's sort of John Chapman's whole deal—or legacy, at least. People telling stories that are hard to confirm."

"See, you get it. There was one person—some *historian* . . ." (Patti uses her hands to form air quotes around the word) "who claimed he knew where every John Chapman orchard was planted, and it's like, 'How *could* you?' Chapman himself didn't even know where every orchard was planted. He didn't keep records. He didn't keep track of a damn thing."

This is true, and is also the basis for one of my personal favorite *unconfirmable*—yet *believable*—legends about Appleseed. Or, in this case, maybe not so much a "legend" as what I would call, if you'll allow me to coin a term, "historical gossip." That Chapman was so bad with paperwork one could easily argue that he lost a not insignificant percentage of the entire state of Ohio.

What we can *actually* confirm, though, is that Chapman bought a 160-acre plot in Ashland County (the same county Patti and I are currently sitting in) but did not record the deed and subsequently lost the entire property. Other nurseries he established were also lost, later, when settlers arrived and laid claim to land while, you know, not leaving to go walking for months or years at a time.

We still have records of nineteen different locations with different sized lots—sometimes only a couple of acres, other times the size of an entire township. Some land was paid for with money, while other land was paid for with seedling trees. You can find the deeds listed in the appendix of *Johnny Appleseed: Man and Myth* by Dr. Robert Price, which shows Chapman's first land ownership in 1797 in French Creek Township, Venango County, Pennsylvania, and his last holding in 1838 in Eel River Township, Allen County, Indiana. All that said, given the aforementioned knack for misplacing paperwork, one can assume that there were many other properties lost to time.

"On top of all that, it's been two hundred years," Patti said.

"Two hundred years is a long time."

"Two hundred years *is* a long time. Some other historian"—again Patti's air quotes come out—"once said, 'Every apple tree was taken down during Prohibition. So your tree can't be that old.' But we have a photo of it standing strong in the 1930s. The tree was already huge, it'd clearly been there for ages."

The FBI did indeed go after cider makers—and thus apple trees and orchards—during Prohibition, which officially started in 1920. The culmination of the temperance movement, which had begun almost a hundred years before. A moral movement, to be sure, but it really got cooking when it intersected with government greed (it's hard to tax Uncle Vito's basement wine, after all, or someone who makes cider in their own backyard).

American apple growers were then forced to innovate—they rebranded the fruit as a healthy *food.* During Prohibition, historian (no air quotes) Howard Means writes, "Apple growers were forced to celebrate the fruit not for its intoxicating values, but for its nutritional benefits . . . its ability, taken once a day, to keep the doctor away."

On the same subject, Michael Pollan writes, "The identification of the apple with notions of health and wholesomeness turns out to be a modern invention, part of a public relations campaign dreamed up by the apple industry in the early 1900s to reposition a fruit that the Women's Christian Temperance Union had declared war on. Carry Nation's hatchet, it seems, was meant not just for saloon doors but for chopping down the very apple trees John Chapman had planted by the millions." Carry Nation (sometimes spelled, less confusingly, as "Carrie") being Caroline Amelia Nation—aka Hatchet Granny—a radical member of the temperance movement who vehemently and *violently* opposed alcohol (even before the supposed popularity of Prohibition), attacking alcohol-serving establishments with, yes, a hatchet. Pollan continues, "That hatchet—or at least Prohibition—is probably responsible for the bowdlerizing of Chapman's story." At least partially so, I would argue.

But with the Twenty-first Amendment, Prohibition failed, and today, hard cider—once more popular than whiskey, wine, and beer in this country—is one of the fastest-growing alcoholic beverages in America.

This upsurge in sales can be credited to many different factors, but it certainly owes a heap of thanks to the reemerging craft beer movement. In a time of massive conglomerates, when my own beloved Budweiser, "King of Beers" (an alarmingly nondemocratic title, come to think of it), is owned by a Belgian company, one can take a little comfort in the fact that—as of a recent count—craft beer accounts for almost 25 percent of the total beer market in retail dollar sales in the United States.

I take a peek back down at my lemonade, which is dwindling by this point, and sadly nonalcoholic—my hangover moving from "I'll never drink again" to "Perhaps a little hair-of-the-dog wouldn't hurt."

"Personally, I was always more impressed with the Underground Railroad stories," Patti says, bringing my wandering mind back to our conversation.

"I'm sorry, what?"

"My relatives John and Jane Harvey were well-known abolitionists, and escaped slaves would come through here on their way to Canada. The story goes that there were some loose floorboards in the house. They would hide the escaped slaves under 'em—like if the bounty hunters would come, they'd hide the freedom seekers under the floor. Then they'd put the floorboards back, put a rug over the boards, and then place a rocking chair over the rug. Then my great-great-great-grandmother would sit there while the bounty hunters were searching the farm. Rocking away, with the escaped slaves hiding underneath her."

"That's wild."

"Then, as soon as the bounty hunters left, everyone got out of there and up to Vermillion—following the river, it's almost straight north. If not Vermillion, anyplace they could try and get across Lake Erie and into Canada. There's other stories, too. One where my great-great-grandfather and his brother, Robert, put coal on their faces and ran through the fields so that the bounty hunters would chase *them* while a few escaped slaves snuck out of the house. Another story is that John and Jane Harvey became so well known that—this is written about in some publication from the mid-1800s—someone came to town pretending to be an abolitionist, trying to befriend John and Jane—"

"Wait, like an undercover slave bounty hunter that was doing a sting operation?"

"That's the story, anyway. Again, they didn't trust the man, so they pretended like they didn't know anything, and eventually had some young ones dress up as slaves and the man gave chase, thus showing his true colors. Eventually he simply left town."

If only it had been so easy everywhere. The Fugitive Slave Act—which required enslaved people be returned to their so-called owners, even if they were found in a free state—was enacted on September 18, 1850, part of the dubiously named Compromise of 1850. The act would not be repealed until June 28, 1864, over a year after Lincoln's Emancipation Proclamation on January 1, 1863. In Texas, they learned of their freedom on June 19, 1865—now known as Juneteeth—when Union troops arrived in Galveston and announced the emancipation. The final, official date for the end of slavery in the United States is generally considered to be December 6, 1865, when the Thirteenth Amendment—"The Abolition of Slavery"—was ratified.

Patti goes on to show me the land grant for the farm—made out to her great-great-great-grandparents John and Jane, the document signed by none other than John Quincy Adams. To own land in that area and that time—especially if you planned on planting fruit trees on the property—you had to be given a grant from the president.

An obvious question arises: Whose land was this, that a newly formed and rapidly expanding country felt the right to issue land grants in the first place?

As Patti shows me the yellowed document, I can't help but think of all the history scattered about the country—and around the world. In attic drawers, filing cabinets, and plastic tub containers in the basement. It reminds me of the quote from Dr. René Belloq, the villain in

Raiders of the Lost Ark, while talking about a watch he's wearing: "It's worthless. Ten dollars from a vendor in the street. But I take it, I bury it in the sand for a thousand years, it becomes priceless . . ."

The items we pass down, from one generation to the next—as if to say, "Look, our legends are true," whether or not they really are. Almost always, they're half-truths at best. Stories mixed with facts. The soul of this country, a wad of myths and barely-agreed-upon rules strapped together to make up these United States of America.

A country built to hold room for—or perhaps cover up, or even purposefully forget—the shifting sands of history. Core tenets, sure—but even those didn't get it right just out of the gate. "All men are created equal."

A country of legends—a country of con artists. At its core, a country of both.

"You want to hear one of my favorite stories?"

"That's why I'm here."

"When I was growing up we had cows here on the farm, but all I wanted was horses. What young girl doesn't want a horse? So I would take the apples from the tree—making sure that the tree was blocking the view from the windows here in the house, so my parents wouldn't see me. Then I'd take the apples down to the cows in the fields and pretend they were horses."

"The apples?"

"No, quit kidding. The cows. I'd pretend the cows were horses, I'd pet their faces and pretend they had big, gorgeous manes. I'd feed them the apples, breaking them up into pieces—they couldn't take big bites out of 'em, like a horse could. I'd even climb up on their backs, and pretend we could race through the fields."

I too was a child of imagination. I believe most of us were. No wonder we keep telling ourselves stories as we get older—trying to make sense of the world.

"Another story I have—I can't prove this, but I believe it. Every storm, I've told you, took a few of the trees around the farm, but these ones have lasted. They've even been hit by lightning. I swear, every time lightning strikes near here, it hits those trees, and never touches the house."

"Let's hope that stays true," I say, while knocking on wood. Participating in my own belief—my own superstition.

John Chapman famously wouldn't graft trees, only planting them from apple seeds. Some people say it's because Chapman refused to believe that man could improve upon God's creation; others say it's because he loved the trees so much—like his love of animals—that he refused to cut and hurt them. In a way, I think those two stories are telling the same tale, just using different words. But not grafting trees is a risky game.

You see, planting a seed from the most delicious apple in the world doesn't ensure you will replicate another tree that bears that exact apple. In fact, planting seeds is nature's version of Russian Roulette—let's call it Apple Roulette. Apples can grow almost anywhere, and if you're planting a seed, they can be cross-pollinated by any other apple in the area, thus resulting in a different type of apple entirely. The only way to come close to replicating a specific species is through grafting.

Pollan writes, "More than any other single trait, it is the apple's genetic variability—its ineluctable wildness—that accounts for its ability to make itself at home in places as different from one another as New England and New Zealand, Kazakhstan and California. Wherever the apple tree goes, its offspring propose so many different variations on what it means to be an apple—at least five per apple, several thousand per tree—that a couple of these novelties are almost bound to have whatever qualities it takes to prosper in the tree's adopted home."

I ask Patti about the trees at the Johnny Appleseed Welcome Center in Leominster, Massachusetts. There had been a sign that said they were grafted from the last known John Chapman apple tree, which is in her front yard.

"If the sign there says it was grafted from our tree, then they almost certainly were. One gentleman sells trees planted from our seeds here as a novelty. Many others have grafted from this tree. One astronaut, who was working at Urbana College, arranged to have seeds from this tree go to space."

"What? Did they?"

"Yup. In 2019 seeds from this tree went to space."

"What type of apples are they? Do you know?"

"Rambo apples."

The same as the trees at the Leominster Johnny Appleseed Welcome Center, seven hundred or so miles to the east from where we are sitting. The Rambo apple often has a greenish-yellow skin—though Patti's are green, through and through. They ripen in early to late fall, depending on the region, and are pretty average sized. In *Varieties of Apples in Ohio* (1915), this apple is called "little old-fashioned Rambo" and is described as being found "in almost every old orchard in Ohio." The Rambo looks, well, like an apple.

The Rambo seeds were possibly brought to America in 1637, to the colony of New Sweden along the Delaware River (in present-day Delaware, New Jersey, and Pennsylvania), by Peter Gunnarsson Rambo, a Swedish immigrant. His grandson recounted that he brought apple (and other) seeds with him in a box. The first Rambo apple tree could likely have grown from one of these seeds.

I remember how the Rambos in Leominster called to mind John Rambo, from *First Blood* (yes, the first Rambo movie was not, in fact, called *Rambo*). Turns out I wasn't far off the mark. According to David Morrell, the author of the novel that *First Blood* was based on (also called *First Blood*), he took the name for his antihero from a bag of apples his wife had brought home from a roadside stand—although whether they were Rambo apples or Summer Rambos (confusingly a different type of apple altogether), we'll never know. Morrell says he had previously been influenced by the French poet and soldier Arthur Rimbaud—whose last name is pronounced "Rambo"—and then when he saw the Rambo apples, with that actual spelling? He immediately chose John Rambo as his protagonist's name.

"You know, it's funny you mention *Field of Dreams*," Patti says, as she walks me out. "Dwier Brown, the actor who played Kevin Costner's dad in that film? He grew up around here. He and I acted in a few shows together when we were growing up. There's also the Johnny Appleseed Amphitheater."

"What's that?"

"Oh, they built this giant stage over in Ashland. They had a show—a musical even, that they performed, all about John Chapman. Plus they wanted to have visiting artists and performers. But it shut down a while back, sometime around 2005."

"I'll have to go check it out."

"Pretty sure it's private property."

"Right," I say, unconvincingly.

"Do you want to take one?"

Patti had kindly walked me out of her house and into the front yard.

"They aren't fully ripe yet, but you're welcome to take a few if you like."

She is gesturing at the apples, hanging from *the* tree. When I hesitate, she pulls one down for me, a quiet *snap* as it disconnects, the wood now simply a stem.

"Here." Patti tosses me the apple, then guides my hand over to grab a few myself. In the end, I'm holding four apples.

"They won't last forever, but now you have a souvenir."

I thank her again for being so welcoming and for the lemonade, not to mention the apples.

"You're always welcome. Like I said, the tree is everybody's tree."

A li'l reminder of my time here, of John Chapman's supposed last surviving arboreal mark on this earth. Apples born of a tree whose seeds have now been to space, in my hands. Not knowing what to do with the fruits, I stash them in my glovebox.

It dawns on me that, given the nature of how apple trees are grown (chaotic, from seeds, as Chapman chose to do, *or* more uniformly, by grafting, which he did not), the likelihood that the tree in Patti's front yard is both a Rambo apple–producing tree *and* the last living tree planted by John Chapman would have to be an incredible black swan event.

Then again, sometimes a man can predict his own home burning down in Stockholm when he is 250 miles away. Miracles do happen. Other times, they're cons—it's often up to those of us who come afterward to decide for ourselves what to believe.

I wave to Patti and hop in Rabbit's driver's seat and pull away from the farm. I tell myself that I'll visit Patti again, maybe in a year, doing another circle out this way, just like John Chapman used to do.

27

I CALL MY MA again while I'm driving away from the Harvey-Algeo farm. I say I want to continue our conversation from earlier in the day, but really it's something about Patti and her affinity for the land—the way she's proud of her heritage—that reminds me of how disconnected I have always felt from my grandparents' farm. Maybe it was the circumstances of my birth—the coldness I always felt when the family gathered on holidays, as if I belonged enough to be there, but not enough to feel the warmth of my grandparents' affection (what little of it there was to go around).

I know how much pain my ma was in when she lived on the farm, both as an adult and when she was growing up, and I'm concerned that, in spite of that, she's chosen to go back there again. I want to ask her, "Why? Why do this to yourself?" But instead she tells me about the wildlife on the property—they've seen a moose!—and boxes of old photos she's sorting through while my grandmother's centennial body sleeps in the other room. I remember thinking that there were always photos of the other grandchildren up on the walls, and none of me.

"Hey Ma, I gotta go. Call you soon, okay?"

"Okay, Isaac. I love you."

"Love you too, Ma."

The cell service was getting spotty, but that isn't why I got off the phone. Up ahead of me is something I've never seen before: a young Amish man driving a buggy.

Now, to be clear, I've seen plenty of Amish horses and buggies—on this trip and throughout my life—but I have never seen a buggy like this one. The vehicle only has two wheels, and no roof. It is neither boxy nor clunky, as I've come to expect Amish carriages to be. The best way I can describe it is, a convertible buggy. A . . . sexy buggy?

I start to pass the young man and his contraption. "It's okay to talk to the Amish, right?" I try to remember. I toss my phone in my glove compartment, like I wasn't driving a motor vehicle or wearing modern clothing, or breaking who knows how many other Amish rules, and take my foot off the gas as I roll down my window.

The young man turns and gives me a large, strong grin. Maybe that's customary, but he also just looks like a kid having fun. I notice that his hat has a strap that ties under his still youthful beard.

"How goes it?" The Amish man—teenager?—yells over my engine and the clopping of his horse.

"Good, I guess. I've never seen a, uh, buggy like that before."

"You're not familiar with harness racing, then?"

"Can't say that I am. What is—"

Before I can finish he shouts out, "I'll show you."

The reins in his hands snap loudly and quickly—but only once—and his horse instantly accelerates from a steady trot into a breaking gallop. For a moment I think about giving chase, maybe even racing him, before the headline "Jeep Driver Splatters Young Amish Man in Ohio" flashes in my mind. But even if I had pushed my gas pedal to the floor, I wouldn't have caught up with him. It's my first time driving on this winding strip of pavement—whereas this young man clearly knows these roads like the back of his hand. In the time it takes me to have these few thoughts in succession, he is gone.

I have been beaten in a street race by an Amish kid.

Before moving on, I visit the Beyond Measure Market. The place is a grocery store owned and operated by MAP, or Mission to Amish

People, a "nonprofit organization helping young girls who have left their Amish communities land on their feet."

A sign near the front of the store reads:

"Imagine leaving your home with no job, no money, no credit card . . . and no place to live. Now imagine being a young girl in this situation, in this fallen world in which we live. Through your support, MAP Ministry is making a difference in the lives of these former Amish. Your purchase at Beyond Measure Market makes a difference. We are a Market on a Mission, and we thank you for your support."

In front of the surprisingly large grocery store is an even more surprisingly large wooden horse and buggy, along with a sign claiming that it is the "World's Largest Horse & Buggy." The grocery store opened in 2016 on the vast property, along with an apartment building called the New Beginnings Homestead, which "provides housing for young former Amish girls as they train at the store, learn the retail business, make an income, and help pay for their own living expenses." The organization was started by Joe and Esther Keim in 1999, themselves formerly Amish, in hopes of helping young women integrate with the modern world. The Keims believe their work is a calling, saying that the Lord beckoned them to start more than twenty-five years ago.

I think about the young man and his buggy. There's a definite allure there for someone like me—who doesn't truly know the culture, but doesn't hate the idea of a life with no technology. Community-based living. Gather your boys and raise up a barn, maybe do some harness racing in your free time. But, as with so much of this country, the story is more complicated than that. One person's Eden is another person's Sodom and Gomorrah.

I buy some candy, quickly read the prayer above the doorway, and head over to Mansfield, Ohio, which is about twenty-five miles away.

Mansfield lies between Columbus and Cleveland, each city about sixty-five miles apart. It sits on a fork in the Mohican River, and is home to around 50,000 residents in the city proper—and 125,000 or so if you include the surrounding areas. It is the largest city in the region.

Another fun fact about Mansfield is that it's been used as a location for several big-budget Hollywood movies; among the most notable of these were *The Shawshank Redemption, Tango & Cash,* and *Air Force One,* all of which featured the Ohio State Reformatory as a backdrop in pivotal scenes. But *The Shawshank Redemption* is the real hometown favorite, the entire movie being filmed in Mansfield, Ashland, Upper Sandusky, and Butler in 1993—save the movie's famous final scene, which was filmed in St. Croix, US Virgin Islands.

The movie has brought cinephile tourists to the area since its release, and soon the Mansfield/Richland County Convention & Visitors Bureau—seeing an opportunity—created the Shawshank Trail: a self-guided tour around eleven sites in Mansfield, one in Ashland, two in Upper Sandusky, and, for the true completists, yes, one site at Sandy Point National Wildlife Refuge in St. Croix.

The Mansfield/Richland County Convention & Visitors Bureau is now known as Destination Mansfield. There's a website for the self-guided tour (they recommend you take two days, assuming you aren't going to St. Croix), and in 2008 they printed their first Shawshank Trail brochure. They're now on their fourteenth edition.

Outside of town is the Historic Ohio State Reformatory, where the Shawshank State Prison scenes were filmed. The building is massive, gothic, and looming. I take the time to walk the grounds. A place where—even in the sunny days of summer—if someone said to you, "That place is a Four Seasons for vampires," you'd think, "Yeah, sure, that sounds about right." In front of the building is an advertisement, despite fall still being months away, for "Blood Prison: Ohio's Ultimate Haunted House," along with year-long guided tours.

It's no small thing, having one of the best movies ever filmed in your town.

As you're coming into the city, if you're traveling along North

Main Street, near the corner of Harker Street you'll meet a giant sign painted across nine towering white silos that reads "Welcome to Mansfield." Red, white, blue, and yellow—the same colors as the Ohio state flag. The sign was painted in the summer of 2000 by Terry Philpott, Richland Correctional Institution Catholic chaplain and deacon at St. Peter's Church.

Terry told the local paper that when the mayor asked him if he'd do the job, she said, "Terry, you're the only guy I know who's dumb enough to climb that high and do some work like that." He also claimed he had hired someone to stand watch at ground level while he worked on the project, saying, "If anything were to happen to me, his job was to call 911." At 8 a.m. on a Monday morning, he started painting with a roller and industrial enamel paint. "It took two gallons of red, two gallons of blue, and two gallons of yellow," he said. The number of silos matched the number of letters in Mansfield, "which made it easy and convenient."

Terry's handiwork is a bold welcome to Mansfield, if a tad worse for wear now that a quarter of a century has passed. The silos watch over the town like sentries.

I find the Appleseed monument that I'm looking for in South Park, at 100 Brinkerhoff Ave. The park is thirty-five acres and boasts a gazebo, walking trails, a playground, a number of re-created historic buildings, and wide-open green fields. One of those buildings is "The Blockhouse," a re-creation of, well, a blockhouse—a fortification with a wide second floor, and an extremely narrow first floor. These types of fortifications go back all the way to 1398, but were extremely popular throughout the North American frontier—every step of the way west—in the 1600s, 1700s, and through the 1800s. A sign in front of the building tells me that "11 or so were built in the Mansfield area during the War of 1812, to fortify against British and Native American attack."

Entering the park, I find a historical marker that reads "Johnny

Appleseed monument (within this park): John Chapman—better known as 'Johnny Appleseed,' Pioneer, Apple Nurseryman lived in & around Mansfield for twenty years—1810 to 1830."

Mansfield, Ohio—more than anywhere else in America—is the closest place John Chapman had that resembled a home, at least after childhood. Again, he never had a residence, but in his years of walking loops throughout Ohio, Mansfield was an area he returned to again and again. It is also here that he first put his name in the history books.

To break the long and complicated story down quickly—always a danger when discussing history—it was during the War of 1812, and Delaware Native Americans had been forcibly removed from their village, Greentown, in Ashland County and were being held in a detainment camp in Mansfield.

Tensions were high, and the people of Mansfield wanted relief from soldiers and militia who were stationed at Mount Vernon, some thirty miles to the south.

Before John Chapman was famous the way that he is now—an animal-loving, seed-throwing wanderer, posthumously beloved—he gained notoriety while he was still amongst the living. Was he known locally as a Swedenborgian-preaching nurseryman who was a bit of an oddity? Absolutely.

But then came the War of 1812, when he broke into the big time—as Howard Means puts it, "The stage was set . . . for John Chapman to become the Paul Revere of the frontier."

To quote a historical marker in Mansfield:

> The Killing of local shopkeeper Levi Jones stirred rumors of an impending Indian attack. Mansfield's settlers needed help. On the evening of August 9, 1813, Johnny Appleseed is believed to have

embarked from here on a daring overnight journey to the settlements of Clinton and Mount Vernon for reinforcements.

Here is a story that further confuses the oft-repeated notion of Chapman being a "Friend to the Indians." Means points to a 1900 centennial history of Mansfield by one A. J. Baughman:

> As an attack was considered imminent, a consultation was held and it was decided to send a messenger to Captain Douglas, at Mt. Vernon, for assistance. But who would undertake the hazardous journey? It was evening, and the rays of the sunset had faded away and the stars were beginning to shine in the darkening sky, and the trip . . . must be made in the night over a new cut road through a wilderness—through a forest infested with wilde beasts and hostile Indians.
>
> A volunteer was asked for and a tall, lank man said demurely: "I'll go." He was bareheaded, barefooted and was unarmed. His manner was meek and you had to look the second time into his clear, blue eyes to fully fathom the courage and determination shown in their depths. There was an expression in his countenance such as limners try to portray in their pictures of saints. It is scarcely necessary to state that the volunteer was "Johnny Appleseed" for many of you have heard your father tell how unostentatiously "Johnny" stood as "a watchman on the walls of Jezreel," to guard and protect the settler from savage foes.

Means goes on to quote another source who spoke with an early settler claiming to have firsthand memory of the night. "Although I was but a child, I can remember as if it were but yesterday, the warning cry of Johnny Appleseed, as he stood before my father's log cabin door that night. I remember the precise language, the clear, loud voice, the deliberate explanations, and the fearful thrill it awoke in my bosom, 'Fly! Fly! For your lives! The Indians are murdering and scalping at Mansfield!' These were his words. My father sprang to the door, but the messenger was gone, and midnight silence reigned without."

At the time, Chapman would have been in his late thirties. The imminent all-out attack never came, but John Chapman, according to legend, did return with reinforcements the very next day. Still, smaller attacks in the area took place.

The stories of John Chapman's run made the rounds very much when he was alive, raising him from local eccentric to celebrated war hero—all without carrying a gun. Yet, the legend of John's 1812 run is all but forgotten when his story is told in elementary schools across America. It complicates the way America *wants* to remember him. Here is the "Friend of Native Americans" very much picking a side—which in itself is understandable, but it does muddy the waters which America would prefer to keep clear. Again, two things can be true—his relationship with American Indians throughout his life may have been respectful, but when war came knocking he didn't sit on the sidelines, gun or no.

Which stories get remembered, whose stories get sweetened for easy swallowing, and whose get forgotten? This question was on my mind as I stood there, children involved in some sort of summer camp laughing and playing nearby. The monument is a stone obelisk, surrounded by a small iron fence, set back behind the blockhouse re-creation. The words carved into the stone are almost identical to the historic marker at the entrance of the park: "In Memory of Johnny Chapman, Best Known as Johnny Appleseed, Pioneer Apple Nursery man of Richland County from 1810 to 1830."

The stone where the "J" in "Johnny Appleseed" would be has broken off, the monument showing signs of more than a century of wear and tear. It is the first nationally recognized monument to John Chapman.

I will feel a similar disquiet in Dexter City, Ohio—a more southerly part of the state—where I am driving in search of another Johnny Appleseed monument. As previously mentioned, Chapman's father and second family had lived there, though all records would indicate that Chapman rarely visited. Still, many of his relatives are buried in Dexter City, so there's a marker of remembrance for John Chapman.

I pull off and park Rabbit by the side of the road when I get to Dexter City. So many of the Chapman memorials, from his birthplace in Leominster to his supposed grave in Fort Wayne, to his last tree at Harvey-Algeo Farm, can be described this way. *By the side of the road.* I walk to the base of the memorial and sit, doing nothing for a moment like I did at the monument in Mansfield. Eventually, I get on my knees and pray.

Nobody can say how many statues, monuments, or memorials there are to Chapman. Especially if you factor in wood carvings, like the one in Leominster's town hall, or Sunbury, Ohio, where his visage is carved out of a tree trunk. Much like Mark Twain, who seems to have at least one statue in every state he ever set foot in, and a few that he didn't, or the numerous plaques throughout the original thirteen colonies that read "George Washington Slept Here"—or "George Washington Shat Here," if you're staying someplace with a sense of humor. Places like to mark that they've been touched by history. But often when you're there, saying a little prayer at the base of a round stone memorial in Dexter City, Ohio, you get the sneaking suspicion history is actually happening somewhere else.

We have a general idea where Chapman wandered. Massachusetts, Pennsylvania, Ohio, and on into Indiana. But there are rumors of him getting into West Virginia, which borders Ohio, so perhaps that's not so far-fetched. One story even posits he got as far as the Potomac River in Virginia—though that seems unlikely, especially as it would place him there not later in his life, but between his trip from Longmeadow, MA, to Warren, PA. Rather out of the way.

Not when you have a Jeep, though.

The one detour I take off of Chapman's known route across these states brings me to an old friend's house not far from the Potomac in Washington, DC. I've been driving around Ohio looking for Appleseed monuments and statues, but after days of camping, and finding myself in Dexter City, I decide to drive five hours east through West Virginia—one of the most gorgeous states in America, in my opinion—and on through Maryland and then down into Washington. I want to see that old college friend, whose name is Alec, and am desperate to get off the road.

Rabbit stinks of the Allegheny River still, somehow, and my gear is wet and ill cared for. On arrival, Alec's wife gently and politely opts not to hug me, and suggests I take a shower. When I return, my flip-flops have been—again, very politely—moved to the backyard, which is when Alec suggests I throw them out entirely and offers me a pair of his shoes in their place.

"Throw them out, or, you know, burn them."

For the sake of the Earth's atmosphere, we decide that binning them will have to do.

28

AFTER REFRESHING IN Washington, DC—a home-cooked meal with friends restorative for my soul, once I'd properly bathed myself and put on a fresh change of clothes—I made my way back out into Ohio.

I go for hikes in the Mohican State Park—both along the Mohican River and following white markers that lead me to the stunning Gorge Overlook—and camp in the forest, never making a fire, but falling asleep with the setting sun. So much of this country is free to enjoy, if you just go out and explore it. After doing nothing but bumming around in the woods for about half a week, I've finally come up with a plan again: to find the abandoned Johnny Appleseed Amphitheater that Patti mentioned.

I know it's near Charles Mill Lake, somewhere near where Route 511 intersects with Route 39 east of Mansfield in Ashland, Ohio. I've been exploring the area for a while when I pull over for gas and ask the man behind the counter if he has any ideas. His response is, "Have you tried looking it up on Google Maps?"

"I'm sorry, what?"

"It closed a long time ago, but I think it's on Google Maps."

I type in the proper name, Johnny Appleseed Heritage Center, and there it is on the map, some ten or so miles away.

When I arrive, I find a dirt logging road where I can park Rabbit, away from the main highway so as not to draw any attention. I take my pack and walk past an alarming number of No Trespassing signs, although none as fun as one I passed on my way here, a private residence with a sign in its front yard that read "Trespassers Welcome: Dog Food Is Getting Expensive," nor as straightforward as the ones on the islands of the Allegheny River, "Stay the Fuck Off Our Island."

I follow an old entrance road and jump a fence—on which hangs a sign warning that the area is under video surveillance, although I see no cameras nailed into any of the surrounding trees—and then some chains that have been strung up across the roadway. Another sign reads "STOP: Restricted Area, Authorized Personnel Only."

The amphitheater was first dreamed up in 1996, ground was broken in 2001, and the entire place was completed in 2003. When it opened in 2004, the outdoor amphitheater boasted 1,700 seats and was meant for outdoor plays. There were also plans to rent it out for weddings and receptions, or for bands to perform and bring in fans from the surrounding area.

At the core of the amphitheater's business, though, was a play that told the stories of John Chapman's life through song and dance. Patti saw the show when it first opened. But the hope of bringing in sixty-five thousand people annually, well, how best to put it? It helps not to hinge everything on one recurring performance. Attendance petered out quickly, and by 2005, less than a year after opening, the amphitheater—which cost over $4 million to build—was closed.

Location couldn't have helped. I make the long walk from the rural road I drove in on. Mansfield, the closest small city, is fifteen miles away. *I guess not enough people there wanted to watch the same play over and over again,* I think, with an air of sadness.

Eventually I come to a statue of Johnny Appleseed, or that's what I assume it is. The figure's head has been cut clean off. Farther in, I find the abandoned amphitheater. It is gigantic—the place had grandeur, I'll give them that. An incredible outdoor space, although the seats, all 1,700 of 'em, feel rather ambitious out here in the woods.

In *The Botany of Desire,* Pollan spends time with William Ellery Jones, "a fifty-one-year-old fund-raising consultant and amateur historian with a dream: to establish a Johnny Appleseed Heritage Center and Outdoor Theater on a hillside outside of Mansfield." Pollan's book was published in 2001, around the time they would have been breaking ground on the place. Now here I stand, almost a quarter century later. The dream has come and gone, but the structure itself still stands. All metal apple logos and empty seats.

I pour out a little hard cider—which I've rucked-in, stowed away in my pack—on the stage for all the dreamers out there. It really was a gorgeous setting. I could see Bill Jones's vision. But now the low underbrush of the forest and high looming branches continue to creep in and reclaim the land for nature.

As I sit there, a familiar black dog lumbers down the amphitheater stairs, like some surprise guest making a big entrance in a Broadway show. The behemoth is closer to me than it had ever been, though it still keeps its distance. The sight of him no longer alarms me. I don't understand it, but it doesn't feel unexpected.

The dog makes it halfway from the stairs to the stage, then sits down in a position that is recognizable to me by this point: its back straight, its head cocked to one side, the weight of its body resting on its curled-up haunches and straight front legs. With nothing else to do, or maybe nothing left to lose, I fix my gaze on the creature and speak.

"What do you want?"

The dog just sits there, its tail unmoving, same as the rest of its body.

"I get it. You're following me. So if you've got something to say, spit it out."

The dog lies down, its head still alert. The animal's silence upsets me, its unblinking eyes unnerving in a way I can't express.

"What the fuck do you want?" I yell this time. My voice booms off the concrete amphitheater and empty metal chairs and surrounding trees. Birds shout their displeasure and take to the sky. I gaze at them, their many wings fluttering against the evening dusk. When I return my eyes to the ground, the dog is gone.

29

WHAT HILLS THERE were left petered out as I drove through western Ohio and into Indiana.

Indiana is not the start of the Great Plains—in fact, on the Ohio-Indiana border, you're basically still two states away. But it's like a movie trailer for the Great Plains, one that gives away most of the plot, to be honest. Or an appetizer that makes the main course feel almost overwhelming.

I drive through idyllic settings, expansive flat farmlands with a giant barn by an old white oak in the middle of a field, like something out of an Andrew Wyeth painting. The majesty of the landscape only tarnished by the occasional billboard advertising the Warm Glow Candle Outlet off exit 145, with a hunky cowboy wearing nothing but a white ten-gallon hat, his abs glistening in the midwestern sun. What the man has to do with candles is left only to your imagination. Or signs for the Uranus Fudge Factory, with such slogans as "Let's Talk About Uranus" or "Explore Uranus" or "The Best Fudge Is Found in Uranus."

Perhaps the billboards don't diminish the American landscape, though. In a way, maybe they're what makes it. The American part, at least.

I find myself playing a game of chicken with my gas tank as I drive into the outskirts of Indianapolis. The warning light went on miles back, but I had covered so much ground, stuck in that meditative state that anyone who has driven long distances is familiar with.

Stopping for any reason starts to feel like failure. A defeat. So you pass each service area, each exit advertising gas, willing your engine to run on fumes. Images of walking the highway with a plastic gas can in your hand bouncing in your brain. But those harrowing images are somehow not enough to make you actually pull over.

As I mentioned before, I have almost every vice on the planet, save gambling. But when I enter this trance-like state—one that is still new to me, given how long I went without a vehicle as an adult—I feel as if I can completely understand how one might put their entire life savings on black and let the roulette wheel spin. There's something intoxicating in the pushing forward.

I ride that high all the way into "The Crossroads of America," the official state motto of Indiana and nickname for Indianapolis. Which makes sense, as the city is indeed in the middle of the state. The name refers to its being the junction of I-65, I-69, I-70, and I-74.

The *true* geographic center of the United States is about a thousand miles to the west (and a notch north), in Belle Fourche, South Dakota.

Even that has only been true since 1959, when Alaska and Hawaii became states. Before that, starting in 1912—when New Mexico became a state in January of that year, followed by Arizona in February, the last two states to join the Lower 48—the geographic center (and still the geographic center of the contiguous states) was near the town of Lebanon, Kansas, around seven hundred miles west of Indianapolis. Still, none of that stopped Indiana from adopting "Crossroads of America" as its motto in 1988.

Yet, when John Chapman made his way this far west, it was considered the wild frontier by his fellow white colonizers. Indianapolis was itself no more than a wood cabin in the beginning.

I finally capitulate to my gas tank in our imagined game of chicken—as happens every time, eventually—and pull into an Amoco on the corner of East 25th Street and North College Avenue. I consider getting a bite to eat at the nearby restaurant, efficiently named "Steak and Lemonade," or possibly at the chicken and fish shop next door. But the sun is starting to set, and I want to get to where I plan to lay my head this evening.

I have followed the highways down into Indianapolis instead of toward my actual destination, Fort Wayne, for one main reason: the only people I know who live in Indiana are in Indianapolis.

They are also the only people in the state that I can text, same day, and say:

Been on the road for a minute. Tired of sleeping outdoors. Could use a shower too, frankly. Any chance you have an open couch?

My friend Ashley C. Ford and her husband, Kelly (not to be mistaken for my girlfriend of the same name; Ashley and I often bragging about our respective Kellys to each other), do me one better. A warm shower and a whole guest bedroom.

They're waiting on the porch of their adorable, cozy rental as I park Rabbit across the street. We hug, order some food (not from Steak and Lemonade, sadly, that is still a fantasy to this day), Kel rolls a joint, and we sit down.

It is the most comfortable I have felt since my friend Alec and his wife in DC let me sleep in their house despite my awful smell, about two weeks ago.

Ashley was born and raised in Fort Wayne, Indiana. She then moved to Muncie for a bit of school before landing in Indianapolis, where for seven years she lived in the Irvington area—named for Washington Irving, the American short-story writer, who had one helluva run in the early nineteenth century with "Rip Van Winkle" in 1819 and "The Legend of Sleepy Hollow" in 1820. In 2014 she headed out for New York City, where she stayed for over half a decade, before moving right back here to Indianapolis. Ashley is a full-time writer, and Kel works at a local bookshop. When I ask Ashley if she missed

Indiana when she lived on the East Coast, she answers immediately, "All the time. All day, every day."

She takes a pull from the joint Kel lights and hands her, then continues.

"I think because I'm a Black, queer, empathetic person, everybody was always like, 'Man, I bet you wanted to run out of Indiana. I bet you dreamed of the day you would escape.' And to be honest? That was never part of my plan. Ever."

Home is home. I think about Peter, from the Allegheny River, and his concern that so many young ambitious people head to New York City, Los Angeles, Austin, Texas—or even just the cities in their home state. Ashley is indeed ambitious, but she missed the little things when she lived in NYC. A neighbor dropping off zucchini bread, made with vegetables from their own garden. An old friend breezing into town for some weed, a little takeout, and a long-overdue catch-up.

"Some people are great at riding New York's wavelength. But me? I wasn't getting any joy out of it—and we only have so much time, after all."

I think about the newfound value I place on time. Is it something that comes with age? Or is it the idea of time as a finite resource something everyone feels, and I'm just late to the party?

Our delivery arrives and we put it out on plates—piles of steaming noodles and greasy dumplings from a nearby Chinese restaurant, a type of food I've been greatly missing on the road—then continue our conversation as we eat.

"I'm a person who enjoys dawdling," Ashley says while splitting her chopsticks.

"You're a dawdler?"

"I'm a dawdler—and I like other people who enjoy dawdling, too. I like conversations where there's no time limit. It's not meeting someone for a half-an-hour coffee or a forty-five-minute lunch. It's a friend coming over, sitting here on the couch like we are, ordering food, with a whole night ahead of us to do nothing except talk, eat, and be in each other's company. There's no rush, you can take your time and I won't interrupt you other than to give affirmation. 'Oh, that's interesting. Please go on.' "

"No time pressure."

"Where do you have to go, Isaac? What pressures are you under right now?"

I give it a moment of thought before answering. Like a lot in life—and throughout history—the deeper answer is a bit like a Rubin's vase. You know the one, you look at a picture, do you see a vase or two faces?

What pressures am I under right now? On the one hand, not many. You might say I'm bullshitting around the Midwest, sleeping outdoors or on friends' couches, rambling through American history and often overstaying my welcome. But looked at another way, my life has been more gutters than strikes over the past couple years, and it isn't as if I was doing so great before that, either. I've been growing increasingly concerned about my, shall we say, ability to comprehend reality, not to mention my life-altering obsession with somebody who never had a permanent address—but by this point, I'm too stoned to get into any of that.

"I mean, none, really."

"You want to get a good night's rest because you've been sleeping outside like a damn fool, but other than that, there's nothing going on save the three of us. Right here. Right now."

We reload our plates as our conversation continues. Kel talks about how much he loves being back in Indiana and being closer to his family, but also how it allows him to hunt and ride ATVs.

"I love to do that, too," Ashley agrees. "We love all that hick shit."

"Go Hoosiers!" I know the word is the term for Indiana University's sports teams and comes from a demonym for people from Indiana, but I also know that it originally had a negative connotation. A lot of people view Indiana as the hick state of the North, and—while the term is welcomed warmly now—"Hoosier," back in the day, meant an unintelligent or uncultured person. Some folks claim the word originated from 1800s census takers knocking on front doors and saying, "Who's here?"

By 1833 there was a newspaper called *The Hoosier*.

Other people claim that the word might have come from Methodist minister Reverend Harry Hosier, who preached on the frontier during the Second Great Awakening. Reverend Hosier was also known as Black Harry, and had been born a slave in North Carolina and sold north to Baltimore before gaining his freedom and beginning his ministry around the end of the American Revolution. Even though he was illiterate, some people called him the greatest orator in America at the time. But also, yes, it was a term that meant "rough person" or "yokel."

Ashley slurps down a dumpling and continues, "I loved growing up here. I grew up in a mainly all-Black community. That's another thing that happens. I think when people hear I grew up in Indiana, they assume I grew up in an all-white town. I did not. When people assume that, I'm like, 'Bitch, I grew up in a place Blacker than you have ever been.' Indiana's diversity is on the rise—but there's always been a strong Black population in the state. Again, something I ran into when I was out east, this 'idea of Black excellence.' That's great and all, but I'm not striving for Black excellence. I want Black freedom."

"How do you mean?"

"Being excellent is great, but I shouldn't have to be excellent in order to justify my existence. Black freedom to me is: I can be excellent, or I can be *not* excellent. Hell, I can be terrible if I want. I get to exist, and that's enough. Excellent? Not excellent? Doesn't matter. What's important is I can just be. I wanna be who I am and have that be enough."

I think for a moment about the promise of the religion I was raised on. God's unconditional love—no catches or takebacks.

"So where'd you grow up, exactly?"

"I grew up where you're headed to—you're going in the wrong direction, mind you."

"I know."

"But yeah, I grew up in Fort Wayne, on the southeast side of town. Like I said, a primarily Black neighborhood. I grew up immersed in Black culture—which is not to say that white culture didn't seep in. Of course it did, this is America. But in my world, we were primary. And not primary because we were at the top of a list, but primary just because by numbers we were in the majority, you know?"

"Of course."

"But eventually there were more and more white kids at school. I remember the first time I really noticed. Saying to myself in high school, 'Wait a second, this class has a lot of white people in it.' Which was, like, four or five white kids. They were usually working class, living around the poverty line. But in the end we just blended, we all blended in. And I liked that, I liked that mixing of cultures—seeing how they danced different at the school dances. Or cheered different at the football games. So those were the dynamics that I grew up in—different dynamics than what were eventually out in the world. Once I got to college, that's when things got really white. And once I got to New York, well, New York was my first real confrontation with *class*."

Most Black people in Indiana came during the Great Migration, although there were some enslaved people in the area before the Northwest Ordinance prohibited slavery and involuntary servitude in the land that would later become Indiana.

"After the Civil War many Black people came up from the South—many Black people helped build up Indianapolis at that time—and then there was the Great Migration. Then there was some *more* migration, which happened in the 1950s and '60s. Many Black families moved here for manufacturing jobs. Indiana used to do so much manufacturing. So much engineering. That's when my family came up this way. This is why—and it's passed down from generation to generation—so many Black people in Indiana still have a country accent, or an accent from the South. In fact, my grandma is from rural Missouri, so she has a strong rural Missourian accent, which she then passed on to me. Which is why you'll hear a southern twang in my voice, or—depending on who I'm talking to—even a strong country accent. But also, as stated before, like Kel, I love country shit."

I suddenly notice the twang in Ashley's voice. I've never thought before about the midwestern accent being southern-inflected. We keep talking, about the myriad of things she and Kel love about living in a place with *space*. Her plans for her garden. The sun shining on grass in the early morning, and feeling wet dew under her feet, between her toes. Four-wheeling, shooting guns. A schedule that isn't crowded. A life that isn't crowded. All things bucolic, just a short drive away.

"People are supposed to roam around, especially in their younger years. To go 'discover yourself.' So that's what we did, but one of the things we discovered was how much we missed it here. Being away from home intensifies the things you miss. I really missed, well, everything we're talking about."

I drift for a moment: "People are supposed to roam around, especially in their younger years." The years I'm currently inhabiting can't really be described as "young." Kelly—my Kelly, although I'm sure she was on my mind at least partially because I am watching *Ashley's* Kelly chomp into a crispy egg roll—is very much someone I am missing. Over the course of the past year we've gone from dating casually to spending more and more time together. Moving in together. A deep longing hits my heart as Ashley describes what she had missed about living in Indiana, as I empathize and start feeling what, or really who, I am missing back east. I want to call Kelly right there, at that moment, but I don't want to be an impolite guest. I make a mental note to call her more, and tune back in to Ashley's list of things she missed.

"I missed open, empty spaces. I like being able to drive and see the sky for a long time."

"I've been doing a lot of that."

"What do you think?"

"It's beautiful, of course," I say. "Any time I travel around the US—which I've done a lot throughout my life—I'm always struck by our landscape."

"What do you miss most about where you're from when you're out this way?"

"Whenever I'm in the Midwest, I miss the ocean. I don't like being this far from the sea. The ability to look out at all that water."

"See, for me, there's not a lot of difference between watching the waves of the ocean and watching a strong, consistent breeze flow through a field of corn, or soybean plants, or wheat. It gives me the same thing. The same feeling. I used to feel embarrassed about that, but I'm not anymore. You'll see a lot of fields like that when you drive up to Fort Wayne tomorrow. Are you going to go to the festival?" she asked, remembering my itinerary for Indiana, which I had momentarily forgotten.

"The festival?"

"The Johnny Appleseed Festival. They do it every year in Fort Wayne. Tell me you know about the festival, Isaac!"

"I mean, I do now."

"Do you know that I planned my wedding so that the Johnny Appleseed Festival was the day after?"

"I didn't—"

"You would have, if you'd come to my wedding."

I was a workaholic at the time, and had missed their celebration. A lamentable choice, in hindsight.

"So what'd I miss?"

"Other than a great wedding where my uncle made us custom hot sauce? You missed a huge celebration in Fort Wayne, that they do every year for your boy Johnny Appleseed."

"Because he—"

"Because he died there, yes. At least supposedly—I remember there being some controversy about if it was really his grave or not. But that didn't stop us from going to the Apple Orchard in the mall."

"What's the Apple Orchard?"

"It's not there anymore, but at one point in the Glenbrook Mall, there was this place called the Apple Orchard. It was a covered hallway that went from one side of the mall to the other, so that you could just skip right through. They also had a place where you could get treats and caramel apples and kettle corn and stuff like that, so the whole hallway smelled delicious. There were benches with these little fake trees and fake gas lights. In the middle, there was this massive wooden statue of Johnny Appleseed that somebody had carved out of the trunk of a tree."

"Holy shit."

"It was huge. When they closed down the Apple Orchard, everybody was like, 'But what's gonna happen to the big Johnny Appleseed statue?' Everybody was really sad about it, so they put him in the H&M."

"Wait. So there's a giant wooden statue of Johnny Appleseed carved out of a tree in the middle of an H&M in Fort Wayne, Indiana?"

"You bet your ass. Last I checked, at least."

"And the festival?"

"You'll see."

The night is growing late, and we open a bottle of wine. It's the latest I have stayed up in weeks—a far cry from falling asleep with the setting sun like I had in Ohio's Mohican State Park. Ashley's Kelly plays records while the three of us talk more, catching up on old friends and dreams for the future—me promising to visit the Johnny

Appleseed statue in the H&M, and saying that I'll be sure to come back for the festival in the fall.

Eventually Kel brings me to the guest bedroom, which is filled with books and has posters of book covers on the wall. The next morning I wake up, say goodbye to Kel, Ashley, and their beautiful chocolate Lab, Astro, who was so chill the night before that I almost forgot he was there.

The drive to Fort Wayne the next day is beautiful. The sun is shining and I think of Ashley's comment about the fields looking like the ocean. There are billboards again—"We Were Having Big Fun in Uranus"—but now the fudge advertisements remind me of something you might find in New Jersey at the boardwalk. Something silly by the seashore, way out here, so far from the ocean.

30

When I arrive in Fort Wayne, I am worried at first. The route I rode in had me driving through what seemed to be a never-ending strip mall. But now, as I drive into the city center, a bustling downtown opens up before me.

Apparently that downtown has been hard fought over for more than the past two decades. Like many smaller cities in America, Fort Wayne has struggled as industry and jobs left for overseas. But more recently, investments in excess of a billion dollars have been pouring into the area—one of the latest being a $30 million boutique hotel called the Bradley. The city is making use of its waterfront, too—with an area by the river now called Promenade Park—as so many cities throughout the Midwest are starting to do.

I learn all this while sitting at an outdoor bar called the Deck. I'd parked Rabbit by the St. Mary's River, knowing that I'll eventually make camp somewhere by the water—usually the easiest place to remain inconspicuous, especially in an urban area. But I'm well rested after my night at Ashley and Kel's, and there is a gorgeous new city to explore.

Though perhaps the truth is that sleeping outside isn't the exciting prospect that it had been earlier this year—all the more apparent after a night in a cozy, warm bed in Indianapolis.

It's lunchtime, and the Deck is bustling. I set up shop at one end of the horseshoe-shaped bar and make conversation with the waitstaff, who are happy to recommend sites and things to do in Fort Wayne as

I sip on a Purple Haze—a mix of grape-flavored vodka, Blue Curaçao, grenadine, sour mix, and a splash of lemon-lime soda—which the bartender insists I try.

People come and go, but eventually two young men sit down next to me and settle in for an afternoon of drinking. I'm surprised they are even served. They look like children to me—something nobody tells you about getting older. Your peers seem to stay the same age, but those younger than you begin to look *so* much younger. Surely when you were twenty-one, you didn't look like *that* much of a baby, right? When carded, the two toddlers turn out to be twenty-three.

I'm writing down some of the bar staff's recommendations in my notebook, which catches the attention of one of the infants.

"What are you writing?"

"Oh, just some things I want to do while I'm in town."

"Where are you visiting from?"

"Back east."

"What's your name?"

I tell him, and then ask him his. It's Ray, which he tells me is short for Ramirez.

"I'm not from around here either," he says, in the way young men try to be worldly. Something I've been guilty of myself, many times over.

He tells me most of his family lives in Corpus Christi, Texas.

"What brought you up to Fort Wayne?" I inquire.

"Well, I've lived here for a long time. My grandfather was an illegal immigrant." Ray says it matter-of-factly, not with pride, nor with shame or bashfulness. Just stating a reality. "But he was smart."

"How so?"

"He knew the closer you are to the US-Mexico border, the more likely you are to get into trouble. The more cops and Feds are always looking for illegal immigrants, right? So he hauled his ass all the way up here. Took me and my mom and some other family with him. But my parents are legal. I'm legal. We were all born in America. But my grandfather was smart. You can't just get across the border and chill in Texas anymore. You've got to go somewhere else in the country. The Midwest, or out east—where you're from. Or up in California."

"Do you ever get back to see the rest of your family in Corpus Christi?"

"Oh, yeah. I love Texas. I wanna move back there, to be honest."

"You don't like Fort Wayne?"

"No, I do. But it gets too cold in the winter, man. Plus, it's hard on the cars."

"The cars?"

"All the salt, and just the wear and tear. My dream is to get back down to Corpus Christi and live there."

Ray's friend, who has been silently scrolling his phone, doesn't look up, but speaks for the first time.

"Ramirez paints cars. He's real good, too."

I notice that the friend is looking at Instagram, thumbing through images of one incredible car after another.

"You know, my grandfather was an illegal immigrant, too," I offer. "Or maybe it was his father. Family history's dicey."

The friend looks up from his phone, but Ray lightly admonishes me.

"Don't be an asshole."

"From Canada," I explain. "They were Scottish, but snuck in over the border from Canada."

Both of 'em chuckle and shake their heads.

"My grandfather also used to love cars," I persist. "Loved to race them when he was a kid. I didn't hear these stories until I was older, but apparently back in the day he'd take old junkers that he'd fix up on the cheap, and in the winter he and his buddies would wait for the river to freeze over and then go race 'em on the ice."

"Do you like cars, like your grandad?"

"I do. Never raced 'em on the river, but—well, yeah. I like cars."

"I love cars. I love souping 'em up. I love painting 'em. I love showing 'em off."

Ray pulls out his phone and starts showing me pictures—cars he loves. Cars his friends own. Cars he painted. Eventually he and his drinking buddy both show me pictures of their own vehicles. Not as flashy as the others, but getting there.

"Maybe if you raced 'em on the river when it freezes you wouldn't miss Corpus Christi during the winter so much."

"I don't know about all that. But we do race. What are you doing later on?"

I tell him the truth, I don't have a single plan.

"We're doing a car show tonight. Come meet us—I'll text you the location. What's your phone number?"

"Like, in a convention center or something?"

"No, a parking lot." His face says the rest, which I interpret as something like "You silly old fool." "We show off our cars, do donuts and stuff. Drink a few beers. Race. You'll love it."

I give him my number, Ray texts me the details, and he and his friend, whose name I would eventually learn was Joe, pay for their beers and leave.

Not long after, I follow suit, finishing up at the Deck and making camp down by the water, out of sight, like I'd planned. A warm summer evening was setting in, so I decide to walk over to where the pin Ray texted me earlier tells me to go. I don't need to spend my whole night hanging out with twenty-year-olds, but it's been a while since I've partaken in the great American tradition of drinking in a parking lot and messing around in cars.

The scene at the lot could be something straight out of the 1950s, except instead of Thunderbirds, GTOs, and Mustangs you have Acura NSXs, geared-up Honda Civics, Toyota Supras, and, well, okay, also still some Mustangs. The more things change, the more things stay the same. The spirit is there. Alive and well. Young people wanting to go fast and show off the machines they've worked on with their own hands, hoping to catch some interest or attention from their peers.

When I see them with their phones out, recording videos and taking pictures, I ask if they're doing it for social media. I was thinking of Joe, looking at Instagram. Maybe there's an account I could follow.

"No, these are just for us. To show friends—like we showed you earlier today at the bar," Ray replies. "What do you think we're doing? Snitching on ourselves? Posting shit for the cops to see?"

Once the sun goes down, the cars light up. Not simply headlights and taillights, but undercarriages glowing with dark blues and bright greens, exterior lighting running down the sides of their vehicles, or interior lights the deep purplish color of a blacklight or the Purple Haze I drank earlier. The young men take turns peeling out, leaving rubber on the abandoned parking lot pavement. Eventually spreading their vehicles into a wide circle to make room for other cars to do donuts, which in turn become more and more elaborate. I imagine the young Amish man from Ohio here, urging his horse to spin his racing buggy in wild shapes—maybe getting up on one wheel as his hat grazes the pavement—a young person's desire for speed, for a vehicle, for freedom, for an ability to show off transcending culture, space, and time.

The music is loud, played out over expensive car speakers. Ray gave me a beer when I arrived that I am slowly sipping on. Joe nods hello, but the guys mostly cackle with their friends and leave me alone, maybe surprised I've shown up. I wonder if anyone is actually going to race, but figure that's an event that will take place later in the night. Eventually people start mentioning that cops are on their way. I ask Ray what's up—I don't hear any sirens.

"Nah, they know. They always try to come out and break it up. But hey, we're gonna ditch here anyways. Wanna come with?"

The young men are headed to a second location, inviting me along.

"There'll be girls there!" It's the second sentence Joe has ever said to me. And the last.

I tell 'em I appreciate the offer, but I have to call it a night. There comes a time when you realize you are no longer the young man, and you have to leave the young men to do young men things.

I think of my younger years spent driving like a maniac, constantly powered by a voice telling me to *go.* Nights spent driving around in friends' trucks, racing too fast under wide-open skies. I remembered the old men I'd see sitting in bars: I'd look at them fondly and think they must have something figured out—an old drinker stoicism. But now I'm closer in age to those old barflies than the young men leaving me behind in their fast machines, one more rip of hot rubber burned onto the pavement, their hands waving goodbye. Yet I have no secret knowledge. Maybe I'm a little smarter at knowing how to avoid trouble, but that's about it. These days I prefer just to sit at the end of the bar to do nothing other than pass the time.

Which is what I decide to do. Sure, I'm not up for spending the night racing through Fort Wayne, but I'm not excited about going to sleep on the hard ground again, either. Not yet.

31

YOU'RE NOT FROM around here, are ya?"

The bartender puts my beer in front of me, making my dream of being an old man at the end of a bar a reality.

"I'm not," I answer, noticing that it's the second time in one day that someone clocked me as an out-of-towner.

The bar, which is called GnomeTown, is jumping. It is located on the Landing, a commercial area in Fort Wayne that was somewhat deserted for decades—old photos of the area show abandoned storefronts—but now is bustling again, a result of the city's 2000s renaissance. Fort Wayne reminds me of a smaller, more midwestern Nashville. Young people are out, bachelorette parties are kicking off for the weekend, lines form to get into breweries and Instagram-friendly gastropubs like the one I'm already in, making my old-man-at-the-end-of-the-bar status all the more deeply felt.

The man serving drinks is certainly one of them—a young person, though older than the gearheads I've just departed—but his confidence seems to come from something deeper. He is above average height, with closely clipped, jet-black hair, and a mustache that fits him perfectly, but also seems to imply that it might have been grown as a sly joke. One only for himself. Maybe it's the fact that I'm road weary, or the fact that I've been drinking, but I feel the urge to talk to him—to tell him what I am doing here, an urge I didn't have at the bars in Westminster or Warren. So I tell him all of it, as best as I can understand it myself at this point. Following in the footsteps of

Johnny Appleseed. Searching for the man who was once welcome "in every cabin in Ohio and Indiana," as Michael Pollan puts it, because "he was bringing the gift of alcohol to the frontier. . . . Our American Dionysus."

"Well, that sounds completely crazy."

I nod in agreement. It's becoming ever clearer to me, too.

"I'm Isaac," I say, and offer my hand.

"Dakota," he answers, taking it. I notice right away that he's wearing a memorial bracelet—a metal band with a name and rank stamped into it—on his wrist. I recognize the bracelet because of my friend Conner, who, despite our delinquent childhood, ended up going to West Point and is still in the military to this day. He also wears one in remembrance of a fallen comrade.

My eyes move up to Dakota's name tag, which reads "RICHARD."

I raise my eyebrows. He sees my expression change.

"Why would I want customers to know my real name? Besides, it's funny."

"How so?"

"You know, Dick."

I laugh. We continue getting to know each other, until he eventually calls over another person sitting at the bar to join our conversation, indicating the man's hat to me. This other patron—Dakota seems to know him—is wearing a baseball cap with a red apple on it, adorned with a face and a tin cap on its head. The Fort Wayne TinCaps is a Minor League Baseball team that feeds players to the San Diego Padres of all places—and was named as a tribute to Johnny Appleseed. I'm hoping to catch a game while in town and am really starting to respect how seriously Fort Wayne takes John Chapman.

"Are you a fan?" I ask.

"I went to games as a kid; I keep meaning to go now, but, you know—"

"Just like you keep meaning to talk to girls in here," says Dakota, "but every night it's the same. You just end up talking to me." It's clear the man on my side of the bar is a regular—and that Dakota regularly gives him shit.

"But tonight's gonna be different," Dakota continues.

"Why's that?" responds the man. I'll soon learn his name, too—Scott.

"Why? Because tonight, we've got Jack Black."

It takes me a moment to realize that Dakota is talking about me. I've been on the road for months, mostly sleeping outside. My diet hasn't exactly been stellar. Fewer fresh apples and living off the land, and more gas station delicacies like bags of beef jerky and day-old (optimistic estimate) hot dogs. My hair has grown long and my beard big and wild—same as John Chapman's. But if all the artistic renderings of Chapman were to be believed, well, that's where the similarities stop. Where Appleseed is presented as skinny and wiry as the trees he planted, I'm growing as red and round as the fruit that they bore.

When you're young, your body can take being on the road. But as you get older—like any well-used vehicle—the miles start to show.

I don't know if you've ever been given a nickname—I've had a few in my day. But never before have I been given a nickname so quickly, directly after meeting someone, and with as much confidence as Dakota delivers it. And yet there doesn't seem to be one ounce of malice behind it.

Without pausing to gauge my reaction, he goes on,

"When Jack Black is in town, anything is possible."

I would be called Jack Black for the rest of my time in Indiana.

The rest of the night goes as you might expect—Dakota gets his manager to let him split from his shift after chatting up a couple of blond girls who are in town for the weekend. He introduces me to them as Jack Black and refuses to give up the bit, which has the women laughing until they agree to head over to Henry's Restaurant with us.

Henry's has been family owned and operated since 1959, and when Dakota suggests it as the place we should head next, I vaguely remember Ashley mentioning it, too, encouraging me to check it out.

"Henry's is your kind of place, Isaac."

She was right. The restaurant has small but welcoming booths, and the bar is all old wood and hazy glass. There is an ancient bicycle nailed to the wall—and the room is packed with a thrumming weekend crowd. So much so, in fact, that we decide to sit outside.

Once we're at our table, Dakota orders bottles of Budweiser and shots of Jameson with diligent regularity. The staff knows him, and he introduces me to everyone there as, yes, Jack Black. The women he's met and invited along have come from South Bend, where they live—coworkers at a McDonald's who had become friends and are in town for some fun. They tell a harrowing story about being robbed at gunpoint while working there, and then being robbed again, six months later. I have questions.

"So wait, you got robbed at gunpoint, and you kept working there? And then it happened again? And you *still* work there? Do you get benefits? Free Happy Meals?"

The women seem nonplussed—almost casual about the violent recurring affair. "It happens. The place gets robbed. There's a protocol."

"I don't know what to tell you—we've got guns out here, Jack," Dakota says, before steering the conversation to the rules of a game he is having us all play, one where we confess to different embarrassing stories about ourselves and laugh maniacally. In fact, that's how the robberies come up in the first place.

Eventually Dakota's manager joins us, as Henry's stays open later than GnomeTown. Scott gets one of the ladies' phone numbers, with Dakota briefly hyping him up when the two women excuse themselves to go to the restroom. Dakota's manager tells me about his father being on the board of the Johnny Appleseed Festival while he simultaneously tries to extract the phone number of the other girl. She, unsurprisingly, seems more interested in Dakota. So does her friend, if we're being honest. So do we all—if we're being extra honest—which eventually leads to him making clear that he has a girlfriend. He diffuses any awkwardness by turning the attention back onto me.

"Jack, here, of course, is married to Tanya Haden."

When he found the time to look up the name of Jack Black's wife, or if he already knew that very specific piece of trivia, I'll never know. That said, the two blondes aren't interested in me anyway. Some combination of my age and general lack of fitness, my uniform of running shorts and torn Hawaiian shirt, my dirty toes sticking out the front of my slides, and the fact that I've already mentioned how much I've been sleeping outside lately. I don't need to mention I have a girlfriend, too.

"You show Jack your leg?" The manager gestures at Dakota's thigh. It turns out Dakota has recently purchased a tattoo gun—something I wasn't aware you could just do—and likes to "doodle on himself." He pulls up his pant leg and shows me a thigh covered in small black tattoos: the Rolling Stone Tongue eating acid, a ghost, a skull, a UFO, a mountain range, a Band-Aid heart, a gravestone that reads "Bye," and the words "Fuck, Laugh, Die."

I point at a magnifying glass on his upper thigh near his crotch. "You gotta lower expectations before you surpass 'em, ya know?" Dakota says and winks. "But mostly I tattoo tiny reminders of people I meet. Like you. I'd do an apple, but I already have one," he says, pointing to a crudely drawn still life.

"What about a portrait of Jack Black?" I reply.

"Afraid I'm not that good yet. I'll tell you what—" he says, raising his bottle and clinking it against the neck of mine. "I'll do a bottle of hooch, with three *X*s on it for you."

I chuckle while the young women excuse themselves and Scott and the manager offer to walk them out, clearly both hoping to be invited along to wherever they are headed next. Dakota stays with me, ordering one more shot, and closes out the table's tab. The final bill is a small fraction of what we drank, and the waitress smiles flirtatiously at him when she drops it.

"Listen, Jack, I'd invite you to my place to crash for the night, but that girlfriend I mentioned also has a kid—not mine, but I want to do my best, and part of that means not bringing hobos home to sleep on the couch. No matter how much they resemble the guy from *School of Rock*."

I thank him and tell him not to worry about it. I've already set up my camp, which is where I would sleep that night.

But the next day? When I discover there's a home TinCaps game that I can attend, and when I get one of the team's longest-tenured employees to agree to talk with me before the game, I know I'll need a shower. I rent a room at the Bradley Hotel, at Ashley C. Ford's recommendation. It is, in a word, heaven.

". . . But hey, I have a feeling we'll cross paths again, Jack," I remember Dakota's last words to me before downing his final shot. "And I promise to have that tattoo done before we do."

I didn't believe him at the time, but we do cross paths again. And the first thing he does is show me the bottle with three *X*s he has permanently drawn on his thigh.

32

THERE ARE SO many good things to say about Parkview Field. It's big and it's beautiful, and it's right downtown. The tickets are more than affordable, starting at seven dollars, and the food at the field is delicious and plentiful. The crowds are more manageable than at a Major League park. It's an old man's thought (seem to be having a lot of those lately), but sometimes I worry we've let the world get too large, constantly obsessed with making the lines on various charts and graphs go up, up, up. There are maybe 6,500 fixed seats—with more room if you consider standing room, lawn, and luxury boxes—which is the perfect size for a ball field. Yankee Stadium, by contrast, has more than 50,000.

There are plenty of bars and restaurants surrounding the field. I park Rabbit in the lot I've been told to park in—not because I need to drive there, but because I was hoping I could exploit the free parking for a few days, which I do—making me not just a fan of the TinCaps, but also of their lot staff. (One note of warning about Fort Wayne: the city's parking control officers are good at their jobs.)

Michael Limmer, vice president of marketing and promotion for the team—who has been with the TinCaps since 1999, save a brief period between 2006 and 2008 when he was in graduate school for sports marketing—is a tall man with a big wide smile. When I reach out to him, he generously offers to show me around the park. He is one of the organization's longest-tenured employees, and unsurprisingly, the first thing he wants to show me is a tree.

"It's an apple tree, of course. They told us it would only get *yea* high," Limmer sticks his hand out at the level of his head, "but . . ." He gestures at the tree, which reaches far above his head, its branches bearing fruit but also obscuring the sign above the park gate.

"We'd cut it down and plant a smaller one, but I think it's grafted from some original Johnny Appleseed tree, so we can't."

I tell Limmer that I was at that very tree a few days before. The gate swings open and we go inside the park.

"We're the TinCaps, right? So Johnny Appleseed is the theme. We called the merch store the Orchard."

"Like the old Apple Orchard in the Glenbrook Mall."

"So you know the area?"

"No, just have a friend who grew up here."

"We have the J. Chapman's Suite Level Loft, which is right on the first-base line. It's sponsored by the University of Saint Francis."

"A very Chapmanesque saint."

"Our group area is called the Treetops. You get the idea. The theme gave us a lot to play around with. We really embrace the apple. We made sure it was prominent in our logo. When we started doing outreach to the Latino community here in Fort Wayne, we started the Manzanas Luchadoras, the Fighting Apples."

At the Orchard merch area, I marvel at the sheer amount of items emblazoned with the TinCaps' logo. In one of the corners of the room is a bunch of blue-and-gray T-shirts emblazoned with a wizard. Gandalf he isn't, though. More the type of wizard you'd find airbrushed on the side of a van with no windows that you wouldn't want to see near a playground.

"That's Wayne."

"Wayne?"

"Wayne the Wizard. The old mascot."

"So wait, you weren't always the TinCaps?"

"Oh, absolutely not. We were the Fort Wayne Wizards, the name that was picked when the team moved here in 1993—we didn't become the TinCaps until 2008. This team has a lot of history. We became a Padres farm team in 1999; before that we were a Minnesota Twins farm team."

"I mean, that makes a bit more sense than San Diego."

"Before the team was the Wizards, it was in Kenosha, Wisconsin, and before that the team was in Wisconsin Rapids, Wisconsin. Before Wisconsin, the team was in Keokuk, Iowa, and before that it was in Mattoon, Illinois. But that goes back to the '50s, the late '40s, even. The start of the Midwest League, which used to be the Illinois State League."

"But the team's been here for over thirty years, and it's been the TinCaps for—"

"We've been the TinCaps for over fifteen years now."

"So you changed the name when Parkview Field was built?"

"That's right. The field opened on April 16, 2009. The place sold out, and we beat the Dayton Dragons—the team we're playing tonight, actually. The TinCaps won the Midwest League championship in 2009."

"Have you won a championship since?"

"No. But the park really helped revitalize downtown Fort Wayne."

"Everybody keeps telling me how much downtown has changed."

"That's because it has. Previously, back in the 1990s and early 2000s, you had twenty thousand people coming downtown to work—but then, at five o'clock on the dot, everybody left. Same thing on the weekends. A few people would be hanging out, but there wasn't really anything to do. We were looking around and we saw Des Moines, Chattanooga, Greenville, South Carolina—all these markets that had revitalized their downtowns. So we asked 'em, 'How'd you do it?' And they said, 'We put a ballpark there. Sixty to eighty nights a year now, there's something happening downtown, something happening during nonwork hours.' "

"Makes sense."

"Our games are obviously weeknights and weekends—but it brings people in. Now more people are coming downtown for entertainment. You can see the park, you can see the lights at night. More and more businesses started popping up around the park. Then *they* started having entertainment, bands and such. So it really kicked off this area for commerce—an area where there wasn't a whole lot going on outside of work offices at the time. Now you can come downtown and catch a ball game, or see a show, or go out to eat—you have a footprint and usually there's at least five things or more to choose from on any given night."

I look up at the towering scoreboard, its shadow cutting across the field in the afternoon sun.

"So how'd you land on the TinCaps?"

"A lot has happened here in Fort Wayne, so there was a lot for us to choose from when thinking about a new team name and mascot. There was General Anthony Wayne, who the fort was named after. So we could've gone the military route. Fort, military, and generals. That sort of thing. Do you know who Philo Farnsworth is?"

"No."

"Well, he's one of the people credited with inventing television. He was an inventor, and developed a television system complete with receiver and camera. I'm unclear on the specifics, but he produced them commercially here for fifteen or so years, so there was the Farnsworth Television and Radio Corporation here in Fort Wayne, so we thought about something to do with television or invention, or electricity. You know what else was invented here?"

Not gonna lie, I was not expecting this many inventors hailing from Indiana's second largest city.

"The first gas pump was invented in Fort Wayne by Sylvanus Bowser. So that was another idea. Something to do with gas, or fire."

Okay, that could have been potentially badass, I think.

"We had a bunch of 'em. The first video game console, the Magnavox Odyssey, was invented in Fort Wayne, in 1969. There was a plastic rifle, and it was originally called Skill-O-Vision. The Odyssey came out in 1972, first gaming console ever commercially sold."

"So some kind of video game mascot?"

"Like I said, we were thinking of everything. Eventually we came down to four or five finalists, internally. I remember doing a URL search for all five, and 'tincaps.com' was the only one that was open—you didn't have to add 'Fort Wayne' or 'Baseball,' or anything like that."

"So you wouldn't have somebody fleecing you, trying to sell you the URL for twenty thousand dollars or something."

"Exactly. But also, at the time, I was thinking, 'If a seven-letter URL is available, we should probably grab that.' I was young, thinking about how my email at the time was '@fortwaynewizards.com' or '@fortwaynebaseball.com' or something like that. I liked '@tincaps.com.' That felt short and easy. Same for the gas pump mascot, actually—it was 'Octane.' That'd be good. '@octane.com.' "

"But the URL wasn't available."

"That, yes. But also, the Octane logo—it was hard to get something that didn't look like it belonged to an arena football team, or an XFL team, you know? Because it was all chrome and flames. Not to mention—and this gives you a good idea of what goes into choosing a new team name and mascot—it was 2008."

"The recession."

"Bingo. Gas prices kept shooting up. Five bucks a gallon and higher. So you gotta ask, 'Do we want to be associated with gas prices?' "

" 'I can't afford tickets to a game to see the High Price Gasolines—I gotta fill my tank.' "

"Now you're getting it. Like I said, there were others. There was a General Electric plant here that used to provide a lot of jobs, so we were thinking Boltman, or something around electricity—a proton, maybe. I mean, even with Johnny Appleseed we had to get creative."

"How so?"

"Well, the obvious choice would be something to do with apples, right?"

Makes sense, but Limmer doesn't even give me a chance to respond.

"But we had to stay away from anything to do with apples."

"Why's that?"

"A little company out in Cupertino, California."

"Oh wow, I hadn't even thought—Apple. Apple computers."

"You don't want to create a whole new name, image—everything that goes into launching a new name and mascot—only to get sued by one of the most powerful companies on the face of the planet. So we went with the TinCaps. I think we also considered the Crab Apples. Those might've been them: Octane, Crab Apples, TinCaps, and the Generals. And the TinCaps won out."

I figure people must have loved it right away, but Michael corrects the record.

"Oh, absolutely not. People hate change. We got so many messages and emails. The local news channel ran a poll online and nearly 90 percent of the responses—something like over a thousand people—were all negative. We got called idiots, all sorts of things. But it wasn't just that."

"What else?"

"You'll figure this out soon enough. There's a lot of people in this world that care about John Chapman, that care about Johnny Appleseed. And I get it—we care about him, too. We built a whole team around the man's memory. But, well, a lot of historians—or people who like to think of themselves as historians—got mad at the whole 'TinCaps' of it all."

"Because a lot of people don't think he actually wore a pot on his head."

"That's right. So, look, it's funny to talk about it now, but at the time we had put so much effort and money into this. But not only is the local population rebelling at the change, but all of a sudden we're getting phone calls and messages from all across the country. All of these—"

"Chapman fans?"

"Yeah, all of these Johnny Appleseed fans who are telling us why the name isn't historically accurate, and the apple isn't the kind of apples he actually planted."

At this point, I'm in stitches at the absurdity of it all, and Limmer smiles, too.

"Like I said, funny now. But we were sweating. The local evening news would have these armchair historians call in and just tell us how wrong we were about it all."

"In the meantime, you're just trying to relaunch a franchise to go with the new park y'all just poured a boatload of money into downtown to bring some family-friendly entertainment to the area."

"Wish you'd been around, maybe we could have gotten you on the news defending us. But we waited out the storm. The park opened up and people loved it. Then we started winning. Pretty soon, this logo and name that everybody hated became the top-selling logo in Minor League Baseball that year, plus we had over a hundred wins that season. So that probably helped."

I can see how proud Limmer is. "Nice work."

"It was a group effort. A lot of work went into all of it from so many different people."

"Still, it always feels good to be proven right."

Limmer pauses, before allowing himself: "Yes. Yes it does."

Our walk around the stadium is almost over, and realizing how long we'd been talking leaves me to contemplate something else—how much Michael Limmer has to tell me about TinCaps lore.

But he isn't done.

"I remember going to the Johnny Appleseed Festival before we announced the name—and there's a John Chapman reenactor there, on the stage, and he's talking about all the stories that people get wrong about Appleseed, and one of the things he says is, 'You know what's a myth? That I wore a cooking pot on my head.' And my wife and I are elbowing each other. The reenactor is talking about how handles on cooking pots weren't actually invented until eighteen-whatever."

"That's right."

"But my wife and I are saying to each other, 'People know to have fun with it. Nobody's gonna get upset at a cartoon apple wearing a tin pot with a handle on its head.' Whew boy, were we wrong. We announced the name—and this was way before social media had really caught on. So only the name's out there. There are no videos or images circulating around. Everyone's just talking about it, word of mouth, but nobody's seeing the logo or everything else we came up with around the team name. They're just hearing 'TinCaps.' Only fifteen years or so ago, we didn't have the tools we have now to communicate directly with our fans. And the beauty of a small baseball team is that it's personal—it's local."

"Right."

"It's my favorite thing about this whole team—the people. The community. But it also means those people have your phone number."

I laugh and Limmer continues.

"But it all led to one of my favorite moments. We had a meeting with a bunch of the downtown businesses—they get together once a month, and they invited us to the meeting. We were anxious, the name had already been so poorly received by the general public, and the press was having a field day with it. So we present the logo directly to the board, but here's the thing: they were already in. I remember they had an apple with a face drawn on it, and had taken a tuna can and made a little tin-cap hat out of it, placing it on top of the apple. They had apple candy in the center of their boardroom table. We sat down, and they all told us, 'Don't listen to what everybody's saying. We love this idea. TinCaps is perfect. The theme of apples and Johnny Appleseed is perfect. You're killing it. Weather the storm.'"

"Which is what you did."

"Which is what we did. And they were right. That year, we were the number-one-selling farm league team in terms of merchandise sales. Ever since, we've historically been in the top twenty-five more years than not."

"That's incredible."

"Once people saw the new park, and saw the vision for how it was going to help revitalize downtown, they embraced us."

"You proved the haters wrong."

"I appreciate you saying that, but it's not right. We weren't focused on proving people wrong. We wanted to prove to the people who were rooting for us that they were right. We wanted it for Fort Wayne. In those years everyone was saying, 'Nobody ever goes downtown. It's a ghost town, no bringing it back. The team's gonna leave town.' Then we started selling out the ballpark. Then more businesses in the area started opening up. After that, people said it wouldn't last. 'Let's see if they can sustain it once the newness—the novelty—has worn off.' Yet here we are, over a decade later. Still in Fort Wayne."

Michael is passionate about ticket prices staying within a threshold that makes sense for his community, making sure that it's always a place where people from different pockets of the city can find one another.

"I love it when I hear stories about, say, two old buddies who haven't seen each other since high school running into each other at the park. Or kids making friends with other kids who don't go to their school. A place where everyone in Fort Wayne feels welcome, and you can really see the entire city on display."

I think about how the world shut down, only a few years ago, and ask about how that affected operations.

"I mean, same as everywhere. We had to shut down. A buddy texted me during the last home game, though: 'I haven't been to a game since COVID. I forgot how much fun they were.' That really made my day to hear that."

I ask him how many people come to the games now.

"On good years—and there've been more good years than not—we get over 400,000 people over the course of a season. Sometimes it's 375,000 or 380,000. Our first year back from COVID, in 2021, we got over 200,000, which was tough at the time, but looking back I can see that's still pretty good. We're crawling back. As long as we keep giving people a reason to come out, they keep coming back. But COVID was a trip. Every once in a while I'll stumble upon something that was a COVID artifact and I'll just think, it still feels surreal that that happened."

If you build it, they will come. I think of Patti and her *Field of Dreams* pal. In 2024, the team averaged 5,590 guests a game, up from 5,313 in 2023. It was the team's best overall season since 2018. The 2024 average ranked third among the sixty A-ball teams. And Michael says he's here to stay.

"I'm really proud of being here. I'm really proud of the TinCaps. When I worked at the Wizards, I remember thinking, 'Oh, this is a stepping stone to something else.'"

"Right."

"I remember going to Toledo, and to Indianapolis, and walking into their ballparks and saying, 'I aspire to someday work in a ballpark like this.' But now, look at this . . ."

Limmer takes his large, sturdy hand and gestures out at the park. The field crew is getting the grass ready for tonight's game. There are people loading kegs in, and other staffers going in and out of offices.

"I still go to those ballparks, and they're fine. They're nice, and there are plenty of great people who operate those teams. But me? I'm good. I'm where I'm supposed to be, in a facility that, you know, that has its shortcomings—but I just love when the gates open up and everybody comes in. I love seeing them find their seats and get their food. Or if people have issues, I love helping solve those issues. I love getting someone to stay off their phone for twenty minutes. Engage with the real world. Be a part of the community they're in."

Michael Limmer manages to walk me back to the same gate where we entered with perfect timing. He has to start preparing for this evening's game, so he gives me a few names of some nearby restaurants where I can kill a few hours, shakes my hand firmly, and shows me out, right past the same apple tree we walked in under. As I head away from the park, I notice a car full of what looks like people in Yoda costumes driving by.

33

WHEN I RETURN to the park, the sun is setting and the sky is a kaleidoscope of neon pinks. Limmer told me it was *Star Wars* Night—"one of our biggest nights of the whole season." I'm not sure what I thought that would mean, but I'm definitely not prepared for the number of fully costumed people there are in the stands.

Representatives of the 501st Legion are here—the Northern Darkness Garrison of Northern Indiana. They even have a booth, recruiting new members for their worldwide charitable organization, doing good deeds in local communities while dressed up like Stormtroopers and other *Star Wars* characters. Which at the game means posing with throngs of sugar-fueled children grabbing at their intricate—and one would assume expensive—costumes with sticky hands. But no one in the Northern Darkness Garrison seems to mind.

There are all manner of Stormtroopers—Scout Troopers and Death Troopers and Imperial Shocktroopers—some with giant, futuristic-looking guns, alongside Mandalorians, Wookies, rebel X-Wing pilots, a couple of Kylo Rens, and one Count Dooku (or maybe it was Obi Wan Kenobi). There is even an R2 unit, though I can't figure out if there is somebody in that one or if it is simply a remote-controlled model.

The best costume of the night, though, has to go to the Darth Vader who is *also* in a throwback Wizard costume—a blue, star-covered cloak over his black one, and a pointy blue magician's hat on the top of his fearsome helmet, out the back of which—sparing no detail—locks of long gray wizard hair spill out, and in the front a long gray beard.

Overall the stadium has the vibe of a Civil War reenactment but, you know, a galactic civil war that took place long ago in a galaxy far, far away.

Aside from *Star Wars*—or perhaps alongside is a better way to put it—the stadium is packed with children. So many families, sets of fathers and sons, that it reminds me of all the times my da brought me to Fenway when we lived in Boston when I was a child. Buying tickets in the standing rows, the cheapest you could get. This was the 1980s, and the last time the Red Sox had won the World Series was 1918, their next World Series win still over a decade away. My father would always sneak us into better seats, then tell security a story about how it was my first game. My father winking at me—even then, at that young age, I remember thinking the security guard probably caught the wink, too. But who wants to take magic from a child?

I didn't give it much thought back then but those mischievous trips to Fenway clearly influenced my love of the sport—or not the sport, per se, but simply hanging out in baseball stadiums. I wasn't an athletic child, and discovering drinking and drugs at a very young age didn't help. Football, basketball, hockey, soccer—I couldn't be bothered. Even with baseball, I couldn't tell you the names of the pitchers, or who was covering first base. But the chance to visit a stadium? Divine.

In my late teens and early twenties, when I was living in Washington, DC, the Washington Nationals were setting up shop in the capital. They didn't even have their own park yet, so they'd play at RFK Stadium in those early years, where the Commanders played before moving to FedEx Field—now Northwest Stadium—though at the time the Commanders went by a different name. The Nationals' front office was so desperate to fill the stadium with bodies that they practically gave tickets away for free those first few years, and security let my friends and me bring in whole beer coolers filled with cold bottles and large sandwiches, having a full-on picnic in the stands.

When I lived in San Francisco, I would spend my summer Wednesdays going across the bay to the Oakland Coliseum, sitting in the sun and watching the A's play while taking advantage of the dollar hot dog and dollar beer deals the team relied on to sell tickets on a weekday. Or I'd head to the more expensive AT&T Park (now Oracle Park) to catch a Giants game, if I was feeling flush. The worst seats in the house, farthest from the field, were still some of the best views of the bay in the whole damn city. Sometimes D. A. Powell—Doug to his friends, a poet who holds season tickets every year—would take me for a game, his seats close to the field and right by a food stand where they served Ghirardelli-chocolate-smothered ice cream sundaes. I still try to catch a game with Doug every time I'm back in San Francisco during baseball season.

All the glorious ballparks I've been to in America are thrumming with the infectious community spirit that so clearly animates Michael's purpose in life. I watch his parish of Parkview Field fill up with people—not to mention Jedis, Siths, and, yes, a surprising number of Yodas—and it feels just perfect.

"You're cheering for the wrong team."

I had found a seat right behind home plate, but not so close that I couldn't see the rest of the field, and had been rooting for the TinCaps—or so I thought—vigorously and loudly for about an inning. I took my time getting to my section, basking in all the *Star Wars* festivities and watching the TinCaps mascot, Johnny TinCap, don a brown Jedi cloak and have a lightsaber fight with one of the costumed guests.

Star Wars and baseball both make me think about my da. And not simply because of the whole "Luke, I am your father" bit, though of course that's part of it. I'll often watch my neighbor on the North Fork and his son play *Star Wars* in their backyard, pretending to be characters that I don't even know anymore, given how much the cinematic universe has expanded.

How can you not grow nostalgic for your father while contemplating a series that hinges on mourning your father, wanting to get to know your father better after you lionize him, realizing your father made some mistakes (to be fair, big, galactic, genocidal mistakes), then fighting your father and hating him, only to recognize each other's flaws and accept said flaws so that you can save each other in the end—but not before you both team up to throw *his* father figure down the reactor shaft of the second Death Star?

Here at Parkview Field, it really does feel like I'm sitting in a church dedicated to my da, the man who used to tell me stories as I walked with him in the woods so that I would better keep up with him. Smuggle me to better seats at Fenway. The man who diligently recorded all three original *Star Wars* movies off of a television set that his friend owned, because we didn't yet own one—complete with half commercials and late start times, which somehow added to the feeling of fatherly love once he *did* procure an old TV and VCR a year later, so that I could finally watch them. The man who used the space saga to explain the difference between good and evil to me, using "the force" as a metaphor for faith and the Holy Spirit and God's love. When my siblings and I would play, my half brother would be Luke and my half sister would be Princess Leia, leaving me to play Han Solo, the character who, come to think of it, is sort of a John Steinbeck of space: *Charlie and Me*ing his way through the galaxy with his dog—I mean copilot—Chewbacca.

Hell, the man who first brought me to church, which has led to a lifetime of comparing anywhere people gather—bars, music venues, or yes, baseball stadiums—to churches.

That said, in church nobody tends to say, "You're cheering for the wrong team." I mean, not unless you've royally screwed up.

"What's that?" I finally reply, coming out of my nostalgic haze.

"You're rooting for the TinCaps, right?"

The woman is older and doesn't seem upset but isn't smiling, either. She gestures at my hat, which was indeed a TinCaps, well, cap.

"Yeah?"

"Well, you keep cheering for the other team."

I had been rooting for the team in green, assuming that the fiery red jerseys on the other team belonged to the visitors, the Dayton Dragons. On closer inspection, though, those red jerseys weren't fire, but special *Star Wars* Day–themed shirts that had characters emblazoned along the bottom, which I had mistaken for flames.

"Sorry. First game," I say.

"First game here at Parkview, or first game of baseball ever?" With that the woman gives a quick bark-like laugh and breaks out into a rather shit-eating grin. I smile back and begin cheering for the right team.

The pink skies give way to a rich, midnight blue, which eventually blacken to pure night. The game ends and the brilliant stadium lights pop off, their glow lingering against the dark for a few seconds. The TinCaps have eked out a win, 9 to 8. It's been a rewarding year, with a record number of sixty-two former Fort Wayne players making it to MLB, and the team locking their first overall winning season since 2015, along with their first playoff appearance since 2017.

Fireworks explode in the sky as the cosplayers hold up their lightsabers in a neon salute. As I exit the stadium, they invite all the children to clamber onto the field and run the bases in a surprisingly orderly single-file line. The fireworks soon stop and the field lights snap back on with a thick, metallic *thunk*.

I put my foot up on a rail in the standing section and watch the children as they run the bases, dreams of baseball stardom mixed with intergalactic civil war playing in their heads. I stroll out of the park, the fireworks show still shining in my memory. I pull out the little yellow box Matt Sumell had given me—sunshine in my pocket—and eat a couple of the gummy mushrooms, not wanting the light show to end. Holding on to summer.

34

BUT THE NEXT morning, waking up again in my tent, the euphoria of the night long since washed away, I regret my revelry. The sun seems to bleach out my eyes as I pack up my camp. On my way out of town I stop by the Glenbrook Mall, now named Glenbrook Square. It's surprisingly busy—the monument to capitalism and commerce bustling—an apple-themed play area in the center of the mall, some of the last remnants of the Orchard that Ashley had told me about, is filled with laughing, *loudly* laughing children. I wince and do my best to move quickly by.

While searching for the H&M that houses the mysterious wooden Johnny Appleseed, I stop by an Orange Julius. It's been so long since I've been in a mall, I'd forgotten Orange Juliuses even existed. A wave of nostalgia hits me as I suck the cold, sugary, orange and vanilla concoction into my mouth. I've been on the road for two seasons now, often eating trash gas station food, but just as often sampling the local delicacy—the thing you *have* to try while you're in town. Sometimes, though, you simply want the familiar. The *easy*. A fast-food chain that lets you know, however far from home you are, you can still get something that tastes exactly the way you expect it to taste. The Orange Julius scratches that itch, but not entirely. I make a note in my comedown brain to see if I can find a Popeyes in the mall before I leave.

But first, I have to find John Chapman, which I do. The H&M is in a corner of the mall. I walk inside and a young employee greets me.

I probably look like a new set of clothes wouldn't be such a bad idea, but instead I ask for something else.

"I'm sorry, I'm looking for Johnny Appleseed?"

The employee just points, and I head to the room next door.

The statue is, in a word, gigantic. Surprisingly tall. Cut from the trunk of a tree, clearly, it has a large base and stretches upward until it almost touches the store's high ceiling. Chapman is old and has a beard, though not a giant beard, as he is usually portrayed. At his side, a deer that he is petting, with a carving of a raccoon nuzzling his bare feet. He wears a bucket on his head, no pan or tin cap, and a bag for his seeds is slung across his shoulders. He looks worn down, weary and ragged: a slight smile on his face, but his eyes are almost closed to the world. I can relate.

The more-than-ten-foot statue was made by sculptor Dean Butler in the 1970s, and has been at the mall ever since. Even when the Orchard was disassembled, local history enthusiasts petitioned the mall to keep the sculpture on display. Which is how it came to be standing in the middle of an H&M, surrounded by T-shirts, checkered socks, and a rack of discounted cargo pants.

A nearby plaque reads:

> Johnny Appleseed, real name John Chapman, was born in Massachusetts in 1774. For well over 40 years he traveled throughout the Midwest planting apple orchards. Some of these trees are said to still bear fruit today. As settlers moved westward, Johnny gave away and sold many trees so they could establish orchards of their own. Although he was a very skilled nurseryman and owned thousands of acres of apple orchards, he lived a very simple life. His ragged dress, eccentric ways and religious faith attracted attention and he became a familiar figure to settlers. Many legends were told of him after he died, one being that as Johnny traveled he wore his cooking pot on his head as a hat. His respect for all creatures and his role as a peacemaker between the Indians

and settlers are also widely known. Johnny died in 1845 near Fort Wayne, Indiana.

Chapman looks so out of place here, tucked away in a corner of this mall, right by a Sears. But then I remember my hunger for Popeyes and the deep comfort of an Orange Julius. Wasn't Chapman's modern likeness the same balmy, commodified emblem that we go to American malls for? The complexities of an orange's true flavor flattened into something sweet and simple that you can suck out of a straw while going about your day. A blast of syrupy chemicals that tastes good, so long as you don't look too closely at how it was made.

Still, a towering wood carving of a religious wanderer that looks strikingly similar to Bigfoot feels undeniably out of place in an H&M next to a display of cheap earrings, and I'm beginning to feel out of place here, too. As I suck up the last of my Orange Julius, I ask the statue a question out loud:

"What are we doing here?"

I have a loving partner, a warm bed, and a place to live back east. What am *I* doing here, spending my summer sleeping outside, talking to old wooden monuments erected to a man none of us will ever know? I toss my cup away and go looking for some comforting fried chicken. The mall doesn't have a Popeyes, it turns out, but I will find some on my drive back to the East Coast, slamming the pedal into the floor on my way to see my girlfriend and catch the last few days of summer near the ocean.

Still, I know I'll be back in Fort Wayne very soon . . .

· FALL ·

35

JACK BLACK!"

I'm back in town for the Johnny Appleseed Festival. I've spent the day walking all over Fort Wayne—visiting the Fort Wayne Art Museum, the Old Fort with its large wooden blockhouses, Lawton Park, Bloomingdale Park, Promenade Park, and a few different sections of the Bicentennial Heritage Trail. Fall has come to Indiana, and I've followed the changing leaves back west. What only a month ago was a city of warm sun and solidly green trees is now beginning to grow a little more auburn, a little more cozy. After bopping around the city taking pictures of historic buildings and plaques, I of course had to find Dakota, hoping he'd still be behind the bar at Gnome-Town. Which is exactly where I find him.

"Look at this!" Dakota's tattoos have crept down his thigh and are now covering his calf, too. In the center—surrounded by a knife, a television set, a taco, an open book, a forty-pound hand weight, a badly drawn hot air balloon, and what can only be described as a bicycle gone awry—is a bottle of hooch with three large *X*s on it. Not many people have gotten a tattoo in my honor, and the few that have most likely now regret it. But I am nevertheless touched.

"I also invented an apple cocktail for you—I mean, for the festival, is what I told my manager, but—wait right here."

Dakota runs out to his car—a souped-up Subaru, but not like the cars I saw during my first visit to Fort Wayne. This one is covered in mud, with large tires and a giant rack on its roof holding a big shovel, a spade, and other tools for outdoor survival clamped to the side for all to see. When I ask him about this, he simply tells me that he likes to spend time outdoors.

"Like you do. Camping, time alone to myself. I hiked the Appalachian Trail for two months when I got out of the military."

He returns triumphantly to the bar with a handheld blowtorch and sets about making a citrus apple cocktail that is, simply put, to die for—but not before his manager reprimands him for bringing a mini-flamethrower onto the premises.

"I can make it without the burnt orange, but I'd rather figure out how to get Dylan here to talk to the fire department about letting me use this bad boy every day."

A tiny mystery solved. The manager's name is Dylan.

The bar is slower this time, and I sit there while Dylan does paperwork and Dakota trains a new bartender. The rookie keeps lying about what he knows how to do, but Dakota is patiently, gently calling the young man out without embarrassing him. During Dakota's time in the military, I can imagine his competency at leading his fellow soldiers.

"I hear you're a traveler." One of the waitresses, Stacy—who only has a three-top going in her section—comes over to me. I've never been called a traveler before, but I don't mind it. I've spent most of the year on the road. It's what I am. She wants to share something with me.

Stacy shows me a wooden necklace her boyfriend made for her.

"We travel every chance we get—and every time we go to a new state, he paints a new piece for me. Sometimes it's the state flag, or state bird, or state flower, and then he adds the piece to the necklace."

"Jack's no traveler," Dakota cuts in, although he is clearly the reason Stacy knows anything about me in the first place. "He's doing research for his next role."

"Oh yeah?" I humor him. "And what role is that?"

"Easy. You're going to play me." He smiles. "Should we get after it?"

I am enjoying the slow pace of the bar, growing nostalgic for a time when I worked at Zeitgeist, a watering hole in San Francisco. Open 9 a.m. to 2 a.m. every day of the year save one random Monday in January when we'd clean the place. Shooting the shit between rushes, my cranky coworker named Happy Todd teaching me how to measure out cocktails so they fit into the giant pint glasses we served them in, much as Dakota has been doing with his trainee.

But when Dakota says go, you go. As we run out into the night, I wonder whether Dylan has any say in when Dakota comes in or leaves his job at all.

We head straight back to Henry's. Dakota swears I have to try the hamburger and can't believe I didn't order one last time. The giant greasy thing is served on an onion roll, smothered in cheese. After my day walking all over the city I'm famished and ready to declare it the best burger I've had in years. We eat and drink and talk, and he tells me about his time on the Appalachian Trail, and where he likes to camp now when he gets a few days off work, then talks about his girlfriend and her baby, along with his distrust of Indiana Amish.

"Indiana Amish?"

"Pennsylvania Amish are alright, but I grew up around Indiana Amish. A lot of 'em—at least where I grew up—claim not to use modern technology, but will have a building at the end of their driveway—it looks like an outhouse—and in that building is a phone. It's a workaround. No technology in your house, but a little hut for modern conveniences down the lane. Can't stand it."

I think of all the religious workarounds I know about, and decide I am more lenient on the matter.

"I think what you really hate is hypocrisy," I tell him. Dakota sips his beer.

"Well, you ain't wrong about that."

The night goes on. We go from bar to bar. Dakota continues to drink a lot but it doesn't show. His posture is always straight. His eyes focused. His pronunciation clean.

But he begins to open up more, and his stories become more personal. It reminds me of my friend Conner growing up—his father dead and mine growing cold and distant. We used to call these types of conversations heart-to-hearts. We would walk at night, me smoking cigarettes that I'd stolen from his mom's pack or casually passing a joint between us. Two lonely teenage boys not knowing what to make of the world, but at least trying to compare notes.

Even after we grew older we would continue to have these heart-to-hearts, continue to find loving common ground with each other despite our vastly different adult lives. Conner back from a tour in Iraq or Afghanistan visiting me in San Francisco. Drinking enough beers until he was ready to talk about what he wanted, or needed, to talk about. Me listening as he described what it was like, after a firefight, to scoop a friend's brain up and put it into the plastic bags lining his pockets—just so he could make sure more of his friend got home.

Dakota and I get into a heart-to-heart of our own. I talk about my difficult childhood and mental instability. The choices in my life—or the things I didn't choose at all—that have led me to being a person approaching forty who spends his time sleeping outdoors while chasing an American myth.

He tells me about choices that he made while still on active duty—those he regrets and those he doesn't. How he's now trying to be a role model for his girlfriend's kid. He spent most of his childhood in Indiana, and then in and around Fort Wayne. After that, he moved around a bit. Restless. Georgia. Florida. He has always enjoyed inventing cocktails, and likes the reliability of work that comes with being a bartender. He joined the military in 2014, and got out in 2020—which is when he hiked a big hunk of the Appalachian Trail.

Six years of service and then a long, lonely walk.

After that he tried to live in the Northwest for a bit. Two months. He doesn't like big crowds, which is why he passes when I invite him to come to the Johnny Appleseed Festival with me the next day. Eventually he returned to Fort Wayne. He loves the wilderness—when I ask him about the shovels and other tools strapped to his car he tells me, "You should see what's on the inside. Axes. Hatchets. Anything you need to survive in the woods or the mountains."

We talk about tattoos, and how they are sometimes a way of dealing with trauma. Of taking control of your own body—or something even bigger than that—when you yourself feel a little out of control.

I ask about his memorial bracelet—the one I noticed when we first met.

"We always swore we weren't gonna wear these."

He begins to fidget with it, almost absentmindedly. I feel that he's maybe deciding whether he wants to keep going down this road or simply distracting me by moving us along to the next bar, but he stays in his seat.

"There were sixteen guys in my unit. Twelve of them didn't make it back. But we didn't go for that 'Hoorah,' 'Thank you for your service' bullshit."

"Most of my friends in the military don't either."

"So that's four of us out, right?"

"Sure."

"Well, now there's only two of us."

I've spoken enough with Conner about this particular thing to know exactly what he means.

"Suicide," I say. It's a statement. Not a question.

Dakota goes on, explaining that he doesn't believe in medals, claiming to have given all of his to his dead comrades' families.

"If I wore one of these bracelets for every friend of mine who died in combat, I'd have a whole slew of 'em going up my entire arm. But this one, he's the first real friend I lost to suicide."

He talks about not wanting to live past thirty, even though it's already starting to get closer than he's comfortable with. He talks about the issues he has with his body—how hard he used it, for so long, at such a young age. He tells me of an IED that flipped the Humvee he was in, something he blames himself for. He was in command. Wasn't able to push down on the M2 machine gun's butterfly triggers, and it cost them. Since the explosion his back has never been the same.

Then Dakota tells me worse stories. A mission with his friend who committed suicide. Witnessing the brutalization of children at the hands of a warlord, who their American commanders didn't want killed. Dakota and his friend were ordered to hold off, but together made a decision instead to say fuck it.

"We got discharged with honors eventually—only because some guys higher up on the command chain fought to make sure we weren't simply kicked out."

"Do you have any regrets?"

"Regrets? Yeah, I have loads of 'em. But on that particular mission?"

"Yeah."

"It's the thing I regret the most in my life. Why did I wait to act until the third kid? Why the fuck didn't I act for the first two?"

The bar has gone quiet, and the silence around us somehow grows bigger.

"That was my friend's issue, too. The thing he couldn't get over. And that's my second biggest regret."

"What's that?"

"I was working. When he called, I was working. I didn't see my phone. I didn't pick up. We always said we would, but I didn't see the call. But when I saw his number on my phone, after my shift, I already knew what had happened."

"Jesus."

"That's the voicemail he left me—he didn't leave a suicide note for his wife or his kids. But he called me, and that was the gist of it. Couldn't get the images out of his head. Asking himself the same question, 'Why'd we wait until the third kid to act? Why didn't we disobey orders sooner?' "

Dakota goes on, explaining that he's got no cartilage in his knees on top of his back being shot—but that maybe his girlfriend, and the kid, are worth making it past thirty for. I try to remind him of the other things in life that are, too.

"I like talking to you, Jack. Maybe it's because I know you're leaving, but I do hope we see each other again."

The night has grown late, and the early fall air is crisp. We've left the bar and are back where we started, sitting on some benches in front of GnomeTown, which is now closed. But Dakota uses his key and gets us two more beers anyway. We talk more, about the hard things in life, and the lighter things, too.

"I'll pay you back for the beer next time I'm in town," I say.

"I'll take you up on it, only because that means you'll be back in town again."

"You sure you don't want to come to the festival with me tomorrow?" I ask.

"Like I said, Jack, I don't do crowds."

He tosses our now-empty beer bottles in the trash and saunters off into the night.

I haven't seen Dakota since. But I hope to. Someday soon.

36

WHY DID JOHN CHAPMAN push through Ohio and on into Indiana? The man often tried to stay one step ahead of the American settlers' westward expansion. He was in his sixties when he ventured out toward Fort Wayne. There's a joke to be made here about trying to recapture one's glory days. About how—in his lifetime—Ohio had become less wild, and Chapman needed to get to areas that were still a bit unruly. He still lived outside, and walked in all sorts of weather, which may be how he came to find himself at death's door—reciting the Beatitudes from the Bible, "glowing with serenity," as the Worth family put it.

Chapman died on the floor of the Worth family cabin outside of Fort Wayne. The Worths being God-fearing acquaintances who would let him stay with them when he came around, but not necessarily close friends—he spent a total of five weeks with them in his five years in Indiana. Nobody is quite sure of the specific date on which Chapman died, but it was sometime between March 11 and 18, 1845. The Worths reported that Chapman was happy, cheerful, and excited to finally be crossing over after a lifetime of faith.

He lived to old age, especially for the era—his seventies—before an unspecified winter disease took him. Chapman had walked fifteen miles earlier that day.

On the morning of the Johnny Appleseed Festival I wake up a bit groggy from my late night with Dakota. Not wanting to leave my camp exposed during the day, I pack up all my gear and stuff it into

Rabbit—the interior of which is starting to look like a trashed campsite itself.

I walk toward the fairgrounds, which in a—touching? morbid?—display of historical deference are located right by John Chapman's grave. As with all things Chapman, it's more accurate to say his *supposed* grave, as some people believe he's buried elsewhere.

I don't know what to expect from the day. The festival is advertised as the largest Johnny Appleseed Festival in the country, but how big is *that*? Come to think of it, how small is the smallest Johnny Appleseed Festival in the country? I did a little research and came up with a rough estimate of around fifteen or so Appleseed-themed fairs that take place throughout the country every year—stretching from my own home stomping grounds in Leominster, Massachusetts, all the way across the country to Paradise, California, where they've been celebrating Johnny Appleseed days annually since 1888—only seventeen years after the infamous *Harper's* article memorializing and popularizing him.

Mentally, I begin to prepare for an experience like that of fairs I visited in my youth: the loud, colored posters advertising fun and excitement weeks in advance, then the crestfallen feeling when the actual show came to town. Sad animals, if any animals at all, along with rigged games run by less-than-charming con men and loose, ragged tents that smelled of mildew. The only highlight being some overpriced fried dough under a Scarface pile of powdered sugar and a sticky-fingered, awkward makeout session with some person bored enough to say, "Sure, why not?" when you asked them to sit with you behind the industrial-sized popcorn maker.

But as I walk through Headwaters Park—one of those beautiful revitalizations popping up alongside long-neglected riverfront lots throughout the Midwest, with bench swings and food trucks coupled with a lax approach to open containers, as long as the person holding them is a dad or mom guiding a stroller along the walkway—I notice that the street is already backed up with traffic.

Crossing the Martin Luther King Jr. Bridge—decorated with quotes from the man himself—the traffic persists. I notice out-of-state plates mixed in with the long line of pleasant blue-sky-and-tree-illustrated Indiana ones. Michigan, Illinois, Ohio, Kentucky. I even spot a couple from Pennsylvania before my walk is through. At first I wonder if there's a sporting event I'm unaware of, or something happening at Science Central, the museum by Lawton Park (a lovely place for a walk if you're ever in the area)—but when I pass by, I see that the parking lot is empty. No, this traffic is headed somewhere else.

I turn onto Spy Run Ave., named for Spy Run Creek, which in turn was named to commemorate William Wells, a man like Dan McQuay who deserves to have multiple books dedicated to him all on his own. A white man raised by Native Americans who fought on both sides throughout his life—sometimes, you guessed it, spying. Known as Apekonit (Carrot Top) for his red hair, Wells was the son-in-law of Chief Little Turtle of the Miami, whom he fought for during the Northwest Indian War. During the course of that war, though, he became a United States Army officer, and also served in the War of 1812, all of which is really just the tip of the iceberg. William Wells was on fire his entire life.

I'm starting to realize there could only be one event causing this traffic jam: the 48th annual Johnny Appleseed Festival.

As I get closer to the fairground, volunteers flit about trying to guide motorists to parking spots in nearby fields or in the massive lot for the Allen County War Memorial Coliseum—a thirteen-thousand-seat multipurpose arena (home of the Fort Wayne Komets Minor League Hockey team, as well as the Fort Wayne Derby Girls) looming in the distance.

But when I finally reach the fair itself, there are no lines—and no tickets, either. Admission is, and always has been, free. Despite my being *very* on time for open gates, the festival is already under way. People are pouring in, crowding around the pop-up ATMs to withdraw money for all the cash-only vendors. There is an obstacle course for children, along with a wild take on a maypole—a wooden structure that is wound up to a terrifying height and then sprung loose, children in wooden seats screaming as they spin back down to earth—and something called a roundabout and a bucking bronco (no actual animal involved).

There is every kind of apple-themed food you could imagine: apple petals and apple ice cream and apple-glazed wings, apple crisp and apple crisp á la mode, along with fried mushrooms and fried onion stacks and fried pickle chips and turkey legs the size of your head. I wonder what John Chapman—the rumored vegetarian—would have made of all the meat for sale.

There is also, of course, every manner of apple cider (except the alcoholic type), as well as something called Sarsaparilla Surprise, served in giant blue glass bottles (two of which I'm soon lugging around, having guzzled their contents and wanting to use as vases back home). There is a leather worker making belts—I buy one with eagles emblazoned on it—and women in period dress winding yarn on spinning wheels. There are, in fact, people in period dress of all sorts: buckskin outfits, Civil War garb. I hear bagpipes blaring above fifes and drums as multiple marching bands make their way through the fairgrounds.

The festival is huge beyond my wildest imagination. Like some sort of frontier-themed Coachella. I see a group of teens twerking as one of the fife bands marches by, and later I see a woman in period dress vaping.

There are people making candles, and children having the time of their lives playing in a simple pile of hay. An alarming number of dads are wearing T-shirts that read "YOU THINK I'M SCARED OF YOU? I HAVE TWO DAUGHTERS." ROTC is here doing recruitment.

At one point a person goes by on a Segway, and I overhear a wife say to her husband, "That's what ten DUIs look like."

I watch a flintknapper named Ed Mosher make stone knives, one of which I buy. Mosher has been flintknapping—the process of shaping or chipping away at stone to create tools—since 1990. He uses bits of antler to knap his wares, and often for the handles of his knives. I could have watched him work all day.

There are other people there just to make a buck, not that you can blame them. Hipster youth selling wooden swords, shields, and axes by the palletful for two dollars apiece, much to parents' chagrin, the children quickly getting into formation and going to war with one another. Two young blond women selling neon-colored feathers, encouraging children to make five-dollar headdresses out of them, are clearly not worrying about cultural appropriation.

I notice a large historical-looking tent set up for the Johnny Appleseed Society Museum in Urbana, Ohio. I tried to visit the museum when I was driving all over Ohio, but it was closed. In fact, Urbana College was closed permanently in 2020 due to COVID. I stop to talk with the women in the tent, mentioning my failed attempt to see the museum. They assure me that while the college is closed forever, the museum will indeed be back. I sign up for their newsletter and buy a children's book written by Ann Corfman and Nancy Sherwood, and illustrated by Deborah Ullery, titled *Appleseed Values* (Honesty! Compassion! Civic-mindedness! With a grid at the end where child readers can keep track of how much they display his values in their own lives). Nancy is one of the women I am talking with, and she signs the book: "Isaac, Value yourself and others!" I've gotten worse advice. I promise to visit the museum once it reopens—which it does the following year.

I head over to a map, trying to get my bearings. A volunteer encourages me to download the fair's app, a rather futuristic moment in the middle of an otherwise old-timey day. Eventually, though, I find my way to John Chapman's grave, right in the middle of the scrum of the festival. It is covered in apples placed by festivalgoers. A book that reads "Holy Bible," along with an apple, is cut into the stone, which reads " 'Johnny Appleseed' John Chapman He Lived for Others, 1774–1845."

I want to kneel and pray, but so many people are taking photos and putting their apples and flowers on the grave. The air around me was already filled with a somewhat deafening cacophony of people, but then a larger sound booms across the entire fair. A cannon is being fired. I go off to find it.

When I was young, around twelve years old, and had just befriended Conner, he confessed something to me. We'd been close friends for a few months before he let it slip.

"We're reenactors," he said sheepishly.

My child brain, not knowing the word, did what child brains do, and turned it into something to do with tractors, or engines, or maybe both. Reactors?

I finally grasped the concept—that Conner, his younger brother, and his mother would pile into their jalopy of a car and spend money on gas that they could barely afford in order to drive to old Civil War battlefields around the mid-Atlantic states and dress up as Northerners supporting the Second Battery, Vermont Light Artillery regiment and their cannon.

"Our cannon's in this movie, even though we didn't get to go down for it," Conner said to me while popping in the first video of the two-VHS-set that comprised Ronald F. Maxwell's *Gettysburg,* which we then watched stoned out of our minds in his dilapidated living room.

Looking back, it makes sense. Conner loved to play war in the woods, and we would spend days shooting each other with BB guns and firing off bottle rockets at each other. Little did I know he'd learned to play war because of his parents—then just from his mother when his father passed away from cancer, as she did her best to "keep things normal." How his parents, two extremely poor hippies who lived without electricity or running water until Conner was close to middle school age, got wrapped up in reenacting, I'll never know. Except to say that the centennial of the Civil War occurred in the 1960s, and kicked off a lot of the interest in reenacting generally. Another theory: Conner's father grew and sold weed, so it may just have been that he was Second Battery, Vermont Light Artillery's plug.

Either way, Conner eventually showed me the historically accurate Colt 1860 Army revolver his mother kept in her dresser drawer alongside her much more modern .22 pistol, and after pretending I was the Gunslinger for a few minutes—the hero of my favorite Stephen King book at the time—followed by Val Kilmer's Doc Holliday for a few more minutes after that, I agreed to go with them on the next reenacting trip.

Was Conner's ma trying to keep a family tradition alive, trying to make a bit of money to pay her bills, or simply just wanting to see old friends? I can't be sure. But we drove down south of the Mason-Dixon line, and I learned words like FUBAR (Fucked Up Beyond All Recognition) and FARBY, which means something that's "far before" or "far beyond" the appropriate time period, often used as an insult if someone is seen, say, drinking a can of Coke—or doing what I did, and showing up for a reenactment in current-day clothing.

"Hey, *FARBY,* quit it!"

Conner's ma eventually put me in her late husband's uniform, and one of the other reenactors loaned me a historically accurate pup tent—white canvas and wooden stakes—which is how, later that night, alone in my tent, I came to join the club of people on this earth (a small number, to be sure, but maybe not as small as one might think) who have, while wearing a full and accurate replica of a Union soldier's uniform, jerked off.

The boom of the cannon brings me back to present-day Indiana, now in my current uniform of running shorts, a big Hawaiian shirt, and slides. The crowd *oohs and aahs* as some of the reenactors reload their artillery again, while others hand out literature, hoping to recruit more members for their group. I read the large piece of paper handed to me, made to look like money from the mid-1800s: the "Forty Fourth Indiana Regiment," it reads, their website and Facebook page listed beneath.

The cannon fires a second time. The crowd disperses, and I sit under a nearby tree, exhausted. Maybe it's being on my feet all day, along with my walk to the festival that morning—and my long hang with Dakota the night before—or maybe it's the memory of my brief stint being a reenactor myself (we didn't know it then, but that trip was the last time I or anyone in Conner's family would participate in a reenactment). But more likely than not, it's the cider, sarsaparilla, apple petals, and other treats I've been indulging in, which caused a blood sugar spike, and then crash. I rest my head against the trunk of the tree and fall immediately asleep.

37

I AWAKE TO an argument. A young son and his father are bickering over what to do next, or maybe it's that the line for Little John's Root Beer is too long, or maybe it's time to leave and the young boy doesn't want to. I imagine it's difficult being a parent—trying to bring joy to your child, then being the one responsible for taking that joy away in the name of time management.

My body is heavy with festival food, but still I peel myself off the trunk of the tree and head back toward Rabbit and my gear downtown. I'll sleep by the St. Mary's River tonight, only to rise again at sunup and retrace my steps back to the festival grounds. The walk at this point has become a bit monotonous—back, forth, back, forth—but it is a brilliant, brisk fall day, and that helps.

The morning sun is still cresting over the hills when I approach the fairground again. Even the people who worked the various booths the day before and got to camp on-site are just waking up. A group of Amish are splitting wood, beginning a large fire to heat their giant cast-iron cauldrons, where they'll cook enough chicken dumplings to feed all two hundred thousand people who attend the fair annually. It smelled so good the day before that I had two bowls back to back, stunned by how delicious such a simple dish, cooked outside with basic tools over an open fire, could be. It was the best food at the festival, which is really saying something—though it's worth noting that no other vendor has had a seemingly endless supply of teenagers to help them, one would assume free of charge.

"They get a week off from school and get to come to the festival," one Amish elder told me yesterday when I asked how the money was divided up, as if to say, "What other payment is necessary?" I left it at that, but not before buying a beautiful hand-crafted walking stick. It immediately felt like an extension of my body.

But today it is still morning and my wondrous walking stick and I are coming back to the festival for one reason, and it isn't child-labor-law-flouting-yet-definitely-delicious chicken dumplings. Every year on Sunday morning, the festival conducts a Swedenborgian Mass. And this year, Reverend Kit Billings of the New Church in LaPorte, Indiana, has driven down to do the service. Reverend Billings speaks from the stage where, later that day, the Inclognito Cloggers will perform, along with the Applejack Cloggers, the Fort Wayne Suzuki Players, and Reader the Magnificent, plus a slew of Johnny Appleseed impersonators. But there, in the dewy early-morning air, with us—a spontaneous congregation sitting on benches cut from wood, no nave but the sky above—the hum of the fair melts away and it is as if we are at an 1800s revival or Chautauqua.

"As we gather in this sacred space, let us remember the legacy of Johnny Appleseed, a humble servant of God and the Earth, a good man of deep spiritual conviction. In the spirit of his devotion to the Lord and all of Creation, let us join in worship and prayer."

I mutter, "Amen."

"We come together, like the apple trees he planted, rooted in the Earth's fertile soil, reaching for the Heavens with our branches of faith. In the footsteps of Johnny Appleseed, we are reminded that every seed of love we sow has the power to grow and multiply. Every act of kindness we perform has the potential to bear fruit in the lives of others. As we gather today, may we be inspired by his example to cultivate not only orchards, but also the seeds of compassion and kindness within our own hearts and lives. Let us open our hearts and minds to the beauty and wonder of nature, and to the wisdom of the Divine, as we celebrate the interconnectedness of all living things. In the spirit of John Chapman, who loved apples for their nutrition and their symbolism . . ."

"And their alcoholic cider," I whisper.

"—we strive to be stewards of this good Earth, nurturing and protecting the gifts of Creation for future generations. Let us commit ourselves to reflecting on the simple yet profound wisdom of generosity, faith, and reverence for the Earth. O come, let us worship in gratitude for the abundance of life our God gives us every moment of every day."

"Amen," we all say together. Louder this time. We sing "This Is My Father's World," along with, yes, the Johnny Appleseed song, "The Lord's been good to me, and so I thank the Lord . . ."

Reverend Billings read Proverbs 3:1–4 and Colossians 3:12–14, then gives one helluva sermon, titled "The Spiritual Legacy of Johnny Appleseed: Cultivating Fruits of Kindness." The reverend focuses on the importance of being present in the natural world.

By the end, filled with appreciation for nature and John Chapman, and the spiritual experience of sitting outside with strangers from all different backgrounds and walks of life, listening to a preacher whose religion very few or none of us subscribe to, but sensing the truth of the words, of a need to commune with the world—well, I'm moved to tears.

It's an abundant feeling that I haven't felt in some time, perhaps not since going to Mass as a child, when the crowds and singing and small sips of wine left my tiny heart bursting with the grace of God.

As I begin to weep, we say the Lord's Prayer together, and the Reverend Billings brings the service to a close. The crowd breaks into applause, none of us sure if it is an appropriate response, but all of us wanting to give thanks to the preacher for his words. I think back to the grandeur and decadence of the cathedral in Bryn Athyn, Pennsylvania, and can see why Chapman—and those like him, myself included I guess—might prefer the wild church of nature to more populated areas and permanent stone temples.

Reverend Billings comes over, probably a bit surprised by my quiet but abundant tears. He doesn't ask if I am all right, doesn't give me a chance to explain my emotions away: *"You see, I'm writing a book about John Chapman, but really I've just been walking and sleeping outside a lot, and sometimes I worry I'm losing my mind a bit. Mental illness runs in my family, but maybe I'm just feeling overwhelmed at the moment because . . ."*

None of that. He simply puts his arm on my shoulder, squeezes, and then pulls me in for a long embrace.

38

SOMEWHERE IN OHIO, but not as far from the Indiana border as I want to be, I see a giant green sign that reads "Indian Lake." At first I have no intention of stopping. It's not that I have anywhere to be, particularly, but when driving across a good hunk of the country, it's nice to get into rhythm, and then not to disturb that rhythm—stops for gas or an occasional bite to eat being part of the trancelike dance.

When you're walking, you're moving through the world at a human pace. You slow down. You pay attention. Driving is the opposite—it's the speed itself that makes you pay attention. Hurtling across the horizon, traveling faster than any of our ancestors could have imagined. Yet it feels casual. A little Outlaw Country on the radio, your seat conforming to your body as the hours march on. But still, keep your eyes on the road—bouncing from signs to traffic to the skyline—constantly moving. Constantly alert.

The meditation comes from knowing that you're driving a giant metal death machine, but the end result is the same. My busy mind grows quiet. As if my brain needs something—anything—to chew on. To gnaw on. To bite and tear and consume. Reading, another favorite activity, does the same.

But every once in a while the rhythm gets interrupted.

Like the time I was driving in Western Pennsylvania and a burst of torrential rainfall fell from the sky, seemingly out of nowhere, on an up-until-that-very-moment sunny day. I instinctively slowed Rabbit down, which is when a Saab convertible drove by—the top still down in spite of the rain. A white-haired man in an expensive-looking shirt looked over at me—his wife or girlfriend screaming in the seat next to him. The man was still wearing his sunglasses, but I swear we made eye contact. The man was laughing hysterically, he then shrugged, turned his eyes back to the road, and disappeared into the sheets of precipitation.

When you spend a lot of time out on the road, you have dozens of these little encounters. Like the time I was stuck in traffic, assholes ripping down the breakdown lane—further delaying all of us as they cut back into traffic just before reaching the accident that had caused the backup in the first place. All of a sudden, a semi trailer truck put half its ass in the breakdown lane, immediately backing up all the jerks barreling down it. People rolled down their windows, myself included, to shout thanks at the truck driver, who pulled the cord on his airhorn, letting out a blast, and saluted us all.

It's worth mentioning that in all my time driving this year, I've come to see truckers as the unheralded knights of the road. Someone broken down on the side of the highway? Usually it's an eighteen-wheeler that has pulled over to see if they can help—setting out flares for safety if the sun has gone down.

It's these little moments of distraction that can pop you out of the meditative calmness that comes with driving. A man in a convertible in the rain, a heroic truck driver, an Amish teenager in a racing buggy, a giant green sign—almost begging you to stop—that reads "Indian Lake."

I rip Rabbit into a hard right and hit the exit.

After driving through yellow soybean fields I get to the lake. The first thing I notice is the majesty of the water. The flat, undisturbed lake stretching out—pushing into the horizon. A reservoir so big that it momentarily makes me miss the ocean.

The next thing I notice are the street names. Blackhawk Drive, Cherokee Drive, Chinook Drive, Mohawk Drive. You get the idea. This is out on an island—accessible by a small bridge—called Seminole Island, which is next to Tecumseh Island.

Indian Lake indeed.

Across the water I see what looks to be some semblance of a downtown. I head there, hoping to find a place to rest for a bit.

"You're not from around here, are you?"

Here we go again. "Stick out that bad, huh?"

I'm younger than the bartender by two decades at least. But she is beautiful. Surely more beautiful than me, or anyone else at the bar. The rest of us—myself included, with my unkempt graying beard and long hair, tattered Hawaiian shirt, running shorts, and flip-flops—look like the pallbearers at Jimmy Buffett's funeral. She looks like an angel, one who has perhaps lived a little rough, but has been heaven-sent to escort the famously laid-back crooner to the great big Cheeseburger in Paradise in the sky.

She notices me noticing her and gives the slightest little smirk.

"It was more your New York license plate."

She nods at Rabbit, just visible through a skinny window that allows a cut of afternoon light into the otherwise dim bar. As if the jukebox can read my thoughts, Jimmy Buffett starts playing.

The bartender doesn't ask me who I am or why I am here. Hell, maybe she already knows—the answer being, "You know, that really big green sign out on the highway."

She serves me a cold bottle of Bud and I just sit there, falling into that same meditative state as when I'm walking, as when I'm driving, as when I'm sitting in a dimly lit church—or in a bar—taking a li'l communion. Until the third beer, that is, when she tosses me a wooden chip promising me a fourth, on the house. Looks like I won't be getting back to the highway until tomorrow, so I order a shot and offer to buy one for the bartender, too.

We clink glasses and toss the whiskey down.

My lips loosen, I ask about life on the lake—it used to be a real summer draw, she tells me. There was an amusement park and a dance hall, advertised as the "Midwest's Million Dollar Playground," but that all closed down in the 1980s. Still, the lake did bring in tourists, and as the land became more developed people started living here year round. Mostly retirees, like the folks currently populating the bar.

After another shot, I finally ask: What the fuck was with the street names?

"How do you mean?"

"Look, it's Indian Lake. I get that. I'm just now coming from Indiana."

"Uh huh."

"But every street around here—Pocahontas Path, Big Bear Path—have y'all ever thought about . . ."

"Changing them?"

"Yeah."

"To shit like Lakeview Drive and Atwater, and Pirate's Cove? Sunset Lane?"

"To *exactly* shit like that."

"Oh, New York, and to think I was starting to like you," she says, pouring me another shot. "It'll only be well whiskey for you if you keep this bullshit up."

"What'd the kid say?" shouts one of my fellow Jimmy Buffett music video extras from down the bar.

"He asked if we ever considered changing the street names around here."

A long, grumbling murmur covers the far end of the bar. I'm not absolutely sure, but the word "dickhead" seems to barely reach my ears more than once. Looks like I've been downgraded from "kid."

The bartender pours herself a shot.

"Let's start here, New York. Why don't you change the name of Manhattan?"

I pause. "Fair point."

"You're from the East Coast—you want to change the name of Connecticut? How about Massachusetts?"

Now seems like a bad time to mention that Massachusetts is my home state. I think of the large body of water near where I grew up: the Quabbin Reservoir. She goes on. "If we change the name of our streets, we should probably change the name of Ohio itself, right? Drink your shot."

I drink my shot.

"Why not change the name of Alabama, Alaska, Arizona, Arkansas? That's just the A-states, mind you."

She pours another shot after taking her own—pointedly no longer drinking *with* me.

"The Cleveland Indians are now the Guardians. Does that make you feel more comfortable?" She doesn't give me time to respond. The dark murmuring at the end of the bar has turned into grumbling encouragement, almost low-volume cheering.

"What about Washington's football team—the Commanders?" I manage.

"What about 'em?"

"I mean—"

"That was different. That was a slur."

I almost point out that the Cleveland Indians' mascot wasn't exactly *inoffensive,* but as I mull it over, a clear sentence finds its way out of the Greek chorus at the end of the bar.

"She's Native, kid."

I look at the bartender.

"My mother's side. Shawnee. Take your shot."

I wince as it goes down.

"History is violent, cruel, and often stupid. But ignoring it so people feel slightly more at ease in their day-to-day life? That's stupid, too. You want to change the street names? How about doing a little land acknowledgment while you're at it? Another way for white people to say, 'Sorry for all the murder, and land stealing, the Trail of Tears, and forced subjugation.' But that shit is relieving *your* guilt. Doesn't help me, or my ancestors one bit. But sure, change a sports team name, so you don't even have to spend a moment thinking about the past and how shitty and complicated it is. Change the street names—hell, try and make a perfect society where nobody gets offended and there's no mention of anything uncomfortable from the past, ever. Let me know how that works out for you."

I nod, quietly, but she wants more.

"End up naming every damn street in the country Jesus Christ Street, is that what you want?"

Not exactly what I was trying to say, but I shake my head no.

"We done here?"

"Yes."

"Good, now let's get back to flirting, I liked that better."

"Is now a bad time to mention I have a girlfriend?"

The gallery at the end of the bar lets out a collective laugh.

"Slow down, New York. I said I liked flirting with you. You're not getting any."

We go back to talking, and I put money in the jukebox, my song selection of more Jimmy Buffett winning back the gaggle of men at the other end of the bar. Eventually, they ask me if I want to go smoke a joint with them out on the porch, so I do.

All of the men are easily twenty years my senior—probably more—and they go back to calling me kid as we pass the well-rolled joint around, introducing ourselves. At my urging, the men tell me stories about their childhoods spent on the lake. Soon the bartender, who never offers her name, joins us—smoking a cigarette—and I am entrusted with going behind the bar and getting folks fresh beers, carefully marking the sheet of paper that keeps track of their tabs.

I have an armful of Buds and Coors Lights when I hear a crash on the porch.

The noise is quickly followed by "Oh, fuck," and shouts of "Oscar!"

I abandon the bottles on the bar and run back to the porch. A rather large man with rakish long white hair and a prominent goatee has hit the deck. The bartender is at his side—a bottle of water in her hand, which she pours into his mouth.

"Oscar, wake up!" A man—supposedly Oscar's friend—bends over and gives Oscar's potato-sack body a firm shake before slapping him across the face.

"Should I call 911?" I ask, not knowing what to do.

"No!" Comes the quick, unanimous response from almost everyone, the bartender's voice loudest.

The man slaps Oscar again, hard—and Oscar comes to. I say a quick "Thank God" under my breath.

"Oscar, you went out there for a second." The bartender hands him what's left of the water bottle.

"What the fuck am I doing down here?"

"You fell pretty hard, O. You break anything?"

Oscar squeezes parts of his body while slowly getting up, cautiously putting weight on one foot, then the next.

"I've got pills in my jacket, grab those for me?" Oscar is asking his buddy, who then looks at me. I go back into the bar and see a lightweight windbreaker hanging off the back of his chair. Sure enough, a prescription bottle is in the jacket's front pocket. I bring the pills over to Oscar, who thanks me before cracking open the bottle and popping a handful into his mouth, chasing it with a last sip from the water bottle.

"Damn, that was some strong dope."

We laugh at his attempt at humor, but we don't really mean it. Everyone is a little shaken, including Oscar.

"Jokes aside—that could be my ticker. Who's coming with me to the hospital?" Oscar's friend helps him into the parking lot, where they get into a truck and drive off.

"Well, that was a boner killer. Who needs to settle their tabs?"

I pay the bartender, who doesn't ask if I need a place to stay, nor does she tell me to drive safe. She just says, "Be sure to visit again next time you're passing through. Maybe there won't be a minor heart attack, and we can pick up where we left off."

But before I leave I ask, "Why not call 911?"

"Nobody needs the world's most expensive taxi on top of a hospital bill. Hell, bowing out here might be the best option for some of these guys."

I walk around the empty downtown stoned, trying to sober up. There was a time in my life when that would have been what I wanted: simply to party, to have a good time, and then to drop dead on a barroom floor—like Chapman, in a way. That's changing now, as I get older. I value life more, having less of it.

I call my ma, still up in north central Massachusetts with her sister, taking care of their mother. She doesn't pick up. I call Kelly, and she does.

"Sounds like you've been drinking," she says right away.

"Might have been."

"No drinking and driving. You promised."

"I know."

We catch up as I walk past Rabbit, stopping only to grab my sleeping bag. Dusk is turning into night. I don't tell her about the man collapsing—why give her something else to worry about? She's already been so understanding, of all of this. She asks after my ma, and how things are going up there. I tell her the truth, which is that I don't know.

We chat until we both start sounding tired.

"Okay, I have to get ready for bed," she concludes.

"Me too," I say, though I am just staring out at a soybean field.

"I love you."

"I love you, too."

I put my phone into my pocket and lay out my sleeping bag. The sky above me begins to fill with stars. The next morning I'll wake at daybreak in a bright yellow field, walk back down East Lake Drive, climb into Rabbit, and head out from Indian Lake.

39

THERE ARE Johnny Appleseed Festivals throughout the country, but only one has a lumberjack competition. It's another one of those legends about John Chapman that is a bit contradictory. The man apparently refused to graft his trees, but was also heralded as one of the best axmen on the frontier. Howard Means writes, "Like Paul Bunyan, Chapman wielded an ax almost as effectively as King Arthur wielded his magic sword, Excalibur." Means goes on to reference a memoir from 1859 by one R. I. Curtis, in which Curtis writes that "Chapman could chop as much wood or girdle as many trees in one day as most men could in two."

More than reason enough to make another stop back in Pennsylvania, after my sojourn at Indian Lake and drive east through the rest of Ohio.

Indeed, if you will remember back to Warren, wood was very much one of the main drivers of commerce in the area at the time. Chapman's original man crush (okay, maybe more mine), the whiskey-slamming, rafting-down-to-New-Orleans-and-then-walking-back Irishman, Daniel McQuay, was in the area on behalf of the Holland Land Company, transporting lumber down the Allegheny into the Ohio River, and eventually into the Mississippi. Also, this is the younger Chapman we are discussing, so perhaps his aversion to hurting trees didn't emerge until later. In any case, I'm headed back to wood country once again, in the heart of the Allegheny National Forest.

Before arriving in Sheffield, PA, I stop in neighboring Ridgway—the self-appointed "chainsaw sculpture capital of the world." On my way into town, I pass a massive wooden sculpture of the V-J Day kiss in Times Square, an interpretation of Alfred Eisenstaedt's famous photograph published in *Life* with the caption "In New York's Times Square a white-clad girl clutches her purse and skirt as an uninhibited sailor plants his lips squarely on hers." The sculpture is taller than the one-story building it stands next to. Downtown Ridgway has similar smaller sculptures on every corner: here a red cardinal, there a horse. The town had a large number of millionaires in the late 1800s and early 1900s, due to its thriving lumber industry. In fact, at the turn of the twentieth century, Ridgway had more millionaires per capita than any other town in the United States.

I'm a day early for the festival, so I move on from Ridgway and head to an area of the Allegheny National Forest called Hearts Content. There I walk among a stand of three-hundred-year-old white pines. In 1977, Hearts Content was registered as a National Natural Landmark by the National Park Service. The Allegheny National Forest itself is a bit of a miracle, as this entire area was completely clear-cut by logging companies in the 1800s, but the twenty acres that now make up Hearts Content were owned by Wheeler and Dusenbury Lumber Company from 1897 to 1922, and they left these trees intact, deeding them and the land they stand on to the US Forest Service in 1923. Hearts Content remains the only significant old-growth forest in Pennsylvania, and one of a mere handful still in existence on the East Coast.

The area has a gazebo, which has apple trees growing around it, and a variety of trails: there's Tom's Run Loop, Wheeler Loop, Ironwood Loop, and the Hearts Content Interpretation Trail. I hike a few of them before setting up camp in the forest. The next day I walk out of the old woods and finally head down to Sheffield.

I was getting tired. Tired of traveling and tired of being away from home. Tired of long drives and long walks, tired of feeling like an outsider and an observer.

It was one of the ways I related to John Chapman. That condition I mentioned, being a "party monk." Chapman spent so much time alone, roaming and planting, yet he clearly sought out community with others. Staying at people's homes.

I was missing my own home. My community. After a year of being out in the world—and a lifetime, really, of bouncing around—I could feel myself filling up with an urge I wasn't very familiar with: *the desire to settle down.* I wanted to be back by the ocean with my girlfriend and my dogs. I'd seen the ocean of the plains out here. But I missed the salt. I missed the blue.

It's raining when I pull into Sheffield, and the early days of fall—warm, with the lightest perceptible bit of *brisk* (one of my favorite words and temperatures)—have taken a turn for the cold, wet *late* days of fall. No longer is the surrounding Allegheny National Forest bursting with autumn leaves—the leaves are mostly on the ground now, at least up here at 2,050 feet above sea level. Stick season has arrived.

"Well, looks like Al Roker wasn't lying this morning."

I walk into the Shaw House to get out of the rain, and to get my bearings. It's the first bar in Sheffield that I can find, and is already full—on account of the weather, I figure. Folks like myself who are headed to the festival, waiting for the vendors to finish setting up despite the bad conditions.

I order a bottle of Bud and ask the woman next to me if she thinks the festival will still happen, even with, as she has just put it, Al Roker being right this morning on the *Today* show.

"Oh yessir, it certainly will. Rain or shine."

She takes a drag on her cigarette, which is when I realize about half the bar is smoking. A perk of living out in the boondocks, one I remember from my own childhood. Federal and statewide mandates were seen as mere suggestions, to be politely declined if enough local residents got together and agreed—as they clearly have at this bar for years.

"My smokes not bothering ya, handsome?" She has noticed me noticing. I shake my head and smile, unsure if the "handsome" is genuine, or a way of acknowledging that I am not exactly blending in here in Sheffield.

"Anyway, yeah. Those crazy sons of bitches will cut wood in any weather."

The "crazy sons of bitches" are lumberjacks. The Johnny Appleseed Festival in Sheffield features professional lumberjack competitions to celebrate the area's history, Sheffield once being one of Pennsylvania's biggest logging areas. Although it looks a bit like most of the profits went to Ridgway, and Sheffield has grown even rougher around the edges since the lumber business died.

But it's the lumberjacks I'm here for. Apparently the competition brings competitors from "all around the world," or at least that's what's advertised. But just to cut logs, I think? I could do that. I even wrote ahead to see if they would let me participate in the games, but the organizers politely declined. I'd be lying if I said I wasn't still hoping to see if I could swing an ax today at some point, though.

I talk more with the woman, her man quietly sitting next to her.

"Do you like jokes?" she asks.

"Sure."

"What goes in hard and comes out wet and sticky?"

I immediately turn red, and even people down the bar turn to watch my embarrassment.

"Gum, you pervert. Why are you blushing?" The woman bursts

into laughter, which has nothing on her man's—his sounds like it's coming from the bottom of a mountain.

I raise my bottle good-naturedly. Perhaps seeing that I can take a joke, her man speaks for the first time.

"Nice tattoos."

"Thanks," I say.

"You know, I've got a tattoo, too."

"Really?"

"Yep. A hundred-dollar bill, right on my dick."

I turn a brighter shade of red, not knowing what to say.

"Yeah, this girl here," he squeezes the woman, "she loves to blow money."

At this the whole bar falls apart, although they've clearly heard the joke before. I think their laughter has less to do with what was said, and more to do with how red my face has become. They offer to buy me another drink for being a good sport, but I wave off their generosity and head out onto South Main Street.

Like a few other places I've visited, Sheffield reminds me a lot of where I grew up in Athol. I once saw a map of Massachusetts that made fun of each section of the state with designations such as "Townies and immigrants" or "Witches, fishermen, and quaint-ass towns" or "Gaycationland." For the part of the state where I grew up, it just read "There be dragons here." Sheffield also has this vibe. The main drag consists of a few gas stations, a thrift store, the Shaw House Bar, and a distributor efficiently named Sheffield Beer & Ice.

By the river, near one of the gas stations, is a welcome sign that reads "Welcome to Sheffield: The Heart of the Allegheny National Forest" along with a map of the area and a large sign to help you identify the fish you can catch in Tionesta Creek. I pick a place to make camp—figuring it's better to make camp in the rain while there's still some light in the sky, instead of later on when it's both dark *and* wet.

After taking far too long to set up a basic tarp over my campsite by Minister Creek—a tributary of Tionesta Creek—and cursing while my tent poles slipped in the rain, I do my best to anchor my stakes in the already muddy ground. Then it's time for the festival.

A large field in the center of town has been taken over by booths and vendors, *but*—and I want to be clear here, life is not meant to be about comparisons—the Fort Wayne Johnny Appleseed Festival this is not.

It may be the weather, or perhaps how this festival seems smaller—but I feel lonely, despite all the people braving the rain to help support the town fair. The Johnny Appleseed Festival takes place at the Sheffield Memorial Park. There is a cornhole tournament and "Kids Sawdust Pile & Fun Zone," along with a horse pull and a tractor pull and apple pie baking contest. In the firehouse there's a cluster of area wineries giving out samples; some vineyards having opened recently as people look to develop a new economy, based on something other than lumber.

"Do you ride?"

An older woman sitting at a booth and wearing head-to-toe leather looks at me. I quickly glance at the literature in front of her and see motorcycles.

"I used to," I answer honestly. "And I hope to again one day."

"Did you ride alone?"

"Uh, yeah, for the most part."

"Well, you never ride alone when you ride with Him."

The woman hands me a flyer that reads "CMA: Christian Motorcyclists Association."

She then walks me through the flyer, which presents the colors of the CMA. Not motorcycle club colors, like the Chicago Outlaws' black and white, or the Hells Angels' red and white. In the CMA the color gold represents heaven, "Somewhere we all want to go." Black represents sin, "Our Problem—All are sinners." Red represents the Blood of Christ, "God's remedy for sin." The color white represents salvation, "Our response to what Jesus did for us on the cross." And then there's green, which represents growth: "But grow in the grace and knowledge of our Lord and Savior, Jesus Christ."

"So, do you ride with Jesus?" she asks, trying again.

"I try," I say with a small grin, "when He lets me."

I promise to keep the literature and look it over. After almost getting recruited into a Motorcycle Gang for Jesus, I check out the large stage that's been assembled next to the town's bleachers.

So far the only thing that has really impressed me about the Johnny Appleseed Festival in Sheffield—other than the community's clear desire to make the fair a success despite the weather, and a couple of the wines that I sampled—are the apple fries, which are exactly what they sound like—apples, sliced to resemble French fries, and served with caramel or marshmallow dipping sauces. I got both.

But that's about to change. Soon the stage, which has clearly been assembled just for this event, begins to fill up. A voice bellows over the loudspeaker announcing the start of the lumberjack competition.

How best to describe what happens next? Well, for one thing, I immediately realize I will not be swinging an ax that day, and completely understand why the organizers denied my request to join. Strong, broad-backed men along with strong, broad-backed women begin swinging axes that seem to be made of chrome, their metal heads catching rays of sun despite the rain clouds overhead. There is sawing, chopping, and climbing—all in the rain. Hunks of wood fly everywhere at an impressive rate, all while the announcer keeps us in the audience on the edge of our seats. Sheffield's Johnny Appleseed Festival isn't a fair with a lumberjack competition attached, it's a lumberjack competition with a fair attached. I am thrilled. All of a sudden the rain doesn't seem as cold. If these competitors, some of whom are breaking personal records despite the weather, can endure, surely I can. Scarfing down a second order of apple fries helps, too.

In between events I buy some merch, to show my support for what is clearly a well-cared-for annual event. I also speak to some of the competitors, like Martha, from Chadds Ford, PA, who does twenty to thirty competitions a year in both the US and Europe. When I ask her why, she says, "The wood chopping community is a family. Why wouldn't I want to spend time with my family?"

I meet Felixia Banck, a forestry technician and Timbersports athlete from Denmark who boasts hundreds of thousands of followers across her social platforms. She tells me, "I actually had to go to Sweden to first try out Timbersports. That's eleven hours for me. But I loved it. Right now, I'm the only female in Denmark doing this sport. And I'm number two in Europe. So I started out last year doing this sport for real—had two competitions last year. This year, I've had seven Timbersports competitions—been on the podium for every one of them."

"No bullshit?" I say.

"Bullshit, why would I bullshit?" she asks me in a straightforward Scandinavian manner. Her eyes shine with pride, the same shine making the axes gleam despite there being little sunlight.

"Nobody thought I was going to do this," she goes on. "I was a photographer five years ago. So I changed my professional life completely to do tree work—to become a forest worker. Nobody in my life really saw that coming, including myself. But when I discovered Timbersports, I simply fell in love. It's so different. It's so fun."

"Plus, you're good at it."

"It's been a good season for me, yes."

I speak to Sandy Setili, one of the original founders of the Johnny Appleseed Festival. When I suggest that the rain must have been a bit of a letdown, she stays upbeat, saying the wet wood is better for the axes.

"My oldest son, he recently retired, but he was a major in the army. My other son, Nathan, went to forestry school, and while he was there he learned about lumberjack competitions. So he joined the Syracuse Woodsmen's team and started doing Timbersports. After he graduated he went to Australia for six months, because in Australia wood chopping is like football, it's so popular there. Like the Mecca of Timbersports. He learned a lot down there, then he came back—he was doing competitions all over Canada and the United States. So one time, when he was home visiting, he said to me, 'You know, Mom, I grew up in the middle of the beautiful Allegheny National Forest and I cannot compete anywhere close to home.' 'Why is that?' I said. But apparently there weren't any competitions nearby."

"So, wait, you're telling me this was all built so there'd be a nearby lumberjack competition for your son?"

"That's right. I said to him, 'You know, when I was growing up, they had this festival in Sheffield and it was called Johnny Appleseed Festival.' I had some old photographs, so I pulled them out and showed them to him, and Nathan says, 'Mom, could you get this going again?' And I said, 'I bet I could.' So I came to Sheffield and I met with the supervisors and some people told them the idea and they were like, 'We'll support you. Go for it.' So we held a public meeting and we had probably thirty people come to the meeting. And from that we developed our committee and got started."

"No sh—" I catch myself. Sandy was a very sweet woman. "Really?"

"We started very small. Over fifteen years ago. It was just a Saturday, Sunday thing. But my son Nathan, you know, he put the woodsman's part of it together, and soon lumberjacks were coming from all over. It's grown over the years—now we have fifty-one craft vendors and eleven food vendors."

I immediately feel like a judgmental jerk for my thoughts earlier in the day, and say a quick prayer for forgiveness.

"This year we have sixty-five-plus lumberjacks and lumberjills here. We have four from Sweden. We have one from Denmark. We have 'em from British Columbia, Washington State, upstate New

York. They're coming in from everywhere. And it's like that every year now."

The wood has to be white pine or bigtooth aspen or basswood, the last one being what they were using this year, brought to the area in big logging trucks.

"There's a Cochran and Zandy lumber mill just up the road a ways, and they allow us to have our wood delivered there and it comes in logs. Then we have a wild weekend where we work as hard as we possibly can to get all that wood ready for the competition."

While Sandy says all this, log after log—many of them giant—is being sawed and axed to pieces. It dawns on me that Sandy was probably who I was communicating with when I asked to be a part of the competition. I ask her and she laughs.

"I'm sorry," I say. "I don't think I realized how serious a competition it is."

"Oh, I felt bad turning you down, but I knew you couldn't—"

"Keep up with your son and the other competitors?"

"Sure, that's a nice way to put it. But it is serious. It's not just a physical competition. There's a mental game, too. A real chess element to it—when to save your strength, how best and where to place your first. You can't just swing an ax and hope for the best. Plus, there's the insurance to consider."

"I can only imagine."

"A lot of the competitors wear chain mail so as not to get hurt. It's very intense."

"Well, thank you, Sandy. You saved me from showing my butt up there."

At that moment, chainsaws fire up. I didn't even know there were going to be chainsaws involved. All the lumberjacks and lumberjills crowd under a pop-up tent away from the audience, but young children still run up and ask for autographs. They seem like knights at a tournament—extremely hot knights, it must be said, their lean, ax-swinging, trunk-climbing bodies taut and sinewy from their labors—and the crowd adores them. At one point, they cut slits in the sides of tall trunks, and using springboards to climb higher, stand in the air at eight or so feet off the ground, a death-defying stunt. All the while swinging their axes higher and higher as chips fly everywhere. The show they put on is one of the best I've seen all year, the kind of event you feel lucky to have experienced in person, even in spite of the rain.

40

MANY OF THE lumberjacks are crashing at the local firehouse this evening to get out of the rain, which hasn't let up at all. What an incredible way to move through the world: going from town to town chopping wood, showing off your skills with a saw. As a young person, you can dream of becoming a football star or a basketball star—a firefighter! But how do you decide you want to become an all-star at Timbersports?

I'm surprised to discover that many of the lumberjacks are top talent, with huge followings online. The internet can unlock many things; you can watch practically whatever you want whenever you want—including lumberjacks in Denmark. Sports, politics, food, culture from all over the world, right in your pocket—if you know how to search for it correctly.

But the internet isn't everything we thought it would be, all those years ago. When I was younger—and the internet was younger—I never would have guessed that in the decades to come we would all be feeling nostalgic for a past version of being online. The idea didn't exist yet. How could it? Yearning for a space that didn't physically exist, and yet somehow now is gone.

That said, the flip side of the coin is something I think about often. Imagine you're a pianist in a small town: Sheffield, for instance. In days gone by, if you practiced hard enough, you'd get hired for weddings or to play the local bar. You might even get a recurring gig at the town church, if you figured out a few hymns on the organ. If you were good, you could maybe have a little career in the surrounding area. You didn't have to be *the best.* But that idea seems to have shifted over the past twenty or so years. People can look up videos of Ryuichi Sakamoto whenever they want, and he's not even alive anymore. Why should they listen to—let alone pay for—someone like you?

The internet, like many things, is a double-edged sword. It helps creative people reach each other all across the globe, but it also pulls us out of our present—our reality. But if there's a kid out there right now, watching videos on YouTube, dreaming of becoming a lumberjack? It can't be all bad.

The rain continues into the night. I walk to a nearby bar because I don't want to simply be wet at my campsite. The place looks, well, there's no other way to say it, the place looks like it could star in *The Haunting of Hill House,* as the house. Lee House makes Shaw House—the other bar in Sheffield—look like Bemelmans Bar in Manhattan. It reminds me of house parties of my youth, the kind where the parents never came home—and then a hundred years went by. Posters and liquor promotions everywhere, mixing in with the dust and beyond-faded wallpaper.

As I walk in, a bunch of twentysomethings are playing pool on a table that is crooked at best. The bartender and I strike up an easy conversation. She tells me the bar is actually celebrating its 150th year of being open, and points at the lovely original tin ceiling above us. Everything in the place is old—including the bar itself, made of sturdy antique wood. There's gratis shuffleboard in the corner, and the drinks are more than affordable. But that's where the niceties stop. The bartender—who tells me she'd once married a Fitzgerald but was even happier to divorce him—shows me an ancient picture of the place: one of those photos where you can't tell if it's an actual photograph or a drawing or some weird mix of both. Ford Model Ts are parked in front, and Lee House looks like a proper hotel, the kind of place a president might stay while coming out to Western Pennsylvania to win over a few voters.

When I excuse myself to go to the bathroom, I can't help but notice that the next room is—how's the best way to put this?—collapsing in on itself. In the bathroom I find, of all things, a printed-out meme nailed to the wall. It's a picture of Tim Robinson—a still from his show *I Think You Should Leave,* and over his face are the words "Cocaine, You Sure About That?" Right below the picture: a platter full of rapid-response fentanyl test strips.

Back at the bar I overhear the young kids, now done with their pool game, lamenting a friend who OD'd the night before.

"But he'll be okay. They got him to the hospital in time."

"Fentanyl a problem around here?" I ask the ex-Fitzgerald.

"Everything's a problem around here," she replies.

"I come from a similar place."

"I just don't understand it," she plows on. "There's the pandemic, right? The big bad pandemic. We shut everything down—change the way we live. We can do all that for some fancy-ass version of the flu, but not the opioid pandemic? That kid they're talking about, he'll live. But somebody else died just last week. Facebook's only good for remembering friends' birthdays and finding out who OD'd that you went to high school with. Guessing you noticed the test strips?"

"I did."

"We try to be safe here. What else can we do? People are gonna do drugs, but it's gotten so bad. Why can't the government make major moves for *this* pandemic? Get us some real help. Rehab centers. Methadone clinics. Really care about people instead of just let them die. Fuck, given how bad it is here, I can't even imagine how bad it is in the cities. Philadelphia? No thank you."

I have the feeling that Philadelphia, just like any city, or community for that matter—Sheffield included—has parts of town that are comfortable and parts of town that struggle. Same as the country we live in. Addiction doesn't really care about where you live.

"We try to take care of our own here. Try to raise our kids right. I yell at those kids," she gestures at the young group, "if I ever hear 'em say the r-word or the n-word or the f-word." A lovely thought—although, to be clear, she says the actual words.

"Remember Bobby?" one of the kids shouts out.

"We all remember Bobby," the bartender says, "but go on."

The kid goes on to tell the story of Bobby—or the legend of Bobby, might be a better way to put it; it's clear the kids had been drinking all day, so it's a little hard to piece together. But from what I can gather, Bobby was a guy everybody loved. Played sports, popular in school—he'd already moved out of town. Headed west to somewhere in California. But before he left town, *could I imagine?* the kid was asking, his eyes shining as he told his tale, that everyone in town found out Bobby was gay? I, of course, could. But I give the kid a "No shit?" to help move the story along.

"So one night, we were all here. You were here, right, Sandra?"

"I was here, Timmy," the bartender, whose name was apparently Sandra, says.

"So one night, this guy calls Bobby the f-word right here, in the bar, to his face."

"Okay."

"So Bobby puffs up, right? Don't forget, Bobby's a big guy. He's gay, but he's a big guy."

"They do make 'em that way," I say, but my comment is ignored.

"So Bobby, he turns to the guy, and he just whups. his. ass." The kid—Timmy—starts laughing hysterically, urging his buddies to join in.

"That's great," I say.

"But that's not the best part. No, the best part is what Bobby said after. And I'm telling you, he whipped this dude's *ass*. Really put him in the dirt."

"It was a pretty bad beating," Sandra says to me, almost as an aside.

"And you know what Bobby said when he was done kicking the shit out of that dude?" I hope the kid used the test strips in the bathroom. His jaw is starting to lock up a bit.

"What's that?" I offer, letting the frantic storyteller reach the punch line he is desperately grasping for.

"Bobby said, 'I want everyone here to know that a f-word just kicked your ass.'" Timmy punches his fist into the air and his mates start cheering and stomping their feet. "Bobby's a legend!" they yell. "Bobby the f-word!" But they don't—well, you know.

"The best part of that story," Sandra confides to me, "is that Bobby got out of here." She shouts out, "You boys want another round?"

The kids—a mix of boys and a couple of girls—start counting out what money they have left on the bar, trying to figure out what they can still afford. I tell them thanks for the story and to stay out of trouble, then head for the door. In front of the bar, in the dirt parking lot, is an automatic wheelchair, parked as if it were a car.

I walk through the empty town toward my camp. The rain has let up a bit, but it's still drizzling. By Minister Creek, I see a deer in the darkness. It startles, turning its head to look at me. We stand there as the water falls from the sky and stare at each other. Eventually I start to move again, and the animal breaks for the tree line.

The deer was real. The black dog waiting for me back at my encampment is not. But given the weather, it's good to see a familiar face. The dog trots right up to me, and for the first time I lay my hand on its head.

"Hey, boy."

The months on the road are weighing on me, and despite the infectious joy of the lumberjacks and the well-meaning (if a bit offensive) camaraderie of the patrons at Lee House, no "overcoming the elements to find the silver lining of the situation" can make up for my tarp collapsing while I was gone and my tent getting soaked through. It is cold, wet, and miserable.

"You want to turn in for the night?"

The dog doesn't answer, but I leave the front of my tent open so it can follow me in. I squish into my sleeping bag. Wet, sad, and disheartened—both for myself and for the hurt inside America—I finally drift off to sleep, the dog's head resting on my chest.

41

SO, IT'S LIKE you're on a pilgrimage."

I've stuck around a bar after a Browns game ends, eating some onion rings while late afternoon turns to early evening, not in the mood to scout for yet another place to set up camp, and not really looking forward to another long walk. The season has been, for the most part, cold and damp. I've met people out here in the world, but I miss home, and friends I've known longer than a couple of days at most. I've been a leaf on the wind for too long. I want to feel grounded again.

Instead, I'm back in Mansfield, a couple of miles from the Johnny Appleseed monument in South Park that I visited in the summer. I parked Rabbit and searched for anyplace serving food. As I poked around, I noticed a bench in the center of town with a sign on it that read "Movie Site, Shawshank Trail."

I've decided to do Chapman's most famous walk before the weather gets any colder—the one that made him the Paul Revere of the War of 1812. Almost thirty miles each way, longer than two marathons combined, and double my original walk back in the spring that started in Leominster, Massachusetts. I want to do it in two days or less, just like Chapman had.

While I'm sitting at the bar, a man strikes up a conversation with me about the game. I ask him about the team's earthy moniker, wondering why their helmets are orange, and learn that the Browns were named after a coach, *not* the color. The team's first head coach, to be exact. Paul Brown.

I mention that the team's logo seems rather . . . uninspired.

"We love football here," he replies, "so what could be more iconic as a mascot—as a symbol—than just a football helmet?"

He has a point. The team's original mascot, back when the Browns were founded in 1946, was called Brownie, and is best described as a pretty fucked-up-looking Elf on the Shelf. Probably due to his scary appearance, Brownie was de-emphasized in the 1960s, but has been making a comeback as retro jerseys become more popular with modern football fans.

My new bar friend has a story similar to others I've encountered. He moved to the East Coast in his early twenties, but found everything too expensive. After a year or so of racking up debt he moved back home—saving his money now instead of setting it on fire.

"I want to buy a home. Start a family." I think again of Peter, whom I met that summer on the Allegheny, and how this young man's story would hearten him. I wonder if Peter is up the road in Cleveland, if he's a Browns fan. I think about my own family, back in New England, and my girlfriend on Long Island, with our *real* dogs, and our home by the sea.

A couple of women arrive, friends of the man, and they go to play an electronic bar game together. There is maybe some love triangle at play, or perhaps there are even more angles and shapes involved. But who's chasing whom or trying to make whom jealous, I can't quite suss out. Shots are ordered and cigarette breaks are taken. I think about how much I hear about social media and the "antisocialization" of American youth, but this all looks similar to how my friends and I spent our twenties, twenty or so years ago. And we probably looked similar to the youth twenty years earlier, and so on, all the way back to Kerouac's "Boys and girls in America have such a sad time together," twenty or thirty years before that.

The bar is a scene out of *A Fan's Notes* by Frederick Exley, which has one of my favorite descriptions of drinking in any book I've ever read: "Unlike some men, I had never drunk for boldness or charm or wit; I had used alcohol for precisely what it was, a depressant to check the mental exhilaration produced by extended sobriety."

"So, it's like you're on a pilgrimage."

One of the women is talking to me, the electronic game having ended in defeat.

"I hadn't really thought about it that way before, but you're right."

She offers to drive me when I tell her that I'm planning on walking to Mount Vernon, Ohio, the next day. I turn down her kind offer, explaining that I'm foolishly attempting to hike there and back *on purpose*. Yes, I have a car. No, I am not out of my mind. At least not completely.

The two young women eventually invite me back to their place: If I won't accept a ride, I could at least accept a place to crash. They have a couch. I could get a good night's rest before my pilgrimage the next day. But I'm exhausted, and to be honest, tired of talking. Yet I'm tired of camping, as well. And tired of the cold and rain, and of John Chapman, and of chasing the ghost of America or whatever the hell I'm supposed to be doing out here.

I'm sick and tired of myself, above all.

Which is how I come to find myself at what must be the worst motel in all of Ohio.

It's late, and having passed on the young women's couch offer I have nowhere else to go. I remember that first roadside inn back in Westminster, Massachusetts, and how I hadn't slept there despite the sleet and rain. But I'm tired and a li'l bit defeated. I know I'm not going to experience the luxury of the Bradley Hotel in Fort Wayne, where I treated myself to a good, clean bed and one of the best showers of my entire life. But I'll be walking thirty or so miles tomorrow and thirty or so miles back the day after. If there is ever a time to cave and get a room, it's now.

The man at the front desk barely speaks as he takes my credit card, gives me a key, and directs me down the hall. Heading to my room, I notice some doors are wide open and cleaning carts sit abandoned in the hallways. I hear some sort of loud partying happening in another part of the building. The place is a shithole, but what do I care?

I've stayed in shitholes before. I've lived in shitholes before, sometimes for years at a time.

All I need is a bed.

Which turns out to be a good thing, as a bed is pretty much all there is in the room. There are stains on the carpet and on the synthetic-looking drapes. I almost go and get my sleeping bag to sleep on top of the covers, but Rabbit is on the other side of the building and it's been a long walk just to get here.

Sleep is already overtaking me. I get undressed and put my clothes on a little table. I'll be grateful for that table—high above the wall to wall carpeting—in less than two minutes.

That's because in two minutes I've crawled into bed and, well, the sheets do not feel fresh. I have an uneasy feeling, but tell myself I'm overreacting. Tell myself I'm just edgy from having been on the road too long. I almost convince myself—but right before I close my eyes I use the light on my phone to give the bed one final sweep.

Which is when I see it. Right there on my pillow. A bedbug. I freeze momentarily, then jump out of the bed. I throw back the sheets and find a few more. I pull my T-shirt and underwear off and throw them in the trash. I shower and get the rest of my clothes from the table, grateful that I had the foresight not to leave them on the carpeted floor. Glad my laziness ensured that I didn't bring anything else into the room with me.

I'm certainly awake now.

At the front desk I explain what happened, which doesn't take long. It's evident that this sort of thing has happened before. Recently. Often?

"Which room number did you say you were in again?"

When I tell him, the man makes a face which, at least to me, seems to say, "Shit. I knew that was the wrong hallway. I meant to put him in the other wing."

He refunds my charge with the ease and efficiency of someone very familiar with this particular song and dance. I have checked in and checked out in under an hour.

Now I'm standing in the parking lot under the dim light of the motel's flickering sign. I feel an itchiness all over—or maybe just a phantom itchiness.

I don't want to get into Rabbit. Visions of bringing bedbugs into my Jeep and then the five hundred miles back east with me, infesting my girlfriend's home—which we now live in together—flood my brain. After a year of bouncing around on the road, walking all over, sleeping outside, and recognizing how subsequently cool she has been with it all—I was starting to realize I should ask her to marry me. There's no guarantee she'll say yes, given how smart she is. And bringing bedbugs back from a sleazy motel isn't likely to help.

The air is cold, and it's closer to dawn than midnight. My gear is in the back of Rabbit, but I don't want to risk contaminating it. The stingy New Englander in me refuses to throw out a perfectly good tent and sleeping bag.

I want to stay warm, but it is time to go. And I won't take my gear. It will be the most Chapmanesque walk of the entire year. It's unclear whether Appleseed had shoes when he did this journey—at least I have those, I tell myself.

I open Rabbit quickly and take out the hiking stick I bought at the Johnny Appleseed Festival in Fort Wayne, then slam the door shut again. I don't think bedbugs can jump, but I'm not going to take any risks.

Which is how, at 3:30 a.m., with only a walking stick—very much regretting passing on the kind offer to sleep on that couch—I start on the thirty-mile hike from Mansfield to Mount Vernon, Ohio, possibly covered in bedbugs.

I say a prayer of thanks for the sidewalks in Mansfield as I walk out of town. Chapman never had to cross the tangle of highways that I do, which is perhaps impossible during the day—giving a small silver lining to my early departure time. On the other side of the multilane highway a skunk watches me as I pass by. I don't hesitate, thinking, *Spray me if you're going to spray me, friend. Maybe it will help with the bedbugs.*

Step by step I walk down South Main Street past closed chain stores that give way to a Circle K and the Mansfield Fire Department, which in turn give way to darkened suburban houses and then, eventually, wide-open fields. The stars above me are brilliant, but they slowly begin to fade as dawn breaks in the East.

I pass a family of deer and say, "Thank Christ it isn't raining" to nobody in particular, or maybe to the deer, but they give no response. Soon I enter a flow state, the rhythm of my steps quieting my mind.

Onward I go past junkyards and churchyards and cornfields and through a little town whose name I don't know. The sun rises and I welcome its warmth on my face. A lone man is up, feeding his horses. I extend my arm in greeting, and he extends his back. I give the same greeting to some cows, their heads over a fence, watching me as I saunter by. They don't wave back.

I pass a road sign with a horse and buggy on it, and then a barn that's falling apart but has a freshly painted American flag on the side. I pass geese and ducks, and start to realize that this is the most wildlife—especially if you count farm animals—that I've seen on a single walk this entire year.

It's late afternoon when I finally reach Mount Vernon. I have never been more grateful not to be carrying a pack, but even after a year of walking my feet are raw and blistered, having traveled more than a marathon's distance since my predawn departure from Mansfield. I rest on the lip of a fountain's basin in the center of town before making my way down to Owl Creek.

Owl Creek is a tributary of Walhonding River, and is one of the earliest recorded landholdings of Chapman, "who purchased lot 147 and lot 145 from Joseph Walker on September 14, 1809," according to a historical marker at the site. The river is now called the Kokosing, reverting back to its original Native American name, which loosely translates to "River of Little Owls."

There is a concrete bench on the bank of the creek, uncomfortable, surely, for almost anyone who hasn't just walked close to thirty miles. I sit there and watch a large bird circle in the sky, too high up for me to make out what it is.

There is a railway bridge to my right, and eventually I make my way to it, crossing the bridge and sliding down the embankment on the other side. Below I find the usual collection of assorted empty liquor bottles and cigarette butts, along with some youthfully drawn graffiti. I think about going to find some food, but have simply been on my feet for too damn long. For most of the walk, a sweatshirt has been tied around my waist—I unwrap it, then crumple it up to use as a pillow. I mentally begin to recite the Lord's Prayer, but am asleep before I finish.

In the morning I'm shocked that I've slept through the night—and early evening, for that matter. But there's orange in the sky when I open my eyes. Above me, on a branch that I could easily hit if I tossed a rock, sits a bald eagle. It is gigantic, and doesn't notice me as I stare at it, its eyes on the river. Looking for breakfast. I think of the large bird I saw in the sky the day before, and decide that it must have been the eagle I'm looking at now. The branch below its body bends as it launches itself into the air, before quickly diving down into the river and gripping some small, helpless fish in its talons before flying away.

To live in America is to live inside a legend.

Instead of walking back the way I came, I follow a path through a small wooded area that opens up next to a lake. There, I find public—and open—restrooms. My heart is filled with gratitude. I clean up, my whole body aching from yesterday's walk, but still I push on, and stumble upon Ariel Foundation Park.

Perhaps it's my exhaustion, or my gratitude for public restrooms, but I am stunned by the civic park. Even with the blisters on my feet making every step feel almost squishy, I walk the Tree of Life Labyrinth, a thousand-foot winding walkway, a type of meditation path that turns in on itself. I walk it and then retrace it. There is a museum, but it is too early in the morning for it to be open. From a plaque outside I learn that the 250-acre park is "an example of adaptive reuse, created on the former site of a glass-making factory. It offers architectural ruins, lakes, observation tower, walking trails, steel sculptures, a museum, and connections to both the Kokosing Gap Trail and the Heart of Ohio Trail."

I think back on the dream I had for walkways all across America. Here is a stunning example of what could be done with all this land, all these seemingly abandoned sites. The park opened on July 4, 2015, but plans for it began fifteen years before that. I think of Bill Jones and his amphitheater, land that can maybe be reclaimed and put to good use still. I have to have faith. Faith that things seemingly lost can still be saved.

At the heart of the Ariel Foundation Park is the Rastin Observation Tower—a part of what they call the Ruins, what's left of the gigantic glass-making facility that once stood there, which is free and open to the public, for everyone to explore.

The tower stands at 280 feet, with a winding steel spiral staircase that wraps around the outside. It's the tallest structure in Knox

County, and was once a smokestack—built in 1951—that was part of the Pittsburgh Plate Glass Factory. The chimney closed down when the factory did in the 1970s. At 140 feet up, at the end of the staircase, is an observation deck. There are 224 steps up to the deck. I walk each one.

Looking out over what feels like the entirety of the state—at the lands where John Chapman roamed—I know his story isn't the only one. So many other histories are contained here, some immortalized by plaques, others erased, or just long forgotten. Triumphs and tragedies, joys and brutalizations. All of them—Chapman's, my own, everyone's—somewhere in between.

I know it isn't possible, but I feel like I can see all the way to John Chapman's grave in Fort Wayne.

I remember visiting the grave, just a few months ago, the day after the festival cleared out. Everyone gone, all the vendors packed up. The park where the grave resides is small. Insignificant. There was an RV in the dusty parking lot. A modest encampment. A transient home, which felt fitting. It was out of the way, far from the grave. I doubted anyone was going to bother them.

I walked up to Chapman's headstone, the small iron fence around the grave giving it an air of importance, but hitting at only knee level. I remember looking over at the neighboring Allen County War Memorial Coliseum, a giant building, all glass and concrete. A monument to progress, perhaps, and also a giant human cut against the natural landscape. It's easy to assume Chapman would hate it, given how he was always moving away from the European idea of civilization pervading colonial and postcolonial America, but I guess we'll never know for sure.

Hate it or not, there his grave lies, in the shadow of that monolith and its surrounding parking lots. So tiny in comparison. And we don't even know if his bones are down there in the dirt, or if he made it to Swedenborgian heaven, a place, to this day, to which some people still think they're heading. We have no idea about so many things.

Simply existing is to have some faith—whatever shape that faith may take.

Chapman might not have liked that building, or the way this country has become less wild, but he is still very much a part of it—he was, and is, an American legend, a story used to propagate. We have no control over who tells our tales after we die, or the ways in which those tales are told. We have so little control over everything.

I palmed one of the apples Patti had given me from her family's miraculous tree, small and green. I bent over the iron gate and gently placed the maybe-Johnny-Appleseed apple on the headstone of the maybe-Johnny-Appleseed grave.

Here and now, it's still early morning in Ohio, and I still have the thirty-mile walk back to Mansfield ahead of me. Then the more than five-hundred-mile drive with Rabbit back to New York City—seventy extra miles tacked on if I want to drive out to Kelly's house on Long Island. But looking out over this land right now, with all the stories happening below me—all of us simply discrete histories, bouncing off one another constantly and in real time—I know one thing:

I want to live my life wild and free, but I don't want to die on someone else's floor like Chapman did.

I take one last look out at the country unfurling below. Once I turn, once I place that first foot forward, I will be heading back. Heading in the right direction. I say a quick, short prayer—just as I did when I put that apple on John Chapman's grave in the summer—and begin my long journey home.

· WINTER ·

EPILOGUE

I, GIVE ME A CALL. *Dad.*"

It was February. Just shy of a year since my first long walk from Leominster back to my parents' home along the Johnny Appleseed Highway—the day I'd fallen short of my goal and they picked me up at Red Apple Farm.

I looked down at the text from my da and instantly knew without knowing how.

A flash of Dakota jolted through my brain.

"I was working. When he called, I was working . . ."

I did as my da requested, although I already knew what he was going to say.

My mother had killed herself. Hung herself from the rafters of the family barn where she'd grown up—one town over from the house where she and my father had been living. Right on the property where I'd lived as a child, too. Some of the worst years of my life were spent in that drafty cold gray house.

In that same house—now painted yellow—only weeks before, in late January, my father and my mother had discovered my aunt, her sister, dead on the floor. Stage four colon cancer, undiagnosed. She'd been fatigued since the fall. Kept meaning to get to the hospital, but never got around to it.

My father said my aunt had filled the house with branches and rocks and dirt and feathers and other assortments of things from the woods.

"It was like she was trying to bring the outside inside."

My ma's side of the family, with their deep New England roots, always had an appreciation for the pagan. Celebrating solstices and putting real, burning candles on the Christmas tree. I know where my desire to sleep outdoors comes from.

My mother and her sister were living in the area to take care of their mother—with help from two younger sisters who live in Vermont. My grandmother still living on the farm, and who, as of my writing this, is one hundred years old and still alive.

I told my girlfriend, whom I would marry in one month and one day, what had happened. That I had to go be with my father. She would stay and take care of the dogs and join me in a few days.

I showered and climbed into Rabbit and drove north. I was coming from the North Fork of Long Island, so I took the Cross Sound Ferry to Connecticut.

Back on the mainland, as I drove, I fell into the same meditative state I'd been in so often during the past year. I looked out at the ocean, thinking of Ashley C. Ford's oceans of cornfields, soybeans, and wheat.

I had driven this route just a month ago. The same ferry from New York to Connecticut. The same drive north. Conner's mother had fallen ill.

It was January then. Conner flew in from where he is stationed out west to visit his ma, who now lives in a state-run facility for the aging. He called and asked if I wanted to come along. I drove back to the area where I spent my teenage years. Before we went, we linked up with his brother and went to visit their old childhood home, long abandoned. The forest had begun to take the building back. There were tree branches growing in through the windows and some of the walls were beginning to rot. In the living room we found boxes and boxes of old DVDs, treasures from a different time, forgotten now and no longer of any value. We grabbed a few, unsure what we'd do with them, but knowing that you don't leave newly discovered treasure in the woods.

Conner's ma is in a rehab center and mental health facility, an eldercare home for people who didn't financially plan for their golden years. At the end of its driveway we found a pile of discarded, empty nip bottles—someone's last party before going in to get sober.

Every wing had locks with different access codes that needed to be punched in. The place was underfunded, but the nurses were doing their best. Conner's ma recognized us when we came in, then her eyes flickered back into forgetfulness. This happened a few times while we were there, although once she hung in for a minute or two, saying, "My lads. My lads. We had fun, didn't we?" We told her we did, and that we loved her. Conner showed her pictures of his kids. We stood around, not quite knowing what to do.

"These are the parts of life they don't show in the movies," Conner said to no one in particular.

Which is when I noticed an old, single-unit TV/DVD player in the corner of the room. The screen was small and we had to wipe off a layer of dust from the glass, but the machine worked when we plugged it in. I ran out to Conner's rental car and grabbed a couple of DVDs from the box in his backseat. The nurse, when she let me back in, asked if she could bring some of the other residents over to watch when I told her what we were doing. There was no popcorn, but we did bring Conner's ma some chocolates. Conner's brother opened them up and passed them around while Conner sat at the end of his mother's bed. I slid a disc into the tray. It didn't really matter which one. The nurse turned down the lights and I hit Play.

The room grew dark as the MGM lion came on the screen and began to roar.

I thought of Matt Sumell, taking care of his dying father with his brother. His dad would go in July. When he shared the news, he said:

> I'm heartbroken—and frankly a little surprised—to share that my father passed away in the early morning hours of July 10th, after a brief illness and 85 years of self abuse, fast food, alcoholic rootbeer, and in general questionable decision-making. I'll never know if his last words were "thank you" or "fuck you"—but that's perfect, and the truth is it doesn't matter because deep down I know what he meant. I've always recognized his warm and good and funny heart behind the things he said: "Hey shitbird" or "Dipshit" or "Yuh just mad I fucked yuh mother" (true, btw, I am) all meant, in his way, what my last words to him were: that I loved him deeply.
>
> Quick story: When he coached my Little League team he picked the players based on who had the best looking moms. We sucked, but our games were well attended. Go Eagles!
>
> This one-legged, stubborn as a rock, hysterically funny, literal motherfucker with the brightest most vulnerable blue eyes ever will be deeply missed by his three children, two grandkids, his sister Janey, nieces and nephews, co-workers and colleagues, and potentially a couple of old girlfriends but that one's doubtful.

His statement ended with a request for donations to the Montessori School of Mahoning Valley, where Matt's nieces went and his father volunteered, "but in lieu of that, tit pics would be great (it's what he would have wanted)."

Middle-aged men taking care of aging parents. Elderly parents taking care of ancient parents. Mothers outliving daughters—one legit, and one with an asterisk.

When I was up in January, my mother and I spent an afternoon together. She had lost weight, and I noticed a few things that had me concerned, reminded me of when I was younger. When it was just me and her, and she was losing her mind.

We were too late. Had been for some time.

I was, of course, going through an onslaught of emotions. My ma was sick. She had been sick for a long time. But what I tried to hold in my heart—and will do my damnedest to hold in my heart going forward—is that she was brave. Brave for holding the monsters at the gate for as long as she did. But still I gnashed my teeth in anger.

When I arrived back in Athol, one of the first things my father said to me was, "Well, one of us should learn how to use the washing machine."

I was upset at first—until I realized that, technically, he was right.

He was brokenhearted, and simply trying to take care of logistics. There was some fish in the fridge that might go bad. He mixed it up with some eggs and called it dinner.

We sat in silence for the most part, looking at photos of her. She hated to get her picture taken. But you could see how beautiful she was.

We wouldn't find her suicide note until six months later. There were two of them, actually. One still had tape on the corners. She had meant to leave it on the door of the barn, but seemingly forgot it in a manila envelope left among books on her bookshelf, wedged between Virginia Woolf and Sylvia Plath. She wanted to warn her sister, so that she wouldn't be the one to discover her body. On the top of the first note was the Hebrew word *dayenu*. A word that roughly translates into "enough," but can be understood in various ways—as in, "This would have been enough," or the altogether different, "This has been enough."

But at the point of my father's whitefish and eggs, we hadn't yet found them. All my da knew was that she flashed him a smile before she'd left the house that morning. All we had were her favorite poems. Not knowing what else to do, my da and I stayed up and read the poems to each other, back and forth. He in his chair, me on the couch. Until we fell asleep.

My mother's youngest sister had found her. A woman, Rosie, who was helping them ensure that the farm didn't fall into further disrepair, was with her at the time, as well. My ma had gone to the farm early in the morning so she'd be alone before everyone's arrival for the day. But then, she'd forgotten the note she'd meant to put on the door warning them not to come in.

I went to the farm the next day to retrieve my mother's car. When I hugged my aunt, my ma's youngest sister, I cried for the first time. Just a few tears. Her embrace was so much like my ma's. Her body and arms felt the same.

I searched the barn for any sign of a note, but found nothing. My aunt made only one request of me: to take the gray-and-black stepladder my mother had used and get it out of the barn and throw it away. Later that day, I chucked it into a dumpster behind the local Chinese restaurant.

When I searched my mother's car for a note, nothing. But I did find a St. Jude's prayer:

> Most holy Apostle, St. Jude, faithful servant and friend of Jesus, I place myself into your hands at this difficult time. Help me to know that I am not alone. Please pray for me, asking God to send me comfort for my sorrows, bravery for my fears, and healing for my suffering.

I took the car home. Cleaned it out. And found a car dealer willing to take it off my hands quickly because I was willing to let him take advantage of us a bit.

More family began to show up, along with packages of food sent by my friends who lived elsewhere but had heard the news.

My father grew frustrated with the amount of boxes that were arriving, packed with food we couldn't figure out how to cook. And I

On the day my wife and I were married, one hundred turkeys inexplicably appeared on our front lawn. One of our dogs got loose, and chased every single turkey into the trees, their limbs bowing under the weight. As if our dog was saying, "Not today. Your sadness is not welcome here." The day was an amazing elopement on a beach near our house. The two friends who introduced us, a photographer, a reverend, and no one else—save the outline of an old woman who sat in the gazebo in the bluffs, silently watching the ceremony. The only time all day I thought of my mother was when I caught a glimpse of that woman. A ghost? Or, as Chapman would put it, an angel?

Beside the woman, that same black dog—the Irish wolfhound that had been following me around America. The woman stood up after the ceremony and walked away. The dog stayed. I knew it wasn't real, but what it represents was. Those same dark shadows passed on to me. The same way this country that we live in can break you if you look directly at it, but also consume you if you ignore the truth of it, choosing instead only the legend.

Before all that, my father simply asks me, "Do you want to go for a walk?"

We go to the Quabbin Reservoir.

We walk for miles, until we reach the water.

The air is warm. Spring is just around the corner. If only she'd waited a few more days. She loved it when it finally got warm out.

We have been quiet the whole time. No stories. No legends. No making sense of it. No embellished histories or memories.

There will be no monument for my mother, save the wall we put her ashes in, which was already there. She wouldn't have wanted one anyway. John Chapman probably didn't want one either.

Save for turkeys on windowsills, or black bears in driveways, or the silhouettes of old women at weddings.

Save for the wind blowing through the reeds on the shores of the Quabbin Reservoir.

I stand there with my father not talking. Not moving. Simply being.

The sun setting over the water.

Spring will come.

ACKNOWLEDGMENTS

This book is dedicated to Kelly Elaine Farber, my wife, for extremely good reason. Without her, this book would simply not exist. Not only did she help me dream up the concept in the first place, but she was there with me every step of the way—not the actual walking, mind you. But the more difficult parts. The writing. The typing. The reading and re-reading of multiple drafts. The late nights and early mornings. While I lived this project, she also watched over our dogs and our home, a home I would never have without her. I love you, Kelly, you are the shining lighthouse to which I always return.

I would also like to thank Meredith Kaffel Simonoff, the best agent a wayward writer could ever hope for. Thank you so much for all of your guidance, care, and encouragement, along with your seemingly endless willingness to hold on to my anxieties. You have changed my life in so many ways. I will be forever grateful.

Rounding out the trifecta of people to whom this book owes an unquantifiable debt: John Freeman has captained this ship from a few scribblings on a napkin to the tome you now hold in your hands. Not only is John an incredible editor, but he is also a great champion of the human spirit. No matter how lost I was while writing this book—both figuratively and literally—John was there to make sure I didn't get mired in my own fearfulness or penchant for falling into loneliness, both as a person and on the page. Thank you so much, John, for believing not just in this project, but in me.

This book would also not have been possible without the tremendous efforts of the entire team at Knopf. My eternal gratitude goes out to Jordan Pavlin, Hilary Redmon, Gabrielle Brooks (who so elegantly came up with the title, *American Rambler*), Chip Kidd (who dreamed up the book's marvelous cover), Jordan Rodman, Jessica Purcell, Ruth Liebmann, Erinn Hartman, Matthew Sciarappa, Laura Keefe, Anna Noone, Angela Rose West, Kevin Bourke, Rita Madrigal, Marisa Nakasone, Felecia O'Connell, Kristen Bearse, Arianna Abdul, Anne Achenbaum, Patty Flynn, Chris Jerome, Alisa Garrison, Chuck Thompson, Amy Stackhouse, and Sierra Fang-Horvath (who skillfully kept the editorial trains running on time). It has been an absolute honor to work with the incredible people that make up Team Borzoi.

Thank you to mapmaker David Lindroth and sensitivity reader Keli O'Neill.

Thanks also to Meredith's colleagues at the Gernert Company, including Nora Gonzalez, David Gernert, Anna Worrall, Will Roberts, and Rebecca Gardner.

I would also like to thank the many wonderful strangers and friends who opened up their hearts—and their homes—to me while on this journey: Patti Algeo Young, Michael Limmer and the entire Fort Wayne TinCaps organization, Ashley C. Ford and Kelly Stacy, Saeed Jones, Matt Sumell, Dakota, Clay, Piper VanOrd and all the folks at Allegheny Outfitters, Pete, Rosie Clark and the good people at Red Apple Farm, Sandy Setili and Felixia Banck and all the lumberjacks and -jills, not to mention all the unnamed (or name swapped) denizens of Leominster, Westminster, Indian Lake, Mansfield, Warren, and Sheffield, and everyone else I encountered on my travels, including every truck driver who did me a kindness out on the highways of America. Kings of the road. Also, of course, the bartenders.

Thank you to those who provided invaluable quotes on the book at an early stage: Adam Johnson, John Green, Tommy Orange, Cheryl Strayed, Patrick Ryan, Tara Westover, and Colson Whitehead.

Huge appreciation to my early readers: Andrea Morstabilini, Isabella Newmark, John Wray, John Hendrickson, Michelle Paulson, Eric Simonoff, Miwa Messer, Cathy Berner, Stijn de Vries, Jim Sullivan, John Ritzman, Jeremy Derbyshire-Miles, Krystie Yandoli, Scaachi Koul, John Glynn, Casey Sciezcka, and Steven Weinberg.

Leonel Teti assisted with the sections translated into Spanish; *gracias,* Leo.

I want to acknowledge Jason Richman at United Talent Agency for being a fierce advocate of my work and a great friend.

History isn't an easy thing, but I am forever in awe of those people who dedicate their lives—or even a part of their lives—to it. Thank you to Florence E. Wheeler and the historians, librarians, and researchers everywhere who are committed to trying to remember our past, as well as trying to get it right. So many historical societies helped me along my journey. Special shoutout to the docents of the Johnny Appleseed Museum in Urbana, OH, with whom I spoke in Fort Wayne. Julia Schmucker at Bryn Athyn Cathedral was extremely helpful and welcoming as well.

Speaking of history, I owe a debt of gratitude to the following fantastic books, as well as their authors: *The Botany of Desire* by Michael Pollan; *The Core of Johnny Appleseed* by Ray Silverman; *Johnny Appleseed and the American Orchard* by William Kerrigan; *Johnny Appleseed, Man and Myth* by the late Robert Price; and lastly, *Johnny Appleseed: The Man, the Myth, the American Story* by Howard Means—if you find yourself looking for a more straightforward biography of John Chapman, this is the book for you.

It would be a shame not to thank Rabbit, for getting me from place to place safely and in one piece, and to the employee at Eagle Auto Mall of Riverhead who steered me away from the Corvette and toward my beloved Jeep. Also, my two (real) pups, Zorra and Hobbes.

I will forever be indebted to my therapist, Dr. Jenny Kaufmann, who has guided me through such a difficult time in my life.

Portions of this book were written at the Riverhead Public Library,

North Fork Brewery, Riverhead Ciderhouse, Greenport Brewery, Barrow Food House, the Old Mill in Mattituck, NY, and Old Town Bar in Manhattan.

A big bursting heartfelt hug to Michael Fusco Straub and Emma Straub and all the employees at Books Are Magic for their early support of the book, alongside independent booksellers and bookstore owners everywhere.

Lastly, with untold love and thanks to my ma, for everything she did for me, as well as my da, and all storytellers like him.

A NOTE ABOUT THE AUTHOR

ISAAC FITZGERALD is the *New York Times* bestselling author of *Dirtbag, Massachusetts.* He is also the author of the bestselling children's book *How to Be a Pirate* as well as the coauthor of *Pen & Ink: Tattoos and the Stories Behind Them* and *Knives & Ink: Chefs and the Stories Behind Their Tattoos* (winner of an IACP Award). He appears frequently on *Today,* and his writing has appeared in *The New York Times, The Atlantic, Esquire, GQ, The Guardian, The Best American Nonrequired Reading,* and numerous other publications. He lives with his wife on the North Fork of Long Island.

A NOTE ON THE TYPE

This book was set in Arno, a typeface designed by Adobe principal designer Robert Slimbach in 2007. Its namesake is the Arno River, which flows through Florence, the city at the heart of the Italian Renaissance. Inspired by the humanist letterforms of the fifteenth and sixteenth centuries, Slimbach designed Arno with the vitality and readability of Venetian and Aldine book typefaces in mind.

Typeset by Scribe,
Philadelphia, Pennsylvania

Designed by Marisa Nakasone